T.

turn on or before the last date shi

The Medical Library Association Guide to Finding Out about Diabetes

The Best Print and
Electronic Resources

Dana L. Ladd
Alyssa Altshuler

An imprint of the American Library Association

CHICAGO   2013

The information in this book is intended to help the reader locate information about diabetes. It is not intended to replace the advice of a qualified health care professional. While every effort has been made to ensure accuracy and currency of the facts presented, this information should not be used to make decisions about medical care. Please consult with your physician before making any decisions regarding medical treatment.

Contact information and URLs listed in the book were accurate at the time the manuscript went to press.

© 2013 by the Medical Library Association. Any claim of copyright is subject to applicable limitations and exceptions, such as rights of fair use and library copying pursuant to Sections 107 and 108 of the U.S. Copyright Act. No copyright is claimed for content in the public domain, such as works of the U.S. government.

Printed in the United States of America
17 16 15 14 13   5 4 3 2 1

Extensive effort has gone into ensuring the reliability of the information in this book; however, the publisher makes no warranty, express or implied, with respect to the material contained herein.

ISBNs: 978-1-55570-890-0 (paper); 978-1-55570-944-0 (PDF); 978-1-55570-945-7 (ePub); 978-1-55570-946-4 (Kindle).

Library of Congress Cataloging-in-Publication Data
Ladd, Dana L.
  The Medical Library Association guide to finding out about diabetes : the best print and electronic resources / Dana L. Ladd and Alyssa Altshuler.
     pages cm
  Includes bibliographical references and index.
  ISBN 978-1-55570-890-0 (alk. paper)
  1. Diabetes. 2. Diabetes—Bibliography. 3. Diabetes—Computer network resources—Directories. I. Altshuler, Alyssa. II. Medical Library Association. III. Title.

RC660.L135 2013
016.6164'62—dc23

2012028333

Cover design by Casey Bayer. Image © djem/Shutterstock, Inc.
Text design in Minion and Avenir by UB Communications.

♾ This paper meets the requirements of ANSI/NISO Z39.48-1992 (Permanence of Paper).

To Linnea Altshuler Renton
for her extraordinary and tireless efforts
on behalf of the medically underserved around the world

Contents

Part I: Basic Resources for Getting Started

Part II: Diabetes Management Resources

Part III: Life with Diabetes

Part IV: Related Health Complications and Care Resources

Medical Content Advisory Board

Kristin Andrs, NP, BC-ADM, CDE, is a diabetes case manager at Virginia Commonwealth University Health System. Andrs earned her bachelor of science degree and her master of science and nursing degree from Virginia Commonwealth University. Andrs serves as the director of a multidisciplinary diabetes education team within the health system and also serves as a health system consultant for diabetes-related issues. In addition, she is a preceptor for nurse practitioner students in the VCU School of Nursing and teaches diabetes classes to students in the program. Andrs is an active member of the Virginia Diabetes Council and the American Association of Diabetic Educators. She is currently completing an integrative medicine fellowship at the University of Arizona, Tucson.

Brigitte Sicat, PharmD, BCPS, BC-ADM, is an associate professor at the Virginia Commonwealth University School of Pharmacy and actively involved in the VCU Institute for Women's Health where she currently serves as the director of education. She received her pharmacy degree from Virginia Commonwealth University in 1998 and completed both a general pharmacy practice residency and a specialized residency in primary ambulatory care at the Medical University of South Carolina in 1999 and 2000, respectively. Her professional practice includes the provision of pharmacy services in the primary care and endocrinology clinics at VCU Health Systems. She is a board-certified pharmacotherapy specialist (BCPS) and is board certified in advanced diabetes management (BC-ADM). Her practice and research interests include diabetes, women's health, and educational research. She is involved in numerous initiatives dedicated to improving the care of patients with diabetes, including co-organizer of the VCU Health System Diabetes Working Group and co-developer of the VCU School of Pharmacy Diabetes Certificate Program.

Alyssa Wehrmeister, RD, CDE, is a pediatric dietitian and site coordinator of the pediatric diabetes education program at the Children's Hospital of Richmond, Virginia Commonwealth University Hospital. She received a bachelor of science in dietetics from James Madison University and completed a dietetic internship at VCU Hospital System. In 2006, Wehrmeister accepted a position with the pediatric endocrinology department. In addition to her educator role, she is also the director of the division's American Diabetes Association–recognized Diabetes Self-Management Education Program and Richmond's Camp WannaCure for children with diabetes. Her clinical interests include pediatric diabetes, cystic fibrosis–related diabetes, and weight management.

Preface

Diabetes is quickly becoming one of the most pervasive diseases in the United States, affecting men and women of all ages, races, and ethnicities. Depending on the type of diabetes, it can be diagnosed at an early age, or it can be an insidious disease, slowly manifesting itself without people realizing it. With the increasing number of Americans who are currently at risk for the disease due to genetics, poor eating habits, or inactive lifestyles, it is crucial that people receive accurate information to either prevent the disease or manage it. *The Medical Library Association Guide to Finding Out about Diabetes: The Best Print and Electronic Resources* connects librarians and patients with valid and useful resources to empower patients to make informed decisions about their own or their loved ones' health. This comprehensive resource book will provide librarians with a background of key diabetes concepts and aid them and patients in finding reliable information about the disease from a variety of print, audiovisual, and web resources.

For any individual, reviewing the amount of information regarding diabetes can be an overwhelming and unnerving experience simply because what is available is so vast, both in print and online. Many complexities and questions surround a diagnosis of diabetes, such as what type of medication to use and when, what type of diet will support a healthy lifestyle and mitigate symptoms, how much physical activity people can pursue, and how to help care for a loved one with the disease.

While the health ramifications of diabetes are well documented, seeing firsthand the repercussions of someone actively fighting the disease, or having a family member who is diagnosed with it, resonated with us. This book is a result of the authors working with library patrons who have posed questions to learn more about types 1 and 2 diabetes and helpful diet regimens. Too often, people receive their diagnosis and treatment specifics from health care workers who use complicated medical jargon, which the patients or family members do not comprehend or which does not meet their core information needs. When people are better informed about the complexities of the disease and the importance of its prevention and management, they are in more control of their health.

Selection Criteria

The authors' reference interactions with patients in public and consumer health libraries drove the selection of resources and chapter topics, which are reflective of the general population seeking diabetes information. The print, web, and audiovisual resources reviewed, evaluated, and selected for inclusion are based on authorship, authority, reliability, currency, and reading level of the information. A Medical Content Advisory Board—consisting of a pharmacist, a diabetes case manager, and a pediatric dietician—reviewed the medical content of each chapter. *The Medical Library Association Guide to Finding Out about Diabetes* provides patients and their family members a portal to reliable diabetes health information so they can continue to make informed decisions about health throughout all stages of the disease, communicate effectively with health care providers, improve quality of life, and properly manage the condition. Finally, this book provides consumer health and public librarians with a core diabetes bibliography and webliography for collection development purposes.

Organization

The Medical Library Association Guide to Finding Out about Diabetes contains four separate parts, each addressing a major area of concern for the diabetic patient, the family member, or the caregiver of a patient with diabetes. There are twenty-five chapters in the book, each beginning with an overview of a diabetes topic that provides the librarian, diabetes patient, or family member with general background information about the specific diabetes issue. The background information in chapters precedes selected, useful Information Sources sections, which are the primary focus of the book. The Information Sources sections are divided into Selected Print Resources, Selected Web Resources, and Selected Audiovisual Resources. Each entry in these resource lists includes a short annotation describing the types of information within the resource.

Part I, "Basic Resources for Getting Started," provides background information about the three different types of diabetes—type 1, type 2, and gestational—and is a starting point for those newly diagnosed with the condition. These chapters also contain pertinent information for those who wish to prevent diabetes from developing, as well as resources on general management of the condition. Chapter 1, "Essentials," provides a broad overview of key diabetes concepts to enhance background knowledge of the condition, including general information about type 1, type 2, and gestational diabetes. In addition to the general print, web, and audiovisual resources in all chapters, this chapter also includes resources for online glossaries and illustrations. Chapter 2, "Type 1 Diabetes," contains information and resources about type 1 diabetes and its causes, symptoms, diagnosis, and management; Chapter 3, "Type 2 Diabetes," covers the same range of information but for type 2 diabetes. Chapter 4 provides information on prevention and lifestyle changes to avoid diabetes. The focus of Chapter 5 is gestational diabetes and resources for pregnant women on how they can protect themselves and their babies if they do develop the condition. Pediatric diabetes is the concentration of

Chapter 6, which provides a range of information and resources for parents, teens, and children.

Part II, "Diabetes Management Resources," includes information about health and lifestyle changes that may be necessary for patients with diabetes to implement to manage their condition and prevent or delay complications from developing. As with any chronic illness, diabetes impacts patients in their everyday lives, from finances to traveling, at work and school. Drug therapy is the focus of Chapter 7, which covers information about insulin and oral diabetes medications. Chapters 8 and 9 focus on healthy lifestyle changes through diet and physical activity. Because many patients look to alternative treatment methods, Chapter 10 provides reliable information on complementary and alternative medicine (CAM) and further resources for finding CAM treatments. Chapter 11 describes clinical trials and lists resources to help patients identify those trials in which they may be able to participate.

Part III, "Life with Diabetes," contains information patients can use to make living with the condition easier. Because communication is so important, Chapter 12 provides information on how patients can learn to communicate and work with their health care team, and Chapter 13 discusses how to find support through family, friends, and others with diabetes. Because patients with chronic illness often deal with financial and legal issues, Chapter 14 provides pertinent information for patients dealing with financial, insurance, and legal issues related to diabetes as well as resources for finding more information. Chapter 15 explains how to deal with diabetes while at work or school, and Chapter 16 provides tips and resources on making traveling easier.

Part IV, "Related Health Complications and Care Resources," explains how patients can prevent complications of diabetes from occurring and what they can do when complications do occur. Each chapter in this section contains information about a particular complication: "Foot, Skin, and Gum Problems" in Chapter 17; "Diabetic Retinopathy" in Chapter 18; "Cardiovascular Complications" in Chapter 19; "Mental Health Issues" in Chapter 20; "Diabetic Neuropathy" in Chapter 21; "Diabetic Nephropathy" in Chapter 22; "Gastroparesis (Delayed Gastric Emptying)" in Chapter 23; "Ketoacidosis" in Chapter 24; and "Sexual and Urological Problems" in Chapter 25. Each chapter provides an overview of the complication or issue, its risk factors, symptoms, diagnosis, treatment, and prevention, followed by additional resources for finding information.

The goal of *The Medical Library Association Guide to Finding Out about Diabetes: The Best Print and Electronic Resources* is to help patients and family members filter through and discern what is valid information and then distill and apply what is pertinent to their particular situation. This book provides public librarians and consumer health librarians with a background of core concepts to enable them to improve their reference interview with patients or interested family members. The library professional will find much-needed information that is accurate, reliable, authoritative, timely, nonbiased, noncommercial, and written in lay language, so it is easily accessible to consumers of all educational and reading levels. Likewise, consumers can also use this book to answer information needs and guide them to needed resources without the help of a reference librarian.

Part I

Basic Resources for Getting Started

Chapter 1

Essentials

Getting Started

In the United States, diabetes mellitus is the seventh leading cause of death, and approximately 26 million people are affected by the condition (Centers for Disease Control and Prevention, 2012). In Canada, more than 9 million people have been diagnosed with diabetes or prediabetes (Canadian Diabetes Association, 2012). Untreated or improperly managed diabetes can lead to significant complications, resulting in serious illness or even death. Many patients who receive a diagnosis of diabetes will seek information online and from friends to learn more about the disease and to manage their condition effectively. Those seeking information may consult a librarian to assist them in finding reliable and accurate lay-level information about the condition, its treatment and management, lifestyle changes, caregiving, or complications of diabetes.

This chapter provides general information about diabetes to assist the librarian and the general public in finding authoritative information written in lay language. Following an overview of the condition is a description of the types of diabetes and their differences. Readers will gain a better understanding of the symptoms of diabetes, its diagnosis, management, and treatment methods. Subsequent chapters of this book will go into further detail about additional diabetes concepts.

In addition to gaining an understanding of basic diabetes concepts, librarians will learn how to conduct an efficient diabetes reference interview and how to evaluate diabetes websites found online. This chapter also provides general diabetes print and web resources; special resources; links to glossaries, illustrations, and easy-to-read resources; information in other languages; audiovisual resources; and recommended diabetes periodicals. This chapter includes general resources about diabetes as well as additional print, web, and audiovisual resources about specific diabetes concepts.

Diabetes Overview

Diabetes mellitus is a chronic medical condition that results in too much glucose in the bloodstream. *Mellitus* is the Latin word for "sweet like honey," referring to the excess glucose in the blood and urine of a patient with diabetes. *Diabetes* is a general term that refers to a group of diseases that affects the way the body uses blood glucose. In diabetes mellitus, either the pancreas does not make enough insulin or the body is unable to use insulin properly.

Glucose Metabolism

Glucose is the main source of energy for the body's cells. The body not only obtains glucose from food but produces it from the liver. After eating, glucose from food is absorbed into the body's bloodstream. Insulin produced by beta cells in the pancreas acts as a key to allow glucose into the body's cells, effectively lowering the amount of glucose in the body's bloodstream. The secretion of insulin by the pancreas drops as the blood glucose level in the body decreases. The liver also stores glucose in the form of glycogen to use when the body needs it. After periods of not eating, the liver releases glucose into the bloodstream. This balance of insulin and glucose keeps blood glucose levels within normal range.

In people with diabetes, the process of glucose metabolism does not work properly, resulting in excess glucose in the bloodstream and glucose being excreted in the urine. The malfunction of glucose metabolism usually occurs when there is a complete or near-complete deficiency in insulin secreted by the pancreas or when the body is unable to respond properly to insulin (Collazo-Clavell, 2009). The lack of insulin causes glucose to build up in the bloodstream so the body does not derive the energy it requires from food. Over time, excess blood glucose leads to serious health complications.

Types of Diabetes

The type of diabetic diagnosis a person receives depends on the cause of the excess blood glucose. In type 1 diabetes, the immune system mistakenly attacks pancreatic beta cells, the insulin-producing cells in the pancreas, resulting in a complete or near-complete deficiency of insulin. Type 1 diabetes is a chronic metabolic condition, and patients need lifelong insulin therapy to survive. While type 1 diabetes typically occurs in children and young adults, the condition can occur in patients of any age. Of the 24 million people currently diagnosed with diabetes in the United States, only 5 to 10 percent have type 1 diabetes (Mercer, 2012).

Type 2 diabetes occurs when the body's cells become resistant to insulin's action. Type 2 diabetes accounts for 90 to 95 percent of all cases in the United States (Diabetes Education Online, 2012). In the beginning of this process, the pancreas makes more insulin to overcome the resistance. Over time, the insulin-producing beta cells in the pancreas are unable to secrete enough insulin to compensate for the extra amount of glucose in the bloodstream.

Different from type 1 or type 2 diabetes, gestational diabetes is a type of diabetes that can occur in pregnant women who did not have type 1 or type 2 diabetes before pregnancy. Although the body makes more insulin during pregnancy, the placenta secretes hormones that block insulin action, and the attendant weight gain makes it difficult for the body to meet its insulin need. Controlling blood sugar during pregnancy is very important to prevent a difficult birth and birth defects and to keep the baby and mother healthy. Gestational diabetes usually subsides completely after giving birth; however, patients are more likely to develop type 2 diabetes later. Of gestational diabetes patients, 60 percent will develop type 2 diabetes within ten years after giving birth (Davis, 2009).

There are other, rarer forms of diabetes. Diabetes can be caused by genetic defects in beta cells or insulin secretion, diseases of the pancreas, endocrine diseases, certain drugs, or infections. This resource deals primarily with the most common types of diabetes: type 1, type 2, and gestational diabetes; it is important to be aware of the differences in the etiology of each type.

Symptoms

Symptoms of diabetes may develop over a short period of time or gradually over a longer period of time. People with type 1 diabetes tend to develop symptoms suddenly. Some people, particularly with type 2 diabetes, experience no symptoms. The most common symptoms of diabetes include frequent urination, unusual thirst, extreme hunger, unusual weight loss or gain, sores that are slow to heal, frequent infections, extreme fatigue, and irritability. Some patients may experience blurred vision, dry and itchy skin, or tingling in the hands and feet. Patients experiencing symptoms should consult a physician to obtain an accurate diagnosis so proper management of the disease can begin immediately.

Diagnosis

Blood tests are used to diagnose diabetes and determine what type of diabetes the patient has. Patients will have a glycated hemoglobin (A1C) test, a random plasma glucose test, or a fasting plasma glucose test to determine if they have diabetes. The A1C test indicates the average blood sugar level over the past two to three months. The random plasma glucose test, done without fasting, can take place at any time during the day and measures the amount of glucose in the blood at a given time. More than one abnormal random blood sugar test result of greater than 200 mg/dL, along with symptoms of the disease, indicates the patient has diabetes.

The preferred diagnostic method is a fasting plasma glucose test: the patient takes this test, usually in the morning, after fasting for at least eight to ten hours. In patients with diabetes, extra glucose remains in the blood even after fasting. Those individuals with a fasting plasma glucose higher than 126 mg/dL after taking two separate tests receive a diagnosis of diabetes. To determine which type of diabetes the patient has, another test checks the patient's blood for the presence of autoantibodies common in type 1 diabetes. The presence of ketones, a waste product created when the body breaks down fats for energy, in the urine also suggests the patient has type 1 diabetes.

Management and Treatment

There is no cure for type 1 or type 2 diabetes; however, the disease is treatable and controllable with medication and lifestyle changes. The goals of treatment are to keep insulin levels as close to normal as possible to prevent or delay complications. Patients with type 1 diabetes must take insulin to survive. Some people with type 2 diabetes can lower their blood glucose to within normal limits through diet and exercise. Those who are unable to lower their blood glucose to within normal range through eating a healthy diet and exercising regularly will need medication to keep their blood glucose level in the normal range and to prevent further complications.

Effective diabetes management includes medication therapy in conjunction with lifestyle changes such as diet and exercise. Diabetes patients need to eat a diet that includes plenty of fruits, vegetables, and whole grains and avoid foods that are high in calories with low nutritional value. Exercise and physical activity are also essential for anyone with diabetes. Physical activity helps to lower blood glucose and blood pressure and to burn calories. Doctors recommend that patients be active every day, participate in aerobic exercise, and stretch. Before beginning any exercise program, patients should consult with their doctor.

Complications

Patients with diabetes need to monitor their blood sugar levels frequently to ensure levels are in the appropriate range to prevent both short- and long-term complications. Blurred vision, tiredness, frequent urination, and extreme thirst may result if insulin levels rise too high. If they reach extremely high levels, a condition called hyperglycemic hyperosmolar state (HHS) develops, resulting in dangerous dehydration. Diabetic ketoacidosis (DKA) may also develop when glucose levels get too high. Diabetic ketoacidosis results when the body becomes starved for energy and breaks down its muscles for the energy it needs. The breakdown of the muscles causes a buildup of blood acids called ketones. Diabetic ketoacidosis is a dangerous condition that can be fatal if left untreated.

Another short-term complication is hypoglycemia, or low blood sugar. Those taking insulin also need to be aware of the signs of hypoglycemia, which results when blood sugar levels fall too low. Some of the symptoms of hypoglycemia include confusion, shakiness, dizziness, sweating, headache, anxiety, and hunger. Patients should check blood glucose levels often and be aware of the signs of hypoglycemia so they can quickly treat it by ingesting a form of sugar. Many patients carry glucose tablets to take when they experience hypoglycemia. If glucose tablets are not available, then it is important to find foods that contain at least 15 grams of carbohydrates that are mostly sugar or simple carbohydrates but do not have a lot of fat. Fruit juice, hard candy, pretzels, crackers, raisins, and honey can also raise glucose levels quickly. If not treated properly, a person with hypoglycemia may get worse and lose consciousness, resulting in the need for immediate emergency attention.

Patients with uncontrolled diabetes are more likely to experience serious health complications. Long-term complications will develop over time due to high blood glucose levels. These patients are at an increased risk of heart disease, stroke, kidney failure, high blood pressure, eye problems (retinopathy), nerve problems (neuropathy), and gum disease.

Working with the Health Care Team

Proper management of diabetes is essential to avoid short- and long-term complications of the disease and to have a good quality of life. Those with any health condition including diabetes should become actively involved in their health care. Patients should work with their health care team to learn how to manage their disease effectively. Patients with diabetes may see a variety of health care providers, including endocrinologists, family practice doctors, dietitians, eye doctors, and others. It is essential for patients to establish a good rapport with their health care providers so they feel as though they can communicate easily with them. Asking questions about their health is very important to understanding the medical aspects of diabetes and its associated treatment and management so patients will be compliant with their prescribed therapy. The National Patient Safety Foundation's "Ask Me 3" is a wonderful resource for patients (and providers) that provides tips for communicating and encourages patients to ask three questions (National Patient Safety Foundation, 2012):

1. What is my main problem?
2. What do I need to do?
3. Why is it important for me to do this?

Additional tips for clear communication can be found on their website, http://www.npsf.org/for-healthcare-professionals/programs/ask-me-3/.

Patients should also strive to learn more about their condition through reading quality print and web resources to fill in any knowledge gaps and become as familiar as possible with diabetes. Librarians can be instrumental in encouraging patients to become active participants in learning about their condition.

Conducting the Diabetes Reference Interview

Often patients may approach the librarian for information after they receive their diagnosis or after they have tried to search for information on their own. Patients may be very upset and emotional about their diagnosis, making communication with them more difficult. Many people will have a question about their diagnosis

Reference Interview— Questions for the Librarian to Ask

- Is the patient a child or an adult?
- Who will be reading/viewing the information (adult, child, senior)?
- What type of diabetes does the patient have? (If the patient is pregnant, clarify the type of diabetes—preexisting type 1 or type 2 diabetes or gestational diabetes.)
- What has the patient learned about diabetes so far?
- What else would the patient like to learn about the condition?
- What type of information would the patient like to find—websites, books, printouts, videos, audio?

but are unsure how to phrase the question properly, so they end up not asking their intended question. Librarians should provide the patient with a safe, welcoming environment and listen thoroughly to what the patient says to them. After listening to the patient, the librarian should make sure to ask open-ended questions. Open-ended questions will help the librarian obtain additional information about the knowledge level of patients so they can connect them to the resources that will fulfill their information needs.

Be aware that patients may be experiencing some confusion about what type of diabetes they have. Medical jargon is often new to many patients, and they may forget or not understand what they were told by their doctor. Also, patients tend to think of "diabetes" as one disease, so librarians should ask patients which type of diabetes they are diagnosed with and, if patients do not know the specific type, then refer them to their doctor's office to obtain this information. In this case, librarians can suggest that patients call the clinic and ask about their specific diagnosis. In addition, librarians can give library coupons or information prescriptions to patients or health care providers. Library coupons and information prescriptions provide information about the location and hours of the library and contain a section for health care providers to fill in the name of the diagnosis, condition, treatment, test, or therapy for which the patient wishes to receive information. The health care provider can fill in the coupon or information prescription and the patient can bring the completed coupon back to the library to receive information.

When assisting women who are pregnant with finding diabetes information, it is important to ask questions to discern what type of diabetes they have. Gestational diabetes occurs in women who did not have type 1 or type 2 diabetes before pregnancy. The librarian should find out if the woman has a diagnosis of gestational diabetes, or if she is pregnant and also has type 1 or type 2 diabetes.

A disease called diabetes insipidus shares some common symptoms of diabetes mellitus, but diabetes insipidus is a rare disease in which the kidneys are unable to conserve water, leading to increased thirst and urination. Even though diabetes mellitus and diabetes insipidus share the term *diabetes* in their names, they are two entirely different and unrelated diseases. While conducting the reference interview, it is important to make the distinction between the two diseases to determine whether patients are seeking information about the more common diabetes mellitus, which patients often refer to as "sugar diabetes," or about diabetes insipidus.

Also, while conducting the reference interview, it is important to ask about the age of the patient and for whom the information is intended. Often a parent will approach, asking for information, and will ask only a general question, such as "Do you have any information about diabetes?" It is also important to ask which type of diabetes has been diagnosed and whether the patient is a child or an adult, so you can connect the person with the most appropriate resources.

Asking patrons who will be reading the information (e.g., an adult or a child) allows you to select information at the appropriate level. To refine the resource search further, you can ask them if they would prefer to read books, look at websites, or view videos, and then ask what level of information they feel most comfortable accessing—lay level, intermediate, or professional materials. Also, because diabetes can cause vision problems, you may want to ask patrons if they would like large-print materials. For additional information on conducting the reference interview, see the National Network of Libraries of Medicine's "Reference Interview Resources," found at http://nnlm.gov/archive/healthinfoquest/help/interviews.html.

Evaluating Websites

The websites found in this book provide patients with reliable, authoritative, and unbiased information. Often, though, patients insist on searching with Google or another search engine to find information. Librarians should strongly encourage patients who would like to conduct further research to become knowledgeable about conducting online searches, especially when searching for something as important as health information.

A Google search of the term "diabetes" yields more than 61 million results. Reading even a fraction of those results is a daunting task, and often many of the results may be sites of poor or dubious quality. Librarians and patients searching for information on the web should use methods to filter the search results to select only quality websites. Patients should learn how to evaluate any medical site they find online before using it to make health decisions.

One way to narrow a search is to use the search engine's Advanced Search tool. Users can often narrow their searches by combining search terms. Instead of entering the general term "diabetes," users should instead try combining "type 1" and "treatment" along with the term "diabetes" to narrow their results to information about type 1 diabetes treatment. The Advanced Search tool also allows limiting results to certain domains, such as .gov or .edu, which can narrow the search further and eliminate commercial sites.

It is important for online searchers to know that anyone can develop a webpage and not all sites are created equally—some sites contain inaccurate and harmful information and others may contain biased information aiming only to sell a product. Also, it is important to note that users should not use blogs, electronic discussion lists, and online support sites as a source for diabetes health information. Blogs are usually written by laypeople, and these people may be suffering from the condition and looking to share their story and experiences with diabetes, so the medical information may not be reliable. Likewise, electronic discussion lists and online support sites for diabetes are usually composed of laypeople with diabetes. Again, the medical information that patients provide may be inaccurate. In general, it is a good idea to avoid using these types of sites as sources of health information.

When a search result looks relevant, it is important to evaluate the website before using the information to make any medical decisions. Evaluation should focus on six components of the site: purpose/motivation, authorship, accuracy, currency, navigability/ease of use, and spelling/grammar.

1. Purpose/motivation: Find out the author's or sponsor's purpose or motivation for the site. Usually this can be found in the "About Us" section of the site. Check to see who actually sponsors the site and if it is a commercial (.com), organizational (.org), educational (.edu), or governmental (.gov) entity.

2. Author: Look for the author's credentials. Is the author qualified to write about diabetes information? Check to see if there is a qualified review board to examine the information provided on the site.

3. Accuracy: Verify the accuracy of the site by checking it against information found in print resources and other reputable online resources.

4. Currency: The information contained in the site should be current. Pages should be updated frequently to reflect current medical practices on the topic. Usually webpages contain a date at the bottom of the page.

5. Navigability/ease of use: The site should be easy to navigate between pages and links and generally easy to use.

6. Spelling/grammar: It is good practice to avoid sites with multiple spelling and grammar errors.

For additional information on evaluating websites, consult the following sites:

- FamilyDoctor.org—"Health Information on the Web: Finding Reliable Information," http://familydoctor.org/familydoctor/en/healthcare-management/self-care/health-information-on-the-web-finding-reliable-information.printerview.html
- Medical Library Association—"Resources: A User's Guide to Finding and Evaluating Health Information on the Web," http://www.mlanet.org/resources/userguide.html

- MedlinePlus—"Guide to Healthy Web Surfing," http://www.nlm.nih.gov/medlineplus/healthywebsurfing.html

Summary

It is important for those with diabetes to become familiar with the condition and their specific type of diabetes. Proper management of diabetes can help prevent complications from occurring. Librarians assisting patients should also become familiar with the different types of diabetes to aid in conducting the reference interview. Most important, librarians should direct patients to reputable sites for finding information online and teach those who wish to search online how to evaluate websites so they can find reliable information about their condition.

Information Sources

Selected Print Resources

➤ American Diabetes Association. 2010. *Diabetes A to Z: What You Need to Know about Diabetes—Simply Put*. 6th ed. Alexandria, VA: American Diabetes Association.
This resource provides information on a variety of diabetes-related topics for those who are newly diagnosed and those who want to learn more about a specific topic. Listed alphabetically, topics include A1C testing, employment rights, healthy eating, insulin, medications, pregnancy, sleep, stroke, and weight loss, among others.

➤ American Diabetes Association. 2011. *American Diabetes Association Complete Guide to Diabetes*. 5th ed. Alexandria, VA: American Diabetes Association.
This book provides basic information about the different types of diabetes, as well as information about diagnosis, symptoms, testing, management, insulin, glucose monitoring, healthy eating, exercise, complications, and coping.

➤ Beaser, Richard. 2005. *The Joslin Guide to Diabetes: A Program for Managing Your Treatment*. New York: Fireside.
Patients will find this a valuable resource for finding information about understanding the types of diabetes, as well as specific information on therapy, diet, exercise, glucose monitoring, complications, insulin, special challenges, and living well with the disease.

➤ Bryer-Ash, Michael. 2011. *100 Questions and Answers about Diabetes*. Sudbury, MA: Jones and Bartlett.
In question-and-answer format, this book explains what diabetes is and the differences between type 1 and type 2. Patients can learn more about diabetes complications, treatments, glucose monitoring, living with the condition, special situations, and caring for a family member. The book also offers additional resources.

➤ Collazo-Clavell, Maria. 2009. *Mayo Clinic The Essential Diabetes Book: How to Prevent, Control, and Live Well with Diabetes*. Rochester, MN: Mayo Clinic.
Patients can learn more about diabetes, including information about both type 1 and type 2 and their differences. Chapters cover prediabetes, prevention, symptoms, risk factors, complications, glucose control, healthy eating, physical activity, insulin therapy, testing, and special issues.

➤ Levin, Marvin E., and Michael A. Pfeifer. 2009. *The Uncomplicated Guide to Diabetes Complications*. 3rd ed. Alexandria, VA: American Diabetes Association.
Beginning with a general overview of diabetes and prediabetes, this resource provides information on acute complications and chronic complications of diabetes. The acute complications section informs about DKA, HHS, lactic acidosis, and low blood glucose. The chronic complications section includes information about cardiovascular, eye, nerve, kidney, gastrointestinal, fatty liver, sexual, skin, bone, and oral complications. There is also information about metabolic syndrome, polycystic ovary syndrome, cancer, sleep disturbance, infections, Alzheimer's disease, and psychosocial complications associated with diabetes.

➤ Mertig, Rita Girouard. 2011. *What Nurses Know…Diabetes*. New York: Demos Health.
Following an overview of the types of diabetes, this resource provides information on diet and physical activity for those with diabetes. It also covers information about diabetes medications, glucose monitoring, and avoiding complications.

➤ Stachowiak, Julie. 2011. *The Diabetes Manifesto: Take Charge of Your Life*. New York: Demos Medical.
The authors not only provide information about diabetes but also give patients tips and self-management skills for living with the condition. Patients can learn ways to take charge of their condition and live a healthy life.

➤ Warshaw, Hope. 2009. *Real-Life Guide to Diabetes: Practical Answers to Your Diabetes Problems*. Alexandria, VA: American Diabetes Association.
This resource provides a variety of information for patients about understanding the condition. It covers eating healthy, staying active, taking medications, and avoiding complications. The book also contains information about finding a health care team and support and details on preventing and delaying long-term diabetes problems.

Selected Web Resources

General

➤ American Diabetes Association, http://www.diabetes.org/
The American Diabetes Association website provides patients an overview of the different types of diabetes. In addition, the site contains information about statistics, treatment, care, parents and kids, medication, complications, glucose

control, genetics, A1C, and living with diabetes. Those with diabetes or living with someone with diabetes will find the ADA an excellent starting point for learning about the condition.

➤ Canadian Diabetes Association, http://www.diabetes.ca/
Patients can find information about the different types of diabetes and learn how to manage their condition through medications, checking blood glucose levels, and following a healthy lifestyles program. For more comprehensive information, the site links to additional fact sheets about insulin therapy, and managing glucose and the highs and lows of blood glucose levels. Users of the site can also learn more about daily life with diabetes.

➤ Centers for Disease Control and Prevention—"Diabetes Public Health Resource," http://www.cdc.gov/diabetes/consumer/index.htm
The CDC provides links to a variety of diabetes health information including prediabetes, eating right, staying healthy, being active, financial concerns, and complications. This site also contains information about diabetes research and statistics.

➤ Centers for Disease Control and Prevention—"Take Charge of Your Diabetes," http://www.cdc.gov/diabetes/pubs/tcyd/index.htm
This resource covers diabetes control, glucose management, vaccinations, pregnancy, and women's health. It also provides information about diabetes complications such as diabetic eye disease, kidney problems, heart and blood vessel problems, nerve damage, foot problems, and dental disease. Also included are glucose log sheets, test goals, sick day records, a glossary, and a diabetes information resource list.

➤ Cleveland Clinic—"Diabetes Basics," http://my.clevelandclinic.org/disorders/Diabetes_Mellitus/hic_Diabetes_Basics.aspx
Included in this site is information about diabetes basics, prevention, types, diagnosis, treatment, management, diet, and complications. The site also contains a glossary of terms and links to diabetes resources.

➤ Diabetes Education Online, http://dtc.ucsf.edu/
Created by the University of California Diabetes Teaching Center, the website provides online instruction and resources for people with diabetes. The section on the types of diabetes provides information about understanding diabetes, health management, and diabetes treatment. Self-assessment quizzes are provided at the end of each section.

➤ Diabetes UK, http://www.diabetes.org.uk/
A U.K. nonprofit organization devoted to treatment and care of people with diabetes, the website provides a range of information about diabetes. The website contains information for the newly diagnosed, an overview of the condition and

living with diabetes, information about healthy eating and physical activity, managing diabetes, complications, and treatments.

➤ dLife, http://www.dlife.com/
This site provides a wealth of information for patients with diabetes. Included in the site is information about the types of diabetes, living with diabetes, avoiding complications, drugs and treatment, nutrition, and physical activity. There are also links to a variety of videos.

➤ Joslin Diabetes Center—"Joslin's Library: Managing Your Diabetes," http://www .joslin.org/info/managing_diabetes.html
A teaching and research affiliate of Harvard Medical School, the Joslin Diabetes Center provides website users with a variety of useful information about diabetes. Patients can read about the types of diabetes, learn more when newly diagnosed, and view information on insulin, high glucose, diet, nutrition, complications, monitoring glucose, and living with diabetes.

➤ Lab Tests Online—"Diabetes," http://labtestsonline.org/understanding/conditions/ diabetes
Lab Tests Online provides information on a variety of tests for various conditions, including diabetes-related testing. The main section on diabetes contains an overview of the condition, information about the three types of diabetes, signs and symptoms, and treatment. Of importance on this site is the section on diabetes-related tests. This section contains additional information to help patients under-stand the different tests they may need, including glucose, A1C, hemoglobin, random urine samples, microalbumin, ketone, kidney function, insulin, C-peptide, and lipid tests. The website contains information about why each test might be needed, how the test is conducted, and what the test result means.

➤ MedlinePlus—"Health Topics—Diabetes," http://www.nlm.nih.gov/medlineplus/ diabetes.html
Produced by the National Library of Medicine and the National Institutes of Health, MedlinePlus provides information about the different types of diabetes, hosts an interactive tutorial, and includes videos and handouts that cover everything from prevention to different aspects of living with diabetes.

➤ National Diabetes Education Program, http://ndep.nih.gov/
This site is a partnership of the National Institutes of Health and the Centers for Disease Control and Prevention. Users of this site can find a broad variety of diabetes publications.

➤ National Diabetes Information Clearinghouse, http://www.diabetes.niddk.nih.gov/
The site, a service of the National Institute of Diabetes and Digestive and Kidney Diseases and the National Institutes of Health, provides a broad range of diabetes information topics starting with an A-to-Z list of subject areas. Readers can obtain

an overview of diabetes; learn about prediabetes, treatment, meal planning, medications, glucose monitoring, and complications; and access links to patient organizations and interactive tools. The site provides a link to easy-to-read publications and Spanish-language resources.

Ethnic Groups Affected by Diabetes

➤ Centers for Disease Control and Prevention—"Native Diabetes Wellness Program," http://www.cdc.gov/diabetes/projects/diabetes-wellness.htm
The page provides links to a variety of resources including handouts and videos. Many of the resources focus on prevention of type 2 diabetes.

➤ Indian Health Service—Division of Diabetes Treatment and Prevention, http://www.ihs.gov/MedicalPrograms/Diabetes/
Much of the information on this site is aimed at the health care provider, yet patients can also find useful information. There are links to patient education materials, online magazines, and fact sheets.

➤ National Diabetes Information Clearinghouse—"Diabetes in African Americans," http://diabetes.niddk.nih.gov/dm/pubs/africanamerican/index.aspx
This page contains a variety of information useful to African Americans with diabetes, including resources on sickle-cell trait and diabetes, risks factors for type 2 diabetes, prevention, and kidney disease.

➤ National Diabetes Information Clearinghouse—"Diabetes in American Indians and Alaska Natives," http://diabetes.niddk.nih.gov/dm/pubs/americanindian/index.aspx
This page contains a variety of publications useful to American Indians and Alaska Natives interested in finding out about diabetes. Publications contain information about risk factors for type 2 diabetes, prevention, and managing diabetes.

➤ National Diabetes Information Clearinghouse—"Diabetes in Asian and Pacific Islander Americans," http://diabetes.niddk.nih.gov/dm/pubs/asianamerican/index.aspx
This page provides links to a variety of information pertaining to Asian Americans and Pacific Islanders with diabetes. Users of the site can find information about preventing diabetes, controlling diabetes, managing diabetes, and preventing complications.

➤ National Diabetes Information Clearinghouse—"Diabetes in Hispanics/Latinos," http://diabetes.niddk.nih.gov/dm/pubs/hispanicamerican/index.aspx
This page provides links to information on diabetes in the Hispanic and Latino population. The site links to a wide range of publications covering information on diabetes statistics, risk factors, controlling diabetes, and preventing complications. The information is available in both English and Spanish.

Children and Diabetes

See CHAPTER 6, CHILDREN AND DIABETES

Older Adults and Diabetes

➤ National Institute on Aging—"Diabetes in Older People—A Disease You Can Manage," http://www.nia.nih.gov/health/publication/diabetes-older-people-disease-you-can-manage
The page provides information about diabetes, prediabetes, symptoms, and diagnostic tests. The articles present information about managing the condition that is aimed at older adults. In addition, the site discusses Medicare and how to get more information on services that Medicare covers. The site contains links to other useful resources as well.

Women and Diabetes

See also CHAPTERS 5, GESTATIONAL DIABETES, AND 25, SEXUAL AND UROLOGICAL PROBLEMS

➤ WomensHealth.gov—"Asian-American Women and Diabetes," http://www.womenshealth.gov/minority/asianamerican/diabetes.cfm
Women of Asian heritage with diabetes will find this page helpful. The site contains an overview of diabetes and tips on living with the condition and proper management. It also contains links to additional information about diabetes.

➤ WomensHealth.gov—"Diabetes: Frequently Asked Questions," http://www.womenshealth.gov/faq/diabetes.pdf
This informational handout, aimed at women, explains type 1 and type 2 diabetes and prediabetes. It also covers risk factors, testing, symptoms, management, care, blood glucose, and prevention.

Glossaries

➤ American Diabetes Association—"Common Terms," http://www.diabetes.org/diabetes-basics/common-terms/
This page contains an extensive list of diabetes-related terms and definitions. The list of terms is alphabetical, and users of the site can click on the letter range to view a list of words beginning with that letter.

➤ Canadian Diabetes Association—"Diabetes Dictionary," http://www.diabetes.ca/diabetes-and-you/what/dictionary/
Users of the page can find a list of diabetes terms and their definitions. The list of terms is alphabetical, and users can click on the letter beginning the word they wish to find.

➤ Cleveland Clinic—"Glossary of Diabetes Terms," http://my.clevelandclinic.org/disorders/Diabetes_Mellitus/hic_Diabetes_Glossary.aspx
The page provides an alphabetical list of common diabetes terms. Users of the site can scroll to find the term they wish to define.

➤ Medspeak Diabetes—"Deciphering Diabetes Medspeak," http://www.mlanet.org/pdf/diabetes1.pdf
This online brochure created by the Medical Library Association acquaints patients with common diabetes-related terms that are important for anyone with the condition to understand. The brochure also contains a list of additional diabetes websites.

➤ National Diabetes Information Clearinghouse—"Diabetes Dictionary," http://www.diabetes.niddk.nih.gov/dm/pubs/dictionary/
The page contains diabetes-related terms and definitions. Users of the site can click on the letter of the alphabet for the term they wish to define and will find a listing of terms beginning with that letter. There is also a pronunciation guide available.

Illustrations

Illustrations can greatly enhance print information and aid the layperson in understanding more about the anatomy, condition, or procedure being described.

➤ Diabetes Education Online—"Resource Materials: Illustrations," http://dtc.ucsf.edu/learning-library/resource-materials/#illustrations
This page contains links to a variety of handouts and illustrations. Included are illustrations showing the effect of insulin.

➤ Learning about Diabetes—"Handouts: Free Patient Downloads," http://learningaboutdiabetes.org/handouts.html
Users of this page can find a variety of illustrations. Topics include type 1 diabetes, type 2 diabetes, risk, healthy eating, medications, blood sugar, being active, prevention, and saving money.

➤ Mayo Clinic—"Diabetes," http://www.mayoclinic.com/health/diabetes/DS01121/TAB=multimedia
This page contains images, videos, and slide shows that are useful for showing to patients with lower literacy.

➤ MedlinePlus—"Diabetes," http://www.nlm.nih.gov/medlineplus/ency/article/001214.htm
Provided on this page are links to a variety of images. Patients can find handouts of images of the endocrine gland, diabetic retinopathy, the islet of Langerhans, blood tests, the pancreas, insulin pumps, glucose tests, diabetic blood circulation of the feet, food and insulin release, and monitoring.

Easy-to-Read Resources

➤ Healthy Roads Media—"Diabetes," http://www.healthyroadsmedia.org/topics/
diabetes.htm
Aimed at patients with low literacy, this page contains information about diabetes.
Handouts are very basic and written at a low reading level. There are short audio
clips of the handouts available as well. Diabetes topics include basics, diet and
exercise, medicine and glucose, pregnancy, risk factors, complications, insulin
dosage, injections, eye problems, nerve problems, and foot care.

➤ Learning about Diabetes, http://www.learningaboutdiabetes.org/
This website contains a variety of informational handouts and brochures on
diabetes written at a very low reading level. There are also illustrations available.

➤ MedlinePlus—"Diabetes—Introduction," http://www.nlm.nih.gov/medlineplus/
tutorials/diabetesintroduction/htm/index.htm
Patients can view this tutorial as an audiovisual interactive presentation or
download it as a PDF file to read online or print. The tutorial covers basic information about diabetes, symptoms, treatment, control, and complications.

➤ MedlinePlus—"Easy-to-Read," http://www.nlm.nih.gov/medlineplus/all_easy
toread.html
This page provides links to health information that is easy to read. Users can click
on the letter *D* and then scroll down the list to "Diabetes" to view the variety of
easy-to-read diabetes information. The site has general diabetes information
about both type 1 and type 2, as well as diabetes risk, prevention, pregnancy,
complications, medications, diet, and physical activity.

➤ National Institute of Diabetes and Digestive and Kidney Diseases—"Easy-to-Read
Publications," http://www2.niddk.nih.gov/HealthEducation/HealthEzToRead
This webpage links to a variety of handouts that are written in easy-to-read language.
Handouts include information about diabetes risk, medications, prevention, healthy
eating, gestational diabetes, physical activity, and type 1 and type 2 diabetes.

➤ Ohio State University Wexner Medical Center—"Patient Education Home,"
https://patienteducation.osumc.edu/Pages/Home.aspx
Patients can start by typing "diabetes" into the search box. This results in a list of
easy-to-read diabetes handouts. Topics include understanding diabetes, exercise,
pregnancy, medications, risk factors, insulin, meal planning, stress, glucose, and
low blood sugar.

Information in Other Languages

Multiple Languages

➤ Diabetes UK—"Diabetes Information in Different Languages," http://www
.diabetes.org.uk/Guide-to-diabetes/Information-in-different-languages1/

This page includes information about diabetes in more than twenty-two languages. There are links to information in languages such as Arabic, French, Hindi, Italian, Polish, Portuguese, Somali, and Turkish.

➤ Healthy Roads Media, http://www.healthyroadsmedia.org/
The website contains a variety of diabetes-related topics. Information can be found in many languages, including Amharic, Bosnian, Karen, Somali, and Spanish.

➤ MedlinePlus—"Diabetes—Multiple Languages," http://www.nlm.nih.gov/medline plus/languages/diabetes.html
MedlinePlus provides information about diabetes in more than two dozen languages, including American Sign Language, Chinese, French, Hmong, Japanese, Russian, Somali, Spanish, Thai, and Vietnamese. Topics include general information about diabetes, controlling diabetes, diabetes prevention, risk, using a glucose meter, and preventing complications.

Sign Language

➤ DeafMD—"Diabetes Mellitus, Type 1: What Is It?," http://www.deafmd.org/pub/ topic/Diabetes-Mellitus-Type-1/What-is-it, and "Diabetes Mellitus, Type 2: What Is It?," http://www.deafmd.org/pub/topic/Diabetes-Mellitus-Type-2/What-is-it
These pages provide information about type 1 and type 2 diabetes in American Sign Language. Written transcripts of the videos are also available.

Spanish

➤ American Association of Diabetes Educators—"AADE7™ Self-Care Behaviors Handouts," http://www.diabeteseducator.org/DiabetesEducation/Patient_Resources/ AADE7_PatientHandouts.html
This webpage provides self-care handouts written in English and in Spanish. Handouts cover topics such as healthy eating, being active, glucose monitoring, medications, reducing risks, and coping.

➤ DiabetesAtWork.org—"Fact Sheets," http://www.diabetesatwork.org/NextSteps/ FactSheets.cfm
Users of this site can find informational fact sheets in both English and Spanish. Spanish information includes information about diabetes type 1 and type 2, living with diabetes, controlling diabetes, and preventing complications.

➤ The Hormone Health Network—"Diabetes," http://www.hormone.org/Diabetes/
There are links to English and Spanish handouts from this webpage. Information includes exercise, glucose monitoring, insulin, nutrition, gestational diabetes, prediabetes, type 1 and type 2 diabetes, screening, and diabetes in children.

➤ Joslin Diabetes Center—"Newly Diagnosed," http://www.joslin.org/info/newly_ diagnosed.html
A section titled "En Espanol" contains links to information in the Spanish language.

There are question-and-answer pages and links to information about what diabetes is and how diabetes is diagnosed.

➤ Learning about Diabetes, http://www.learningaboutdiabetes.org/
Patients can download brochures about diabetes in the Spanish language. Brochures include information about what diabetes is, understanding blood sugar, exercise, healthy eating, and foot care.

➤ National Institute of Diabetes and Digestive and Kidney Diseases, http://www2 .niddk.nih.gov/HealthEducation/EnEspanol/default
This is an excellent resource for finding information written in the Spanish language about diabetes. The site contains an introduction to diabetes that includes information about the different types of diabetes. In addition, there are sections on treatment, complications, prevention, and also links to additional resources.

➤ Ohio State University Wexner Medical Center—"Patient Education Home," https://patienteducation.osumc.edu/Pages/Home.aspx
By typing "diabetes" in the search box and clicking on the "Select Other Language" drop-down menu, site visitors can find a variety of diabetes-related information in the Spanish language. Topics include diabetes basics, meal planning, medications, sick days, glucose, low blood sugar, insulin, pregnancy, complications, and many others.

Selected Audiovisual Resources

➤ American Association of Diabetes Educators—"AADE7™ Videos and Guide-books," http://www.diabeteseducator.org/DiabetesEducation/Patient_Resources/ VideosGuidebooks.html
The webpage contains videos and guidebooks for patients, their families, and their friends. The videos are short, covering self-care behaviors such as healthy eating, being active, monitoring, taking medication, problem solving, reducing risk, and healthy coping.

➤ Canadian Diabetes Association—"Healthy Living Series," http://www.diabetes .ca/diabetes-and-you/healthylivingseries/
These interactive learning modules allow users to work at their own pace to learn more about diabetes and living a healthy lifestyle. Modules include *What Is Diabetes?*; *Diabetes Care*; *Small Changes for Healthy Living*; *Diabetes and Mental Health*; and *Smoking and Diabetes*.

➤ *Diabetes: Common Condition*. 2005. Sherborn, MA: Aquarius Health Care Media. This 30-minute video covers general information about diabetes, complications, and management.

➤ Healthy Roads Media—"Diabetes," http://www.healthyroadsmedia.org/topics/ diabetes.htm

The site provides short audiovisual materials on a range of health topics, including diabetes. Clips include information on diabetes basics, controlling diabetes, complications, insulin, medication, and care.

➤ Insider Medicine, http://www.insidermedicine.com/
Insider Medicine offers short video clips on topics of interest to patients with diabetes.

➤ *Introduction to Diabetes: The Game Plan.* 2009. 3rd ed. Hunt Valley, MD: Milner Fenwick. Available at http://www.milner-fenwick.com/products/db75/index.asp. This short, thirteen-minute film provides general information about diabetes, including basics, diet, physical activity, medications, monitoring, and health care collaboration.

➤ MedlinePlus—"Interactive Health Tutorials," http://www.nlm.nih.gov/medline plus/tutorial.html
Under the heading "Diseases and Conditions" users of the site can scroll down to "Diabetes." Available media include tutorials about diabetes with an introduction and information on eye complications, foot care, and meal planning. Each tutorial includes a slide show with audio and the option to view and print the text version of the slide show.

Selected Periodicals

➤ *Diabetes Forecast* (ISSN: 0095-8301)
A monthly magazine by the American Diabetes Association, *Diabetes Forecast* provides articles pertinent to those with the disease. The articles mainly focus on healthy living through wellness, diet, and exercise. Patients can find articles and information about subscribing at their website: http://forecast.diabetes.org/.

➤ *Diabetes Self-Management* (ISSN: 0741-6253)
This bimonthly periodical by R.A. Rapaport Publishing provides up-to-date information on diabetes and diabetes-related topics such as nutrition, exercises, and drugs. Interested readers can access subscription information, articles, and recipes from their website: http://www.diabetesselfmanagement.com/.

References

Canadian Diabetes Association. 2012. "Diabetes and You." Canadian Diabetes Association. Accessed July 3. http://www.diabetes.ca/diabetes-and-you/.

Centers for Disease Control and Prevention. 2012. "Diabetes Data and Trends." Centers for Disease Control and Prevention. Accessed August 9. http://apps .nccd.cdc.gov/DDTSTRS/default.aspx.

Collazo-Clavell, M. 2009. *Mayo Clinic The Essential Diabetes Book: How to Prevent, Control, and Live Well with Diabetes.* Rochester, MN: Mayo Clinic.

Davis, E. 2009. *Gestational Diabetes: A Guide for Pregnant Women.* AHRQ Effective Healthcare Program. Rockville, MD: Agency for Healthcare Research and Quality. http://www.ahrq.gov/.

Diabetes Education Online. 2012. "What Is Type 2 Diabetes?" University of California, San Francisco. Accessed August 9. http://dtc.ucsf.edu/types-of-diabetes/type2/understanding-type-2-diabetes/what-is-type-2-diabetes/.

Mercer, A. 2012. "What Is Type 1 Diabetes?" Diabetes Monitor. May 15. http://www.diabetesmonitor.com/education-center/diabetes-basics/what-is-type-1-diabetes.htm.

National Patient Safety Foundation. 2012. "Ask Me 3." National Patient Safety Foundation. Accessed July 3. http://www.npsf.org/for-healthcare-professionals/programs/ask-me-3/.

Chapter 2

Type 1 Diabetes

Introduction

Previously referred to as juvenile-onset diabetes or insulin-dependent diabetes, type 1 diabetes is an autoimmune disorder. In type 1 diabetes, the immune system mistakenly attacks pancreatic beta cells, the insulin-producing cells in the pancreas, resulting in no insulin being produced by the pancreas. Of the 24 million people currently diagnosed with diabetes in the United States, only 5 to 10 percent have type 1 diabetes (Mercer, 2012).

Type 1 Diabetes Overview

Type 1 diabetes is a chronic metabolic condition for which patients need lifelong insulin therapy to survive. Typically, diagnosis of type 1 diabetes occurs when the patient is a child or young adult, but adults can also develop type 1 diabetes (Mercer, 2012). It is important for patients to become familiar with the causes, symptoms, diagnosis, and treatment, as these aspects of the disease differ in some cases from those of the other types of diabetes.

Causes

Unfortunately, the entire spectrum of factors that causes type 1 diabetes is not known by the medical community. Type 1 diabetes affects both males and females equally and is more common in Caucasians than in other ethnic groups. Heritability may be an issue, as there appears to be a 10 to 15 percent increase in the incidence of type 1 diabetes when there is diabetes in the family history. There are strong indicators that a person with a family member who has diabetes is more likely to develop diabetes than a person without a family history.

Researchers have identified certain mutated genes that make people more susceptible to developing type 1 diabetes. In very rare cases, an illness or injury to the pancreas may cause the development of type 1 diabetes. Other possible risk factors include viral exposure, autoantibodies, low vitamin D levels, and other diet-related issues. Some researchers believe a viral, environmental, or other trigger in an individual who is genetically susceptible may cause the immune reaction that starts the destruction of pancreatic beta cells (MedlinePlus, 2011).

Symptoms

Symptoms of type 1 diabetes typically develop over a short duration and can mimic those of other conditions. Although some people are asymptomatic, the most common symptoms of type 1 diabetes include frequent urination, unusual thirst, extreme hunger, unusual weight loss, extreme fatigue, nausea, vomiting, and irritability. Some patients may experience blurred vision, dry and itchy skin, or tingling in the hands and feet. Any person experiencing these symptoms should consult a physician to obtain an accurate diagnosis, so proper management of the disease can begin immediately.

Diagnosis

To determine whether a patient has diabetes, a medical provider will run simple blood tests for diagnostic purposes, including a glycated hemoglobin (A1C) test and a random plasma glucose test or a fasting plasma glucose test. The A1C test indicates the patient's average blood sugar level during the past two to three months. Patients with an A1C value greater than or equal to 6.5 percent receive the diagnosis of diabetes. The random plasma glucose test, which can take place at any time during the day because it does not require fasting, measures the amount of glucose in the blood at a specific time. A random blood sugar test result that is greater than or equal to 200 mg/dL is abnormal and, when occurring along with classic symptoms of the disease, indicates the patient has diabetes. The patient may also have a fasting plasma glucose test, which is the preferred diagnostic method. This test usually takes place in the morning—and only after the patient fasts for at least eight hours. Extra glucose remains in the blood even after fasting in patients with diabetes. Those with a fasting plasma glucose higher than or equal to 126 mg/dL after two separate tests receive the diagnosis of diabetes. The American Diabetes Association recommends that an additional test take place on a different date—and which must also have abnormal results—to confirm the diagnosis of diabetes (American Diabetes Association, 2011).

To determine which type of diabetes the patient has, blood tests will look for the presence of autoantibodies common in type 1 diabetes. The presence of ketones, a waste product when the body breaks down fats for energy, in the urine can also indicate the patient has type 1 diabetes rather than type 2 diabetes; however, ketones sometimes are present in patients with type 2 diabetes.

Treatment

Although type 1 diabetes has no cure, treating the disease correctly with insulin therapy can be an effective means to control it. The two main goals of treatment are to keep blood glucose levels as close to normal as possible and to prevent diabetic ketoacidosis (DKA). Insulin therapy occurs either as an injection under the skin using a syringe or an insulin pen or through an insulin pump. Types include rapid-acting, short-acting, intermediate, and long-acting insulin. Depending on the individual situation, the patient's doctor may prescribe other medications, such as aspirin therapy, high blood pressure medications, and cholesterol-lowering medications, in addition to insulin (Mayo Clinic, 2012).

Effective diabetes management includes insulin therapy in conjunction with lifestyle changes, such as improving diet and committing to regular exercise. Patients with diabetes need to eat a diet that includes plenty of fruits, vegetables, and whole grains and avoid foods that are high in carbohydrates with low nutritional value. Regular exercise and physical activity are also essential for anyone with diabetes. Physical activity helps lower blood glucose and blood pressure and also helps burn calories. Doctors recommend that patients be active every day, including stretching, walking, and doing other aerobic exercises. Before beginning any exercise program, patients should consult with their doctor.

Patients need to take an active role in managing their type 1 diabetes by frequently monitoring their glucose levels; working with their health care team; and regularly visiting their physician, dentist, and eye care specialist. Because high glucose levels cause many of the associated type 1 diabetes complications, proper management of diabetes is essential (Canadian Diabetes Association, 2012). If patients experience high glucose levels for an extended period of time and do not seek treatment, serious complications such as coma or death can occur. Patients with uncontrolled diabetes are more likely to experience complications such as heart disease, stroke, kidney failure, high blood pressure, eye disease, nerve damage, and gum disease.

Patients with diabetes need to frequently monitor their blood sugar levels using a glucose meter to ensure levels are in the target range. In addition, the A1C test indicates the average blood sugar level for the past two to three months. The A1C test is used to monitor how well patients are controlling their blood sugar levels by measuring the percentage of blood sugar that is attached to hemoglobin. In the normal range, this test result should be less than 5.7 percent (Mayo Clinic, 2012). Even if patients are taking insulin correctly and eating appropriately, factors such as food intake, sickness, exercise and physical activity, hormonal fluctuations, alcohol use, and even stress can affect blood sugar levels. Blurred vision, tiredness, frequent urination, and extreme thirst may result if blood glucose levels are too high. Patients may then need to take an extra dose of insulin to lower the blood glucose level to a normal range. Conversely, hypoglycemia can result if blood sugar levels fall too low. Symptoms of hypoglycemia include feeling tired; being unable to speak clearly; sweating; feeling hungry; experiencing anxiety, weakness, dizziness, or twitching; having seizures; and becoming pale. Some people with hypoglycemia may lose consciousness. Proper management and control of glucose levels can help prevent or delay the complications associated with diabetes.

Summary

Type 1 diabetes is an autoimmune disorder resulting from the inability of the pancreas to produce insulin. Diagnosis usually occurs in childhood but can also take place in adults. Those with type 1 diabetes need lifelong insulin therapy. Researchers are uncertain of the exact causes of diabetes, but certain ethnic groups and family history may be associated with the condition. While the symptoms of diabetes can mimic other conditions, people should be aware of the symptoms of type 1 diabetes, which include frequent urination, unusual thirst, extreme hunger, unusual weight loss, fatigue, nausea, vomiting, and irritability. Those with symptoms should seek medical care to obtain a proper diagnosis. It is important for those diagnosed with the condition to manage their blood glucose levels. Keeping blood glucose levels as close to normal as possible helps prevent complications associated with type 1 diabetes from developing.

Information Sources

Selected Print Resources

➤ American Diabetes Association. 2010. *Diabetes A to Z: What You Need to Know about Diabetes—Simply Put*. Alexandria, VA: American Diabetes Association.
Although this book is helpful for patients with either type 1 or type 2 diabetes, patients newly diagnosed with type 1 diabetes will find this resource useful. The book covers topics such as glucose management, complications, coping with diabetes, diet, physical activity, insulin, smoking, and medications. Entries for each topic are a brief one to three pages and are listed alphabetically. Those new to the condition may have many questions about diabetes. Using this resource, newly diagnosed patients can quickly turn to a topic of interest to learn more without being overwhelmed with information.

➤ American Diabetes Association. 2011. *American Diabetes Association Complete Guide to Diabetes*. 5th ed. Alexandria, VA: American Diabetes Association.
This book provides basic information about the different types of diabetes, as well as information about diagnosis, symptoms, testing, management, insulin, glucose monitoring, healthy eating, exercise, complications, and coping.

➤ Beaser, Richard. 2005. *The Joslin Guide to Diabetes: A Program for Managing Your Treatment*. New York: Fireside Publishers.
Patients will find this a valuable resource for finding information about understanding the types of diabetes, as well as specific information on therapy, diet, exercise, glucose monitoring, complications, insulin, special challenges, and living well with the disease.

➤ Bryer-Ash, Michael. 2011. *100 Questions and Answers about Diabetes*. Sudbury, MA: Jones and Bartlett Publishers.

In question-and-answer format, this book explains what diabetes is and the differences between type 1 and type 2. Patients with type 1 can learn more about diabetes complications, treatments, glucose monitoring, living with the condition, special situations, and caring for a family member. The book also offers additional resources.

➤ Collazo-Clavell, Maria. 2009. *Mayo Clinic The Essential Diabetes Book: How to Prevent, Control, and Live Well with Diabetes*. Rochester, MN: Mayo Clinic.

Patients can learn more about diabetes, including information about both type 1 and type 2 and their differences. Chapters cover complications, glucose control, healthy eating, physical activity, insulin therapy, testing, and special issues.

➤ Levin, Marvin E., and Michael A. Pfeifer. 2009. *The Uncomplicated Guide to Diabetes Complications*. 3rd ed. Alexandria, VA: American Diabetes Association.

This resource will help patients with either type 1 or type 2 diabetes. Those with type 1 will find this book beneficial because preventing diabetes-related complications is important. Beginning with a general overview of diabetes and prediabetes, this resource provides information on acute complications and chronic complications of diabetes. The acute complications section informs about DKA, hyperglycemic hyperosmolar state (HHS), lactic acidosis, and low blood glucose. The chronic complications section includes information about cardiovascular, eye, nerve, kidney, gastrointestinal, fatty liver, sexual, skin, bone, and oral complications. There is also information about metabolic syndrome, polycystic ovary syndrome, cancer, sleep disturbance, infections, Alzheimer's disease, and psychosocial complications associated with diabetes.

➤ Mertig, Rita Girouard. 2011. *What Nurses Know... Diabetes*. New York: Demos Health.

Written by a nurse who also has type 1 diabetes, this resource provides beneficial information about the condition to those with either type 1 or type 2 diabetes. Following an overview of the types of diabetes, this resource provides information on diet and physical activity for those with diabetes. It also covers information about diabetes medications, glucose monitoring, and avoiding complications.

Selected Web Resources

➤ American Diabetes Association—"Diabetes Basics: Type 1 Diabetes," http://www .diabetes.org/diabetes-basics/type-1/

The American Diabetes Association website provides patients with a brief overview of type 1 diabetes. In addition, the site contains information about statistics, treatment, care, parents and kids, medication, complications, glucose control, genetics, A1C, and living with diabetes. Those newly diagnosed with type 1 diabetes will find the ADA an excellent starting point for learning about the condition.

➤ Canadian Diabetes Association—"Type 1 Diabetes: The Basics," http://www .diabetes.ca/diabetes-and-you/living/just-diagnosed/type1/
Patients can find information about type 1 diabetes and learn how to manage their condition through insulin therapy, checking blood glucose levels, and following a healthy lifestyles program. For more comprehensive information, the site links to additional fact sheets about insulin therapy, and managing glucose and the highs and lows of blood glucose levels. Users of the site can also learn more about daily life with diabetes.

➤ Diabetes Education Online—"Type 1 Diabetes," http://dtc.ucsf.edu/types-of-diabetes/type1/understanding-type-1-diabetes/
Created by the University of California Diabetes Teaching Center, the website provides online instruction and resources for people with diabetes. The section on type 1 diabetes provides informational sections about understanding diabetes, health management, and diabetes treatment. Self-assessment quizzes are provided at the end of each section.

➤ Diabetes Monitor—"What Is Type 1 Diabetes?," http://www.diabetesmonitor .com/education-center/diabetes-basics/what-is-type-1-diabetes
Patients and family members can learn about a variety of diabetes-related topics on the Diabetes Monitor website. Included in the site are articles about understanding and managing type 1 diabetes. Patients can learn about diabetes symptoms, supplies, treatments, diet, and lifestyle.

➤ dLife—"Type 1 Diabetes," http://www.dlife.com/diabetes/type-1
This resource provides an array of beneficial information for patients with type 1 diabetes. The section on type 1 provides information about the condition and its causes. Users of the site can learn more about the symptoms of type 1 diabetes and its warning signs. In addition, information is available about diagnosis of type 1 diabetes, as is information about blood tests and the meaning of the test results. The site also details type 1 diabetes treatment, as well as insulin, insulin injections, and lifestyle changes. The site also provides information about many of the complications associated with the condition, including vision, heart, kidney, sexual, oral, digestive, skin, nerve, and sleep effects.

➤ Hormone Health Network—"Hormones and You: Type 1 Diabetes," http://www .hormone.org/Resources/Patient_Guides/upload/FS_DIA_Type1_Diabetes_EN-web-2.pdf
The Hormone Health Network provides a one-page handout with an overview of type 1 diabetes. The handout explains differences between type 1 and type 2,

symptoms, diagnosis, treatment, and glucose monitoring. A Spanish language version is also available.

➤ Joslin Diabetes Center—"Common Questions about Type 1 Diabetes," http://www.joslin.org/info/common_questions_about_type_1_diabetes.html
A teaching and research affiliate of Harvard Medical School, the Joslin Diabetes Center provides website users with a variety of useful information about diabetes. Patients can view the frequently asked questions about type 1 diabetes, learn more about the disease when newly diagnosed, and view information on insulin, high glucose, diet, nutrition, and living with diabetes.

➤ Mayo Clinic—"Type 1 Diabetes," http://www.mayoclinic.com/health/type-1-diabetes/DS00329/
The Mayo Clinic website provides information on a variety of health-related topics, including diabetes. The discussion about type 1 diabetes provides a succinct overview of the condition followed by information about symptoms, causes, risk factors, complications, tests, diagnosis, treatment, drugs, diet, exercise, blood sugar monitoring, and support.

➤ MedlinePlus—"Type 1 Diabetes," http://www.nlm.nih.gov/medlineplus/ency/article/000305.htm
MedlinePlus provides a detailed overview of type 1 diabetes. Patients can find out about the condition, causes, symptoms, diagnosis, treatment, management, and care.

➤ National Diabetes Information Clearinghouse—"Your Guide to Diabetes: Type 1 and Type 2," http://www.diabetes.niddk.nih.gov/dm/pubs/type1and2/index.aspx
Patients will find this easy-to-read guide an excellent starting point for learning about their condition. The guide explains the differences between type 1 and type 2 diabetes; describes the signs and symptoms of the disease; provides information on disease management through insulin, diet, and physical activity; and supplies tips on living with the disease.

Selected Audiovisual Resources

➤ Canadian Diabetes Association—"Introducing the Healthy Living Series: Take Charge of Your Health Now!," http://www.diabetes.ca/diabetes-and-you/healthylivingseries/
Patients can access interactive learning modules on a range of topics. Modules include diabetes basics, care, and healthy living with diabetes.

➤ Joslin Diabetes Center—Joslin Interactive Learning Center, http://www.joslin.org/ape/CourseListing/OnLineCourseListing.asp
The Learning Center contains a selection of interactive audio tutorials covering topics such as "What Is Diabetes?," "An Overview of Diabetes," and "Managing Blood Glucose."

➤ Patient Education Institute—"Diabetes—Introduction," http://www.nlm.nih .gov/medlineplus/tutorials/diabetesintroduction/htm/index.htm
Published by the Patient Education Institute and accessed through MedlinePlus, this interactive audiovisual tutorial provides an explanation of diabetes. A short section discusses type 1 diabetes. The tutorial also provides information on controlling diabetes through insulin therapy, diet, and exercise, and describes complications associated with the condition and signs of hypoglycemia.

References

American Diabetes Association. 2011. *American Diabetes Association Complete Guide to Diabetes*. 5th ed. Alexandria, VA: American Diabetes Association.

Canadian Diabetes Association. 2012. "Type 1 Diabetes: The Basics." Canadian Diabetes Association. Accessed July 4. http://www.diabetes.ca/diabetes-and-you/ living/just-diagnosed/type1/.

Mayo Clinic. 2012. "Type 1 Diabetes." Mayo Foundation for Medical Education and Research. January 25. http://www.mayoclinic.com/health/type-1-diabetes/ DS00329/.

MedlinePlus. 2011. "Type 1 Diabetes." MedlinePlus. Updated June 28. http://www nlm.nih.gov/medlineplus/ency/article/000305.htm.

Mercer, J. 2012. "What Is Type 1 Diabetes?" Diabetes Monitor. May 15. http://www .diabetesmonitor.com/education-center/diabetes-basics/what-is-type-1-diabetes .htm.

Chapter 3

Type 2 Diabetes

Introduction

Once known as adult-onset or non-insulin-dependent diabetes, type 2 diabetes occurs when the body's cells become resistant to insulin or there is not enough insulin. Type 2 diabetes accounts for 90 to 95 percent of all diabetes cases in the United States (Diabetes Education Online, 2012). Usually, type 2 diabetes begins with insulin resistance, where the blood glucose cannot enter the cells to make energy. In the beginning of this disease process, the pancreas makes more insulin to overcome the resistance. Over time, the insulin-producing beta cells in the pancreas are unable to secrete enough insulin to keep up with the amount of glucose in the bloodstream (Beaser, 2005).

Type 2 Diabetes Overview

It is important for those who are at risk for the condition or who have been diagnosed with type 2 diabetes to become more familiar with the disease. Learning about the causes, symptoms, diagnosis, treatment, and associated complications can help patients better manage their condition and prevent complications from occurring.

Causes

The exact causes of why someone develops type 2 diabetes are not fully known. A person's risk for developing type 2 diabetes increases with age and by being less active, being overweight or obese, and having a family history of diabetes. Race is also a risk factor for developing type 2 diabetes. Those of African, Asian, Native American, Latino, and Pacific Island descent have an increased risk for developing the condition. People with prediabetes and women who had gestational diabetes are also at risk for type 2 diabetes. Genetics plays a large factor; 10 to 15 percent of children with a parent with diabetes will also develop type 2 diabetes (Diabetes Education Online, 2012).

Symptoms

Symptoms of type 2 diabetes may develop slowly over time, and some people may not experience any symptoms. When symptoms occur, they include increased thirst, urination, and hunger; weight loss; fatigue; blurred vision; sores that are slow to heal; frequent infections; and patches of darkened skin. Because proper treatment and management of the condition is essential to prevent health complications, patients should seek medical care if they experience any of the symptoms common for type 2 diabetes (American Diabetes Association, 2011).

Diagnosis

Individuals over age forty-five should have a routine screening for type 2 diabetes, especially those who are overweight. The diagnostic blood tests that can determine whether a patient has diabetes include a glycated hemoglobin (A1C) test and a random plasma glucose test or a fasting plasma glucose test. The A1C test indicates the average blood sugar level over the past two to three months. Patients with an A1C value greater than or equal to 6.5 percent receive the diagnosis of diabetes. The random plasma glucose test, which can take place at any time during the day because it does not require fasting, measures the amount of glucose in the blood at a specific time. A random blood sugar test result that is greater than or equal to 200 mg/dL is abnormal and, when occurring along with classic symptoms of the disease, indicates the patient has diabetes. The patient may also have a fasting plasma glucose test, which is the preferred diagnostic method. This test usually takes place in the morning—and only after the patient fasts for at least eight hours. Extra glucose remains in the blood even after fasting in patients with diabetes. Those with a fasting plasma glucose higher than or equal to 126 mg/dL after two separate tests receive the diagnosis of diabetes. The American Diabetes Association recommends that an additional test take place on a different date—and which must also have abnormal results—to confirm the diagnosis of diabetes (American Diabetes Association, 2011).

Management and Treatment

Some with type 2 diabetes can lower their blood glucose to within normal limits through diet and exercise. Those who are unable to lower their blood glucose to within the normal range through diet and exercise will need medication to keep their blood glucose level in the normal range and to prevent complications. The goals of treatment are twofold: immediately lowering of high blood glucose levels and preventing complications from occurring over time.

Alpha-glucosidase inhibitors, biguanides, meglitinides, sulfonylureas, and thiazolidinediones are some of the common classes of medications used for lowering blood glucose levels. If the patient continues to have poorly controlled diabetes, the doctor may prescribe insulin. Because patients with type 2 diabetes are at increased risk of developing other health complications, doctors may also prescribe additional medications such as angiotensin-converting enzyme (ACE) inhibitors, statin drugs, and aspirin to prevent heart and kidney disease. Those patients who lose weight through diet and exercise may not need to continue medication if their blood glucose levels return to normal.

Patients with type 2 diabetes should continue to eat a healthy diet and participate in regular physical activity even if they are on medications. Maintaining a proper weight is important, and some patients find as they approach a normal weight they may no longer need medications to control their blood glucose level. For more information about diabetes management and treatment, *see* PART II, DIABETES MANAGEMENT RESOURCES.

Complications

Patients with type 2 diabetes are at an increased risk of developing heart disease, kidney disease, neuropathy, stroke, and retinopathy. Regular doctor's visits are important: patients should visit their general physician as well as their dentist, podiatrist, and ophthalmologist regularly. In addition, patients should take care of their feet and check them every day for injury. People with diabetes are more likely to develop foot problems from nerve damage and blood vessel damage. Because diabetes weakens the body's immune system, infections in the feet can become worse, leading to amputations.

Patients who properly manage their diabetes can reduce the risks of long-term complications. Good management means that patients should monitor their blood glucose levels daily and have their A1C levels measured regularly. People with diabetes also have a greater chance of developing high blood pressure and high cholesterol. It is important for those with type 2 diabetes to control their blood glucose, blood pressure, and cholesterol to prevent or delay the complications associated with the disease. For additional information about diabetes-related complications, *see* PART IV, RELATED HEALTH COMPLICATIONS AND CARE RESOURCES.

Prevention

In the United States, 54 million people are at risk for developing type 2 diabetes. Many of those people can prevent or delay the onset of type 2 diabetes by eating a healthy diet and participating in regular exercise most days of the week. Studies demonstrate that people with prediabetes can lower their risk of developing diabetes by losing 5 to 7 percent of their body weight. For more information about prediabetes and diabetes prevention, *see* CHAPTER 4, PREDIABETES AND TYPE 2 DIABETES PREVENTION.

Summary

Type 2 diabetes accounts for most of the new cases of diabetes diagnosed. Type 2 diabetes begins with insulin resistance, where the blood glucose cannot enter the cells to make energy. Over time, the pancreas is unable to secrete enough insulin to keep up with the amount of glucose in the bloodstream. Symptoms of the condition usually develop slowly. Treatment and management of the condition is essential to prevent health complications, so patients should seek medical care if they experience any symptoms common for type 2 diabetes. People with type 2 diabetes can sometimes manage their condition through leading a healthier lifestyle by eating healthy and engaging in physical activity. There are medications available as well, and sometimes type 2 diabetes patients may need insulin to keep their glucose levels under control.

Information Sources

Selected Print Resources

➤ American Diabetes Association. 2009. *Type 2 Diabetes: Your Healthy Living Guide: Tips, Techniques, and Practical Advice for Living Well with Diabetes.* Alexandria, VA: American Diabetes Association.
Beginning with an introduction to type 2 diabetes, this resource explains the causes and symptoms of the condition and provides advice for dealing with the emotions associated with a diagnosis of diabetes. The resource also discusses how to manage the condition through diet, exercise, and medication. The book also provides an overview of the complications that can develop.

➤ American Diabetes Association. 2011. *American Diabetes Association Complete Guide to Diabetes.* 5th ed. Alexandria, VA: American Diabetes Association.
This book provides basic information about the different types of diabetes, as well as information about diagnosis, symptoms, testing, management, insulin, glucose monitoring, healthy eating, exercise, complications, and coping.

➤ Barrier, Phyllis. 2011. *Type 2 Diabetes for Beginners.* 2nd ed. Alexandria, VA: American Diabetes Association.
This book provides excellent information for those newly diagnosed with type 2 diabetes. It focuses on lifestyle changes such as eating a healthy diet and incorporating physical activity and exercise into the patient's daily routine. It also explains the different types of medications available to treat the condition.

➤ Beaser, Richard. 2005. *The Joslin Guide to Diabetes: A Program for Managing Your Treatment.* New York: Simon and Schuster.
Patients will find this a valuable resource for information about understanding the types of diabetes, as well as specific information on therapy, diet, exercise, glucose monitoring, complications, insulin, special challenges, and living well with the disease.

➤ Becker, Gretchen. 2007. *The First Year: Type 2 Diabetes: An Essential Guide for the Newly Diagnosed.* New York: Marlowe.

This resource provides day-by-day instructions for one year for those newly diagnosed with diabetes. It covers information about type 2 diabetes, blood glucose levels, talking with friends and family, diet, drugs, finances, depression, and complications.

➤ Bryer-Ash, Michael. 2011. *100 Questions and Answers about Diabetes.* Sudbury, MA: Jones and Bartlett.
In question-and-answer format, this book explains what diabetes is and the differences between type 1 and type 2. Patients with type 2 can learn more about diabetes complications, treatments, glucose monitoring, living with the condition, special situations, and caring for a family member. The book also offers additional resources.

➤ Collazo-Clavell, Maria. 2009. *Mayo Clinic The Essential Diabetes Book: How to Prevent, Control, and Live Well with Diabetes.* Rochester, MN: Mayo Clinic.
Patients can learn more about diabetes, including information about both type 1 and type 2 and their differences. Chapters cover complications, glucose control, healthy eating, physical activity, insulin therapy, testing, and special issues.

➤ Colvin, Rod, and James Lane. 2011. *The Type 2 Diabetes Handbook: Six Rules for Staying Healthy with Type 2 Diabetes.* Omaha, NE: Addicus.
This book provides an excellent overview of type 2 diabetes for those who are newly diagnosed or for those who want to learn more about managing the condition properly. The resource contains information about diabetes basics, diet, physical activity, glucose levels, medications, and diabetes-related complications. The book also includes meal plans, a glossary of terms, and a resource directory.

➤ Drum, David, and Terry Zierenberg. 2005. *The Type 2 Diabetes Sourcebook.* 3rd ed. New York: McGraw-Hill.
Patients with type 2 diabetes will find this to be an excellent resource for finding out more about their condition. It begins with an overview of diabetes and how it affects the body. The book provides information on diagnosis, treatment, glucose testing, medication, lab tests, complications, diet, and exercise. Additional subject areas include living with the condition, mental health, managing stress, diabetes care, pregnancy, and finances.

➤ Hieronymus, Laura. 2008. *8 Weeks to Maximizing Diabetes Control: How to Improve Your Blood Glucose and Stay Healthy with Type 2 Diabetes.* Alexandria, VA: American Diabetes Association.
This title offers a step-by-step guide to managing type 2 diabetes. Those newly diagnosed with the condition will learn about the disease and how to eat healthy, be physically active, monitor their glucose level, learn about medications, and cope with type 2 diabetes.

➤ Levin, Marvin E., and Michael A. Pfeifer. 2009. *The Uncomplicated Guide to Diabetes Complications.* 3rd ed. Alexandria, VA: American Diabetes Association.

This resource will help patients with either type 1 or type 2 diabetes, and patients with type 2 diabetes will find the book useful in helping prevent complications or dealing with existing complications. Beginning with a general overview of diabetes and prediabetes, this resource provides information on acute complications and chronic complications of diabetes. The acute complications section informs about diabetic ketoacidosis (DKA), hyperglycemic hyperosmolar state (HHS), lactic acidosis, and low blood glucose. The chronic complications section includes information about cardiovascular, eye, nerve, kidney, gastrointestinal, fatty liver, sexual, skin, bone, and oral complications. There is also information about metabolic syndrome, polycystic ovary syndrome, cancer, sleep disturbance, infections, Alzheimer's disease, and psychosocial complications associated with diabetes.

➤ Metzger, Boyd. 2006. *American Medical Association Guide to Living with Diabetes: Preventing and Treating Type 2 Diabetes: Essential Information You and Your Family Need to Know.* Hoboken, NJ: Wiley.

Although the focus of this title is prevention of type 2 diabetes, those already diagnosed will benefit as well. In addition to comprehensive information on diet and lifestyle, this book provides an overview of type 2 diabetes and information on acute and chronic complications of type 2 diabetes.

➤ Peters, Anne. 2006. *Conquering Diabetes: A Complete Program for Prevention and Treatment.* New York: Plume.

This resource covers information about both type 1 and type 2 diabetes but mainly focuses on type 2 diabetes. Written by a doctor, the author incorporates patient stories within the text and covers many aspects of diabetes, including information about insulin use in patients with type 2 diabetes.

➤ Warshaw, Hope. 2009. *Real-Life Guide to Diabetes: Practical Answers to Your Diabetes Problems.* Alexandria, VA: American Diabetes Association.

This resource provides information about understanding diabetes, healthy eating, being active, monitoring glucose, using diabetes medications, and avoiding complications. Those newly diagnosed with diabetes will find this a useful and easy-to-read resource for learning about the condition.

Selected Web Resources

➤ Aetna InteliHealth, http://www.intelihealth.com/IH/ihtIH/WSIHW000/35072/35072.html

Although a commercial website, Aetna InteliHealth partners with Harvard Medical School and Columbia University to provide authoritative health information to patients. Users of the site can find general information about type 2 diabetes, including an overview, symptoms, health complications, tests, diet, exercise, medicines, glucose control, and care.

➤ Canadian Diabetes Association—"Type 2 Diabetes: The Basics," http://www .diabetes.ca/diabetes-and-you/living/just-diagnosed/type2/
Information is provided in both English and French languages. The site provides an overview of type 2 diabetes, information on managing diabetes, working with your health care team, and support. Separate sections provide information on daily management, insulin use, and health complications.

➤ DiabetesAtWork.org—"Fact Sheets," http://www.diabetesatwork.org/NextSteps/ FactSheets.cfm
DiabetesAtWork.org, an organization devoted to keeping diabetic employees healthy, provides a variety of patient fact sheets (in English and Spanish languages) explaining diabetes, with several fact sheets containing information pertinent to patients with type 2 diabetes, including one titled "Diagnosed with Type 2 Diabetes, Now What?"

➤ Diabetes Education Online—"Type 2 Diabetes," http://dtc.ucsf.edu/types-of-diabetes/type2/
Created by the University of California Diabetes Teaching Center, the website provides online instruction and resources for people with diabetes. The section on type 2 diabetes contains information on understanding type 2 diabetes, health management, and treatment. The site also contains a glossary of terms.

➤ Diabetes Monitor—"The Warning Signs of Type 2 Diabetes," http://www.diabetes monitor.com/education-center/the-warning-signs-of-type-2-diabetes.htm
The article provides information about type 2 diabetes and explains how most people with type 2 diabetes do not know they have the condition. Included is a list of ten warning signs of having type 2 diabetes.

➤ The Hormone Health Network—"Type 2 Diabetes Screening," http://www .hormone.org/Resources/Patient_Guides/upload/type-2-diabetes-screening-bilingual-071309.pdf
The Hormone Health Network provides a succinct overview in PDF format of type 2 diabetes. The handout provides a an introduction to type 2 and predia-betes and explains why screening for diabetes is important.

➤ Joslin Diabetes Center—"Joslin's Library: Managing Your Diabetes," http://www .joslin.org/info/managing_diabetes.html
A teaching and research affiliate of Harvard Medical School, the Joslin Diabetes Center provides website users a variety of helpful information about diabetes. Patients with type 2 diabetes can view the frequently asked questions about type 2, learn more when newly diagnosed, view information on medication, high glucose, diet, nutrition, and living with diabetes.

➤ Mayo Clinic—"Type 2 Diabetes," http://www.mayoclinic.com/health/type-2-diabetes/DS00585
The Mayo Clinic site provides information on a variety of health-related topics, including diabetes. Its page about type 2 diabetes provides an overview of the condition followed by information about symptoms, causes, risk factors, complications, tests, diagnosis, treatment, drugs, diet, exercise, blood sugar monitoring, alternative medicine, prevention, and support.

➤ MedlinePlus—"Type 2 Diabetes," http://www.nlm.nih.gov/medlineplus/ency/article/000313.htm
MedlinePlus provides a detailed overview of type 2 diabetes. Patients can find out more about the condition, causes, symptoms, diagnosis, treatment, management, and care. Additional type 2 diabetes resources are available on the site.

➤ National Diabetes Information Clearinghouse—"Your Guide to Diabetes: Type 1 and Type 2," http://www.diabetes.niddk.nih.gov/dm/pubs/type1and2/index.aspx
Patients will find this easy-to-read guide an excellent starting point for learning about their condition. The guide explains the differences between type 1 and type 2 diabetes; describes the signs and symptoms of the disease; provides information on disease management through insulin, diet, and physical activity; and supplies tips on living with the disease.

Selected Audiovisual Resources

➤ American Association of Diabetes Educators—"AADE7™ Self-Care Behaviors Videos," http://www.diabeteseducator.org/DiabetesEducation/Patient_Resources/VideosGuidebooks.html
People with type 2 diabetes will find this collection of two-minute videos useful for learning ways to properly manage their condition. Video title topics include eating healthy, being active, monitoring glucose levels, taking medications, problem solving, reducing risk, and coping in a healthy way.

➤ Healthy Roads Media—"Diabetes," http://www.healthyroadsmedia.org/topics/diabetes.htm
The site provides a variety of short audiovisual material on a variety of health topics, including diabetes. Clips include information on diabetes basics, controlling diabetes, complications, insulin, medication, and care.

➤ Joslin Diabetes Center—"Online Learning Center," http://www.joslin.org/ape/default.asp
The site provides users with a variety of interactive audiovisual tutorials. Titles include "What Is Diabetes?" and "Treating Type 2 Diabetes with Oral Medications," along with others focusing on managing blood glucose and monitoring. Some tutorials require online registration.

➤ NIHSeniorHealth.gov—"Videos: Diabetes: Preventing Type 2 Diabetes," http:// www.nihseniorhealth.gov/videolist.html#diabetes
While targeted at seniors, this five-minute video about preventing type 2 diabetes is beneficial for anyone who is at risk for developing diabetes and would like to learn more about how to prevent the condition.

➤ Patient Education Institute—"Diabetes—Introduction," http://www.nlm.nih .gov/medlineplus/tutorials/diabetesintroduction/htm/index.htm
Published by the Patient Education Institute and accessed through MedlinePlus, this interactive audio-visual tutorial provides an explanation of diabetes. A short section discusses type 2 diabetes. The tutorial also provides information on controlling diabetes through insulin therapy, diet, and exercise, and describes complications associated with the condition and signs of hypoglycemia.

References

American Diabetes Association. 2011. *American Diabetes Association Complete Guide to Diabetes*. 5th ed. Alexandria, VA: American Diabetes Association.

Beaser, R. 2005. *The Joslin Guide to Diabetes: A Program for Managing Your Treatment*. New York: Simon and Schuster.

Diabetes Education Online. 2012. "Type 2 Diabetes." University of California, San Francisco. Accessed August 9. http://dtc.ucsf.edu/types-of-diabetes/type2/.

Chapter 4

Prediabetes and Type 2 Diabetes Prevention

Introduction

Both prediabetes and insulin resistance can lead to the development of type 2 diabetes. Knowing the warning signs of prediabetes and insulin resistance is important for those who may be at risk for developing type 2 diabetes. Unfortunately, patients often do not seek information about the symptoms of type 2 diabetes until they receive a diagnosis of illness, or until a loved one is diagnosed; however, type 2 diabetes is often preventable. People at high risk for type 2 diabetes can prevent or delay diabetes by losing weight through a healthy diet coupled with regular exercise. This chapter outlines some of the risk factors for developing prediabetes and insulin resistance and provides information about healthy lifestyle changes that individuals can incorporate into their lives to reverse prediabetes and prevent type 2 diabetes and its associated complications. An annotated list of prediabetes and diabetes prevention resources follows this overview.

Prediabetes and Insulin Resistance

Diabetes is an ancient disease, traced back to approximately 1552 BC when it was noted by a physician that frequent urination was a symptom (Defeat Diabetes Foundation, 2011), but only recently has it become epidemic in the Western world. This increase in incidence is due to a population with an ever-increasing obesity problem, poor nutrition, and inactive lifestyles. More than 57 million adults in the United States have prediabetes, according to the U.S. Department of Health and Human Services (National Diabetes Information Clearinghouse, 2011). Prediabetes, also known as impaired glucose tolerance or impaired fasting glucose, occurs when blood tests reveal that a person's blood glucose levels are elevated but are not quite high enough for the individual to receive a diagnosis of diabetes.

The problem is different for a person with insulin resistance. With insulin resistance, the pancreas makes insulin, but the body does not use the insulin properly. Insulin is necessary for glucose to exit the bloodstream and enter the cells for use as energy. Insulin resistance begins when blood glucose cannot enter the cells to make energy. In the beginning of this disease process, the pancreas tries to compensate by making more insulin to overcome the body's resistance. Over time, the insulin-producing beta cells in the pancreas are unable to secrete enough insulin to keep up with the amount of glucose in the bloodstream (Beaser, 2005). Both prediabetes and insulin resistance are precursors to developing type 2 diabetes.

Many will develop type 2 diabetes within ten years of being diagnosed with prediabetes. Management of prediabetes and insulin resistance is important to prevent type 2 diabetes from developing, because people with this condition are at an increased risk of serious health complications, including cardiovascular disease and stroke. Patients who make healthy lifestyle changes, such as eating a healthy diet and being physically active on a daily basis, can help prevent type 2 diabetes and its associated complications from developing.

Metabolic Syndrome

Insulin resistance is also found concomitantly with type 2 diabetes, as well as with other health conditions such as high cholesterol, high blood pressure, and metabolic syndrome. Diagnosis of metabolic syndrome, also referred to as insulin resistance syndrome or syndrome X, occurs when a person has at least three of the following conditions:

- Being overweight or obese with a waist measurement greater than 40 inches for a man and greater than 35 inches for a woman
- Having high blood pressure (greater than 130/85) or taking medication for high blood pressure
- Having a fasting blood sugar of more than 110 mg/dL
- Having high triglyceride levels (greater than 150 mg/dL) or taking medications for high triglycerides
- Having low high-density lipoprotein (HDL) cholesterol levels (less than 40 mg/dL for men and less than 50 mg/dL for women)

Insulin resistance or high blood glucose, along with these risk factors, contributes to the development of cardiovascular disease. Leading a healthy lifestyle can prevent metabolic syndrome from developing. Those with metabolic syndrome can reduce their risk of developing cardiovascular disease and other serious health conditions by increasing physical activity and eating a healthy diet (National Diabetes Information Clearinghouse, 2011).

Causes

The exact causes of developing prediabetes or insulin resistance are unknown. Researchers have discovered that some genes are linked to the development of insulin resistance, but it is unclear as to what causes the body to not properly process glucose (Mayo Clinic, 2012).

Risk Factors

The factors that increase the risk of developing type 2 diabetes are the same as the risk factors for developing prediabetes. Being overweight, particularly having too much fat in the abdominal region, and living a sedentary lifestyle both seem to have a causative effect on developing prediabetes. Inactivity plays a large factor in developing prediabetes. The risk of prediabetes increases after age forty-five. If a parent or sibling has type 2 diabetes, the risk of developing prediabetes increases. Additional risk factors include having high blood pressure, high cholesterol or triglyceride levels, cardiovascular disease, and a condition called acanthosis nigricans, which is a dark rash around the neck or armpits (National Diabetes Information Clearinghouse, 2011). Recent studies have demonstrated that inadequate amounts of sleep can also lead to developing prediabetes (Mayo Clinic, 2012). Other risk factors include ethnicity, family history, gestational diabetes, and smoking and alcohol use.

Ethnicity and Family History

Ethnicity also plays a role in whether someone is at greater risk for developing pre-diabetes or diabetes. According to the Centers for Disease Control and Prevention (2011), in comparison to non-Hispanic white adults, Asian Americans are at 18 percent higher risk, Hispanics are at 66 percent higher risk, and African Americans are at 77 percent higher risk of developing diabetes. American Indians and Native Americans are also at higher risk for developing the disease, as indicated by large percentages of both populations being treated for it. Understanding that ethnicity may place certain groups at a higher risk for developing prediabetes or diabetes should help those members become more proactive in preventing the disease.

Like ethnicity, a family history of prediabetes or diabetes also places a person at higher risk. The National Diabetes Education Program (2006) notes four questions patients should ask regarding family history to ascertain whether that factor places them at greater risk for developing diabetes:

1. Does anyone in the family have type 2 diabetes? If so, who is that relative?
2. Has anyone in the family been told he or she has prediabetes?
3. Has anyone in the family been told he or she needs to lose weight or increase activity to prevent diabetes?
4. Did your mother have gestational diabetes while pregnant with you?

In addition, if the patient's mother, father, brother, or sister has type 2 diabetes, the patient has a greater risk of developing the disease.

Gestational Diabetes

Those women who have previously been diagnosed with gestational diabetes are at a greater risk for developing type 2 diabetes later in life. According to the National

Diabetes Education Program (2006), this risk is seven times greater for women who experienced gestational diabetes, and the risk for the children born during this condition is also greater. It is important for women who were diagnosed with gestational diabetes previously to do everything recommended for all adults to lower their risk for developing type 2 diabetes, such as reducing their weight and increasing physical activity. In addition, women who experienced gestational diabetes can also use medications, such as metformin, to help lower their blood glucose and prevent the disease from manifesting.

The National Diabetes Education Program (2006) makes the following recommendations for any woman who is currently diagnosed with gestational diabetes to prevent it from becoming type 2 diabetes after the birth of the child:

- Be tested for diabetes six to twelve weeks after the birth and then at least every three years.
- Discuss blood glucose screening before future pregnancies.
- Achieve prepregnancy weight six to twelve months after the baby is born; if still overweight after this period, endeavor to lose increments of 5 to 7 percent of body weight until normal weight is reached.
- Be active at least thirty minutes per day five days a week.
- Encourage children born to mothers with gestational diabetes to eat a healthy diet and exercise at least sixty minutes per day five days a week.

Smoking and Alcohol Consumption

While a low to moderate amount of alcohol might actually reduce the risk of diabetes, it is documented that heavy alcohol use may increase the risk. According to Collazo-Clavell (2011), heavy alcohol use inflames the pancreas causing it to secrete excess insulin, which leads to increased glucose levels. Likewise, Collazo-Clavell notes that heavy smokers—those who smoke twenty or more cigarettes a day—are twice as likely to develop diabetes than are nonsmokers due to tobacco intake causing increased blood sugar levels as well as resistance to insulin.

Smoking cessation programs are available through the assistance of a certified diabetes educator, and a physician can write a prescription for pharmaceutical interventions, such as nicotine patches or other prescription drugs, to assist in stopping smoking. Many people may be able to reduce alcohol intake successfully on an individual basis; however, if this approach does not work, those at risk should consider attending support groups or counseling to provide further information and assistance.

Symptoms

Generally, most people do not know they have prediabetes or insulin resistance. Symptoms are often insidious, developing slowly over time, which can cause patients to overlook such symptoms. Some symptoms of diabetes include frequent urination, increased thirst, weight loss, frequent infections, blurred vision, and fatigue. In addition to the classic symptoms of type 2 diabetes, some patients may also develop acanthosis nigricans, a condition characterized by darkened, thickened areas of skin. These darkened patches commonly occur in areas such as the neck, armpits, elbows, knees, or knuckles (Mayo Clinic, 2012).

Because those with prediabetes and insulin resistance can usually prevent or delay progression to type 2 diabetes, patients should seek medical care if they experience any of the symptoms of diabetes, particularly if experiencing increased thirst, frequent urination, fatigue, or blurred vision. Individuals who show symptoms of diabetes or who have any of the risk factors previously listed should talk with their doctor about glucose screening (Mayo Clinic, 2012).

Diagnosis

Diagnosing prediabetes early is important so the patient and the health care provider will be able to examine risk factors, identify any complications, and implement a prevention and treatment plan (Levin and Pfeifer, 2009). To determine whether a person has prediabetes, a doctor will perform blood tests. A fasting plasma glucose test or an oral glucose tolerance test can diagnose both diabetes and prediabetes. A random plasma glucose test can diagnose only diabetes, not prediabetes. After a fasting plasma glucose test, those with a fasting glucose level of 100 to 125 mg/dL have impaired fasting glucose and receive the diagnosis of prediabetes. Patients undergoing the oral glucose tolerance test have impaired glucose tolerance when the results show a level of 140 to 199 mg/dL two hours after drinking the glucose-containing beverage (National Diabetes Information Clearinghouse, 2011).

Complications

Left unmanaged, prediabetes can lead to significant health complications. Chiefly, untreated prediabetes can lead to the development of type 2 diabetes. Patients with type 2 diabetes are at an increased risk of developing heart disease, high cholesterol, high blood pressure, kidney damage, kidney disease, nerve damage, stroke, eye disease, and/or blindness. People with diabetes are more likely to develop foot problems from nerve damage and blood vessel damage. Because diabetes weakens the body's immune system, infections in the feet can become worse leading to amputations (Mayo Clinic, 2012). By properly managing prediabetes, the risks of developing type 2 diabetes and other long-term complications can be reduced.

Type 2 Diabetes Prevention

Left untreated, prediabetes may progress to type 2 diabetes over the course of several years. Research shows those with prediabetes can often prevent or delay type 2 diabetes by living a healthier lifestyle that includes eating a healthy diet, increasing physical activity, and taking needed medications. For those who need to lose weight, even a modest amount of weight loss, 5 to 10 percent of total body weight, can have a significant impact on preventing the onset of type 2 diabetes (Canadian Diabetes Association, 2012). Those who are at a healthy weight should work to maintain their weight.

Weight

Being overweight or obese is the primary risk factor for developing prediabetes and diabetes. According to Challem and Hunninghake (2009), one of every two over-weight people in the United States is obese, which increases by eighty times the person's risk factor for developing prediabetes or diabetes compared to a normal-weight person. Further, due to the typical American lifestyle of eating unhealthy foods and being inactive, those Americans born after the year 2000 have a one in three chance of developing diabetes.

The National Diabetes Education Program (NDEP) recommends taking small steps toward eating healthier foods to lose weight. The NDEP suggests that those trying to reduce their weight should take in fewer calories than they burn; eat less fat; and eat smaller portions of high-fat and high-calorie foods. The NDEP website provides a fat and calorie counter to help people make better food choices. Eating a variety of healthy foods from each food group is also important, as is focusing on fresh fruits and dark green and orange vegetables. The NDEP provides tips for selecting healthy items when eating at home, eating out, and when shopping for food.

By working with a registered dietician or diabetes educator, people can receive substantive assistance in developing sustainable healthy eating habits. Most food plans emphasize fresh fruits and vegetables, and limit or eliminate entirely empty calories, such as processed chips, cakes, and sweets. Losing weight not only is a strong preventive measure for prediabetes or diabetes but also helps the body in many other important ways, such as lowering cholesterol and blood pressure, and puts less stress on internal organs, bones, and joints. For more information about diet, *see* CHAPTER 8, HEALTHY DIET AND MEAL PLANNING.

Physical Activity Levels

In conjunction with weight loss, increasing physical activity levels is a strong preven-tive measure against developing prediabetes or diabetes. The NDEP recommends thirty minutes of moderate-intensity physical activity at least five days a week. Those who have been inactive should consult their doctor before beginning a physical activity program. Also, starting slowly and gradually building up exercise endurance is important. There are a variety of low-impact activities that can be done, such as walking, swimming, water aerobics, biking, or dancing. The NDEP suggests starting by taking a five-minute walk on most days of the week and gradually increasing the amount of time up to thirty minutes per walk (National Diabetes Education Program, 2006).

Coupling increased physical activity with a nutritious diet is a powerful preventive combination. According to the American Diabetes Association (2011), it takes only about thirty minutes of light to moderate exercise daily along with a 5 to 10 percent reduction in body weight to lessen the chances of developing diabetes by 58 percent.

The National Diabetes Information Clearinghouse (2011) provides the following additional examples of physical activities that can aid in maintaining a normal body weight if a person performs them often and regularly:

- Walk around while speaking on the telephone.
- Make time to play with the children.
- Walk the dog.
- Do not use the remote control; instead, stand up and walk to the television to change the channel.
- Garden or rake leaves.
- Clean the house.
- Wash the car.
- Take extra trips when doing chores, such as walking up and down a flight of stairs multiple times even though only one trip may be necessary.
- Park at the far ends of parking lots.
- Always take the stairs, not the escalator or elevator.
- Instead of eating during a coffee break, use the time to stretch or go for a quick walk.

For more information on getting physically active, *see* CHAPTER 9, PHYSICAL ACTIVITY.

Medications

The Mayo Clinic's diabetes website recommends that patients with prediabetes properly take their prescribed medications to help prevent the progression to type 2 diabetes. Some prediabetes patients receive prescriptions for oral diabetes drugs, particularly if they are at high risk of developing type 2 diabetes. In addition, patients should also take any prescribed medications for cholesterol and high blood pressure (Mayo Clinic, 2012).

Summary

While patients cannot change some of the risk factors for developing type 2 diabetes, such as ethnicity or family history, many proactive measures can help ameliorate existing high-risk factors for developing the disease or mitigate the chances of developing prediabetes or diabetes altogether. Being conscientious and thoughtful about selecting nutritious, low-fat, and low-cholesterol foods is a major component to reducing weight, as one of the main factors contributing to being at risk for type 2 diabetes is being overweight. Patients can slowly change an inactive lifestyle by incrementally increasing the amount of physical activity they perform on a daily basis. Simple actions like taking the stairs instead of the elevator or escalator; parking far from stores to increase the amount of walking; or taking a brisk walk, jog, or bicycle ride at lunch instead of sitting at a desk can all contribute substantively to reducing the risk of developing diabetes. Before embarking on any type of physical exercise program or changing eating habits dramatically, it is advised that individuals first consult with a physician and a diabetes educator to ensure they are able to safely perform these activities and make these changes to their diet.

Information Sources

Selected Print Resources

➤ Becker, Gretchen. 2004. *Prediabetes: What You Need to Know to Keep Diabetes Away*. New York: Marlowe.
 This resource can help those with prediabetes to prevent the disease from developing into type 2 diabetes. The book includes a background about diabetes, also addressing prediabetes. Following the short course of diabetes, the book provides fifty tips, each of which can be instrumental in preventing the disease. The tips include ways to incorporate exercise into a daily routine; losing weight by eating healthy food and not trying fad diets, which are more harmful than helpful; being mindful and recording important numbers like blood glucose readings and blood pressure; and staying informed about the current scientific literature available regarding diabetes.

➤ Greene, Bob, John J. Merendino Jr., and Janis Jibrin. 2009. *The Best Life Guide to Managing Diabetes and Pre-diabetes*. New York: Simon and Schuster.
 The authors of this book stress that to both prevent and manage diabetes, eating properly and performing moderate levels of exercise are critical. They view drugs and other types of pharmaceutical interventions as a last resort, not the optimal course of action when nutrition and physical activity can help to maintain glucose levels. The book provides a 12-week exercise regimen to jump-start the fitness process, as well as nutritional recipes to incorporate into a healthy daily routine.

➤ Levin, Marvin E., and Michael A. Pfeifer. 2009. *The Uncomplicated Guide to Diabetes Complications*. 3rd ed. Alexandria, VA: American Diabetes Association.
 This title, while covering information on many aspects of diabetes, provides a succinct chapter about prediabetes. Readers can learn more about what prediabetes is, how it is diagnosed, causes, complications, lifestyle modifications, and treatments.

➤ Peters, Anne L. 2006. *Conquering Diabetes: A Complete Program for Prevention and Treatment*. New York: Plume.

Written by a physician who specializes in diabetes, this resource provides substantive information for anyone who has been diagnosed with prediabetes. The author encourages her readers to become experts on diabetes so that they can take control of preventing the disease from occurring. The book provides a risk factor profile, which asks questions about ethnicity, cholesterol levels, exercise and activity levels, age, blood pressure levels, and whether one has had gestational diabetes or has a family member with type 2 diabetes. The book addresses combining proper nutrition with an exercise regimen, along with other advice on how to prevent type 2 diabetes.

➤ Petro Roybal, Beth Ann. 2006. *Prediabetes Wake-Up Call: A Personal Road Map to Prevent Diabetes*. Berkeley, CA: Ulysses.

Written in easy-to-comprehend language, this health writer provides background information on what it means to be prediabetic and how the diagnosis can be positive since it allows a person to make lifestyle changes to prevent the disease from manifesting itself. The book outlines and describes in detail the major risk factors, such as being overweight and inactive. The author emphasizes the importance of preventing the disease because the health complications are serious, such as nerve and blood vessel damage, heart conditions, eyesight concerns, and mobility problems. The book presents true stories interspersed throughout, which helps to personalize the disease and make it more relatable for the reader. The author underlines medical terms that are not commonly known and then lists and explains them in greater detail at the end of the book. Each chapter concludes with questions for consideration, which provide a way for readers to reflect upon their own health and ways to improve it.

➤ Scalpi, Gretchen. 2011. *The Everything Guide to Managing and Reversing Pre-diabetes: Your Complete Plan for Preventing the Onset of Diabetes*. Avon, MA: Adams Media.

This resource is written by a registered dietician who wants to help readers use proper nutrition and a regular exercise regimen to prevent type 2 diabetes. The first section of the book provides a substantive discussion on the condition of prediabetes, its risk factors and symptoms, and how testing can confirm whether one is in a prediabetic state. The second section of the book focuses on setting up an action plan to prevent diabetes, including various exercises and activities to incorporate daily and how proper nutrition is the key to maintaining a healthy weight. The book also presents information on how to eat in restaurants in a healthy manner and how to read food labels properly.

➤ Woodruff, Sandra. 2004. *The Complete Diabetes Prevention Plan: A Guide to Understanding the Emerging Epidemic of Prediabetes and Halting Its Progression to Diabetes*. New York: Penguin.

This book provides suggestions on how to implement lifestyle changes to help prevent type 2 diabetes and progression of prediabetes to diabetes. The book suggests incorporating physical activity and a healthy eating plan as preventive actions. This resource also lists foods and recipes to assist in planning a healthy diet.

Selected Web Resources

➤ American Association of Diabetes Educators—"More Than 50 Ways to Prevent Diabetes," http://www.diabeteseducator.org/export/sites/aade/_resources/pdf/NDEP_AA_50Ways_031809.pdf
This easy-to-understand two-page information sheet provides a food and activity tracker, which can be copied and printed for daily use, and fifty tips on ways to prevent diabetes. Some of the tips include drinking water ten minutes before a meal to reduce appetite, serving food on smaller plates so portion sizes are smaller, delivering messages to coworkers in person instead of by e-mail, getting off the bus one or two stops early to incorporate physical activity into the workday, buying one new fruit or vegetable to try on each trip to the grocery store, reading food labels, cooking with spices instead of salt, and taking time to use relaxation techniques.

➤ American Diabetes Association—"Physical Activity," http://www.diabetes.org/diabetes-basics/prevention/checkup-america/activity.html
This website provides information about how engaging in regular physical activity can help lower the risk for prediabetes and type 2 diabetes. It also includes tips for getting started with exercising and types of exercises that are recommended.

➤ American Diabetes Association—"Prediabetes FAQs," http://www.diabetes.org/diabetes-basics/prevention/pre-diabetes/pre-diabetes-faqs.html
In question-and-answer format, this site covers information about what prediabetes is, diabetes nomenclature, testing, diagnosis, and treatment. It also explains the difference between prediabetes and diabetes and lists information about diagnosis and risk factors. There is discussion on diagnostic tests, such as the fasting plasma glucose test and the oral glucose tolerance test, and treatment options. A unique feature of the site is that it also provides an audio version of the text.

➤ Centers for Disease Control and Prevention—"Prevent Diabetes," http://www.cdc.gov/diabetes/consumer/prevent.htm
With a focus on type 2 diabetes prevention, the site provides information about prediabetes. The site explains diabetes prevention and describes risk factors associated with the condition. It explains that those with risk factors for diabetes should seek testing, and that people can prevent the progression of prediabetes to diabetes through lifestyle changes such as diet and exercise. Additional information about prediabetes is available through the links provided.

➤ DiabetesAtWork.org—"Preventing Diabetes and Pre-diabetes," http://www.diabetes atwork.org/DiabetesResources/DiabetesAndPrimaryPrevention.cfm
This resource provides links to helpful websites that focus on diabetes prevention. For example, there are links to tip sheets on diabetes prevention, prediabetes, proper nutrition, risk factors, and food and activity trackers.

➤ dLife—"Prediabetes," http://www.dlife.com/diabetes/diabetes-prevention/pre diabetes
This site contains information about prediabetes, its risk factors, diagnosis, and treatment. The site begins with an overview describing prediabetes as a precursor to developing type 2 diabetes. There is a link to a page describing the risk factors of prediabetes and the American Diabetes Association screening recommendations for the condition. Another link contains information about the diagnosis of prediabetes and contains information about two blood tests used in diagnosis: the fasting plasma glucose test and the oral glucose tolerance test.

➤ FamilyDoctor.org—"Prediabetes," http://www.familydoctor.org/online/famdocen/ home/common/diabetes/basics/821.html
FamilyDoctor.org provides site users with an overview of diabetes and pre-diabetes, diagnosis, risk factors, and information about the prevention of type 2 diabetes. The site begins with an explanation of the differences between pre-diabetes and diabetes, then lists the risk factors for developing prediabetes, followed by information on how patients with the condition can lower their risk for developing type 2 diabetes. The site encourages eating a healthy diet and engaging in regular daily physical activity to help prevent or delay the develop-ment of type 2 diabetes. The site concludes with links to additional information about prediabetes and type 1 and type 2 diabetes. The information is also accessible in an audio version.

➤ Harvard School of Public Health—"The Nutrition Source: Simple Steps to Preventing Diabetes," http://www.hsph.harvard.edu/nutritionsource/more/ diabetes-full-story/index.html
This website provides an introduction to type 2 diabetes and discusses ways to prevent its development through reducing such risk factors as being overweight, being physically inactive, eating an unhealthy diet, and having an excessive level of alcohol consumption. The site explores these risk factors in detail, with tips on how to moderate and reduce them so that diabetes does not occur.

➤ Healthfinder.gov—"Preventing Diabetes: Questions for the Doctor," http:// healthfinder.gov/prevention/ViewTool.aspx?toolId=44
This information page offers specific guidance on questions patients should pose to their doctor about the risks for developing diabetes. Patients can print the page or write down the questions and then ask the questions at their next doctor's visit.

➤ Healthfinder.gov—"Take Steps to Prevent Type 2 Diabetes," http://www.health finder.gov/prevention/ViewTopic.aspx?topicId=73
This website provides a brief overview of how individuals can prevent type 2 diabetes. The Basics section offers tips as well as additional advice on lowering risk factors. The Take Action section provides specific guidelines to help prevent diabetes from occurring, such as reducing body weight, being physically active, having regular blood pressure and cholesterol checks, consulting a physician, and participating in diabetes screening events.

➤ The Hormone Health Network—"Prediabetes," http://www.hormone.org/ Resources/Patient_Guides/upload/prediabetes-bilingual-071309.pdf
This one-page handout provides information about diagnosis, risk factors, and prevention. The site includes an overview of how prediabetes develops and lists the risk factors that increase the chances of developing the condition. The site also presents information about diagnostic testing along with discussion about the fasting blood glucose test and the oral glucose tolerance test. Blood test result ranges accompany an explanation of whether results indicate a normal, prediabetes, or diabetes diagnosis. The site also includes reasons people with pre-diabetes should take the condition seriously and contains information on lifestyle changes, such as eating healthy and getting regular exercise, to prevent diabetes from developing. A Spanish language version of the handout is also available.

➤ Joslin Diabetes Center—"What Should I Do If I Have It [Pre-diabetes]?," http:// www.joslin.org/info/what_is_pre_diabetes.html
This website provides substantive information on the condition of prediabetes and what one should do if diagnosed with it. The resource explains specific risk factors for developing diabetes, such as being physically inactive, overweight, or previously identified as having impaired fasting glucose; having a family history of diabetes; being a member of an at-risk ethnic group; or having high blood pressure, polycystic ovary syndrome, or a history of vascular disease. Additional sections discuss physical activity and proper nutrition.

➤ Mayo Clinic—"Prediabetes," http://www.mayoclinic.com/health/prediabetes/ DS00624
The Mayo Clinic provides users with an overview of prediabetes and its symptoms, causes, risk factors, complications, tests, diagnosis, treatment, and prevention. Beginning with information on how prediabetes develops, the site contains information on how patients can prevent type 2 diabetes from developing through lifestyle changes. Recognizing prediabetes is important, so the site provides lists of symptoms and risk factors. People with symptoms and risk factors of the condition are encouraged to consult a health care professional. Information on diagnostic testing, such as the glycated hemoglobin (A1C) test, the fasting blood

sugar test, and the oral glucose tolerance test, is available, as is information about treatment and medication.

➤ National Diabetes Education Program—"Small Steps. Big Rewards. Prevent Type 2 Diabetes," http://ndep.nih.gov/partners-community-organization/campaigns/SmallStepsBigRewards.aspx
The National Diabetes Education Program maintains a prevention program for type 2 diabetes. The program consists of messages and communications directed to various communities, such as women who are at risk of developing gestational diabetes, African Americans, Hispanics, Native Americans, Asian Americans, and older adults. There are links to the campaign components, which include articles, fact sheets, and public service announcements.

➤ National Diabetes Information Clearinghouse—"Insulin Resistance and Prediabetes," http://www.diabetes.niddk.nih.gov/dm/pubs/insulinresistance/index.aspx
Readers can learn more about insulin resistance, metabolic syndrome, and prediabetes on this site, which describes each condition. One page contains a list of the symptoms of insulin resistance and prediabetes. The site also provides information about the risk factors of the conditions so those with risk factors and symptoms will be informed about the importance of being tested for prediabetes. Diagnostic testing explanations are available. The site also explains how people diagnosed with prediabetes can prevent the development of type 2 diabetes through lifestyle changes.

➤ National Institutes of Health—"I Can Lower My Risk for Type 2 Diabetes: A Guide for American Indians," http://diabetes.niddk.nih.gov/dm/pubs/amIatrisktype2AI/amerindrisk.pdf
Written specifically for the Native American community, whose members are more than twice as likely to develop diabetes than the general population, the tips to lower risks for the disease are applicable to all ethnic groups. Written in easy-to-comprehend language, it provides a background on both prediabetes and diabetes, the signs and symptoms of diabetes, which factors increase risk for developing the disease, and how individuals can lower their risk factors. A daily food and activity tracker is also available.

➤ Siteman Cancer Center—"Lower Your Risk for Diabetes—Questionnaire," http://www.yourdiseaserisk.wustl.edu/hccpquiz.pl?lang=english&func=home&quiz=diabetes
This is an interactive questionnaire to determine if individuals are at risk for developing diabetes. Questions ask about height, weight, family history of diabetes, smoking habits, exercise levels, waist circumference, alcohol consumption, and ethnicity. The resulting summary is then shown in a bar graph that plots risk factors from low to high risk. The site provides tips on how to lower the risk of developing diabetes and underscores areas where there are positive answers, such as exercising regularly and not smoking.

Selected Audiovisual Resources

➤ American Association of Diabetes Educators. 2006. *Pre-diabetes: Your Path to Preventing Type 2 Diabetes*. Timonium, MD: Milner-Fenwick.
This DVD explains prediabetes to the viewer and emphasizes living a healthy lifestyle to delay or prevent the onset of type 2 diabetes. The video covers information about how to monitor blood glucose, make healthy eating choices, and be physically active. The video explains about oral medications for diabetes, as well as coping and emotional support for dealing with a prediabetes diagnosis.

➤ dLife—"Prediabetes," http://www.dlife.com/dlifetv/video/prediabetes
This short, five-minute video, uses a patient's story of being diagnosed with prediabetes to describe the condition. The video covers information about what prediabetes is, its diagnosis, and management. It emphasizes lifestyle changes to prevent developing type 2 diabetes.

➤ InsiderMedicine.com—"If I Had Pre-diabetes," http://www.insidermedicine .com/archives/If_I_Had_Prediabetes_Dr_Venkat_Narayan_MD_MSc_MBA_ Rollins_School_of_Public_Health_Emory_University_3076.aspx
In this short videotape, Dr. Venkat Narayan explains lifestyle changes someone with prediabetes could undertake to prevent the development of type 2 diabetes.

References

American Diabetes Association. 2011. *American Diabetes Association Complete Guide to Diabetes*. 5th ed. Alexandria, VA: American Diabetes Association.

Beaser, R. 2005. *The Joslin Guide to Diabetes: A Program for Managing Your Treatment*. New York: Simon and Schuster.

Canadian Diabetes Association. 2012. "Prediabetes: A Chance to Change the Future." Canadian Diabetes Association. Accessed July 3. http://www.diabetes.ca/ diabetes-and-you/what/prediabetes/.

Centers for Disease Control and Prevention. 2011. "2011 Diabetes Fact Sheet." Centers for Disease Control and Prevention. Last updated May 23. http://www .cdc.gov/diabetes/pubs/estimates11.htm#7.

Challem, J., and R. Hunninghake. 2009. *Stop Prediabetes Now: The Ultimate Plan to Lose Weight and Prevent Diabetes*. Hoboken, NJ: Wiley.

Collazo-Clavell, M. 2011. "Type 2 Diabetes: Does Alcohol and Tobacco Use Increase the Risk of Diabetes?" Mayo Foundation for Medical Education and Research. July 12. http://www.mayoclinic.com/health/diabetes/AN00548.

Defeat Diabetes Foundation. 2011. "About Diabetes: History of Diabetes in Timeline." Defeat Diabetes Foundation. Updated August 22. http://www.defeatdiabetes .org/about_diabetes/text.asp?id=Diabetes_Timeline.

Levin, M. E., and M. A. Pfeifer. 2009. *The Uncomplicated Guide to Diabetes Complications*. 3rd ed. Alexandria, VA: American Diabetes Association.

Mayo Clinic. 2012. "Prediabetes: Definition." Mayo Foundation for Medical Education and Research. January 26. http://www.mayoclinic.com/health/prediabetes/DS00624.

National Diabetes Education Program. 2006. "Small Steps. Big Rewards. Your Game Plan to Prevent Type 2 Diabetes: Information for Patients." National Diabetes Education Program. http://ndep.nih.gov/publications/PublicationDetail.aspx?PubId=71.

National Diabetes Information Clearinghouse. 2011. "Insulin Resistance and Pre-Diabetes." National Institute of Diabetes and Digestive and Kidney Diseases, National Institutes of Health. Last updated December 6. http://diabetes.niddk.nih.gov/dm/pubs/insulinresistance/index.htm.

Chapter 5

Gestational Diabetes

Introduction

Gestational diabetes is a type of diabetes that can occur in pregnant women who did not have type 1 or type 2 diabetes before pregnancy. Although the body makes more insulin during pregnancy, the placenta secretes hormones that block insulin action, and the attendant weight gain makes it difficult for the body to meet its insulin need, causing a temporary resistance to insulin. When insulin resistance occurs, glucose begins to build up in the bloodstream causing the body to be unable to derive the energy it requires from food. Controlling blood sugar during pregnancy is extremely important to prevent a difficult birth and to keep the baby and mother healthy (American Diabetes Association, 2011a).

Gestational Diabetes Overview

The number of women that develop gestational diabetes is high. Until only a few years ago, the estimate was that up to 7 percent of pregnant women would develop this condition (Davis, 2009). However, the American Diabetes Association recently changed its diagnostic criteria for gestational diabetes. The ADA now estimates, based on the new criteria, that 18 percent of pregnant women have gestational diabetes in the United States (American Diabetes Association, 2011a). Because of this high incidence, it is important for women to be aware of the risk factors, symptoms, diagnosis, management, and associated complications of the condition and learn ways of preventing gestational diabetes from occurring.

Risk Factors

Several risk factors can increase a woman's chances of developing gestational diabetes. Two of the greatest risk factors are being overweight and having a family member diagnosed with gestational diabetes. African American, American Indian, Hispanic and Latina, Asian American, and Pacific Islander women are all at increased risk of developing gestational diabetes. Other risk factors include having a parent, brother, or sister with diabetes; being over age twenty-five; having prediabetes; having previously given birth to a child weighing nine pounds or more; and having had gestational diabetes during a previous pregnancy (dLife, 2010a).

Symptoms and Diagnosis

Gestational diabetes usually starts around the twenty-fourth week of pregnancy when the placenta starts producing large quantities of hormones. Generally, there are no symptoms, making gestational diabetes difficult to detect without diagnostic testing. Symptoms such as increased urination, thirst, hunger, recurring urinary tract infections, weakness, and fatigue may appear in some women with gestational diabetes. Women at high risk for developing diabetes should be tested for the condition during their first prenatal obstetrician visit. The American Diabetes Association's new guidelines highly recommend this early screening due to the increased number of people who have undiagnosed type 2 diabetes. If diagnosed at this stage in pregnancy, the woman would receive a diagnosis of type 2 diabetes rather than gestational diabetes. The ADA recommends screening pregnant women between twenty-four and twenty-eight weeks for gestational diabetes using a 75-gram two-hour oral glucose tolerance test (American Diabetes Association, 2010).

The oral glucose tolerance test requires that the patient fast (have nothing to eat or drink) for at least eight hours immediately prior to the test. To make it easier on the patient, fasting usually occurs overnight and the oral glucose tolerance test takes place in the morning after the fast ends. First, the test measures the patient's fasting blood glucose level, and then the patient drinks a sugary beverage. After drinking, the patient waits for one hour, and then a blood test measures the patient's glucose levels again. The final blood test occurs an hour after that, again measuring glucose levels. The American Diabetes Association recommends diagnostic values of 92 mg/dL or greater after fasting; 180 mg/dL or greater one hour after drinking the sugary beverage; and 153 mg/dL or greater two hours after drinking the sugary beverage (American Diabetes Association, 2010).

Management

Proper management and treatment of gestational diabetes is necessary to prevent problems during delivery. Eating healthy and keeping active are two important elements of a gestational diabetes management plan. A diabetes educator or dietitian can help patients develop a healthy eating plan. Most healthy eating plans for gestational diabetes follow the basic guidelines of limiting sweets and carbohydrates, eating three small meals a day, and including fiber, fruits, vegetables, and whole grains in the diet.

Women should stay active during pregnancy through nonimpact exercises such as walking or swimming. Patients should collaborate with their health care team to develop appropriate physical activity plans. Overall, healthy eating and physical activity will usually help control weight gain, which will then help control gestational diabetes. If healthy eating and physical activity do not ameliorate glucose levels in the bloodstream, further management through oral medications or insulin will then become necessary to manage gestational diabetes and prevent complications.

Women diagnosed with gestational diabetes must monitor their blood glucose levels at home using a blood glucose meter. The health care team will show the patient how to use the meter, check the glucose level, and ensure it is within the appropriate range. The target level for most women upon awakening is up to 95 mg/dL, for one hour after a meal is up to 140 mg/dL, and for two hours after a meal is up to 120 mg/dL. Women should keep a log of their glucose levels to compare the results with acceptable ranges, as well as to monitor the efficacy of their current treatment (National Diabetes Information Clearinghouse, 2006).

Those taking diabetes medication, particularly insulin, need to be aware of hypoglycemia, a condition where blood glucose drops too low. Symptoms of hypoglycemia include becoming dizzy, sweaty, confused, shaky, hungry, and weak. Women noticing these symptoms should immediately eat or drink some form of sugar and then test their blood sugar level. The goal of insulin treatment is to balance insulin intake with food intake and exercise level to maintain normal levels of glucose.

Complications

Without proper management of gestational diabetes, both mother and baby face an increased risk of medical complications. High levels of insulin in the mother's bloodstream can cause macrosomia, a condition where the baby grows larger than normal, often nine pounds or more, due to growing fat as a direct result of the mother's increased glucose. The increased size of the baby causes a difficult delivery. The infant may have respiratory distress syndrome and need oxygen because often the babies are born prematurely due to their increased weight. Gestational diabetes may cause the fetal lungs to develop slowly, resulting in low levels of lung surfactant; surfactant may also be at low levels in babies born prematurely as the surfactant has not had enough time to be produced at optimal levels in the lungs. Insufficient lung surfactant means the lungs are unstable and may collapse during normal breathing. The baby may also be born with hypoglycemia because the pancreas makes more insulin when the mother's glucose enters the baby's body. When the baby is born and no longer has extra glucose from the mother, the baby then has excess insulin, resulting in hypoglycemia (dLife, 2010b).

Although easily treated, the baby may also be born with jaundice, a condition where the skin and whites of the eyes turn a yellowish tint. Patients with gestational diabetes must also monitor for ketones in their urine. The presence of ketones indicates the body is using body fat for energy instead of food. Ketones can be harmful to both the mother and the baby.

The mother is also at higher risk of developing complications including hypertension, which is high blood pressure. Hypertension during pregnancy can lead to a dangerous condition called preeclampsia. Preeclampsia is a sudden increase in blood pressure that can affect the mother's kidneys, liver, and brain. It can result in long-term complications or death for the mother and the baby (dLife, 2010c).

Gestational diabetes often increases the chances of the patient having a cesarean section delivery or having to be induced into labor earlier than normal. The patient needs to work very closely with her health care team to effectively manage blood sugar levels and prevent these complications from developing (Eunice Kennedy Shriver National Institute of Child Health and Human Development, 2012).

Gestational diabetes usually subsides completely immediately after giving birth; however, patients are more likely to develop type 2 diabetes later in life. A full 60 percent of gestational diabetes patients will develop type 2 diabetes within ten years after giving birth (Davis, 2009). Patients can reduce their risk of developing type 2 diabetes by eating a healthy diet, staying physically active, and being tested regularly for diabetes. Children of mothers who had gestational diabetes are at greater risk for becoming obese, having abnormal glucose tolerance, and developing diabetes. The American Diabetes Association recommends screening for women with gestational diabetes six to twelve weeks after giving birth. In addition, the ADA recommends that women who have a history of gestational diabetes be screened for prediabetes or diabetes every three years for life (American Diabetes Association, 2011b).

Pregnant women should work closely with their health care team to diagnose gestational diabetes and to manage gestational diabetes to ensure a healthy pregnancy. Those patients with gestational diabetes should learn more about their condition so they can understand its ramifications for their lives, learn how to eat a healthy diet, stay active or become more active, use their medications appropriately, and regularly test their blood glucose levels.

Prevention

There is no certain way to prevent developing diabetes, but women should plan in advance of becoming pregnant to reduce risks factors for developing gestational diabetes. Women considering becoming pregnant should discuss the risk of gestational diabetes with their health care provider. In addition, women should maintain a healthy weight through eating a healthy diet and staying physically active (dLife, 2010c). For more information about diabetes prevention, *see* CHAPTER 4, PREDIABETES AND TYPE 2 DIABETES PREVENTION.

Summary

Gestational diabetes is a type of diabetes that can occur in pregnant women who did not have type 1 or type 2 diabetes before pregnancy. Librarians serving patients who ask for information about diabetes during pregnancy should be aware that patients may be talking about gestational diabetes. The diagnosis of, management of, and approach to the care of patients with gestational diabetes can be markedly different from caring for patients with type 1 or type 2 diabetes. The librarian should perform a complete reference interview to ascertain whether the patient has been diagnosed with gestational diabetes or was previously diagnosed with type 1 or type 2 diabetes before pregnancy, so the librarian can connect the patient with appropriate health information resources. The resources that follow provide patients additional authoritative information about gestational diabetes so they can stay healthy during pregnancy.

Information Sources

Selected Print Resources

> American College of Obstetricians and Gynecologists. 2010. *Your Pregnancy and Childbirth: Month to Month*. Washington, DC: American College of Obstetricians and Gynecologists.
> This general pregnancy resource provides information for women with gestational diabetes. It explains risk factors and how gestational diabetes can affect pregnancy. It also discusses management of gestational diabetes during pregnancy.

> American Diabetes Association. 2005. *Gestational Diabetes: What to Expect: Your Guide to a Healthy Pregnancy and a Happy, Healthy Baby*. 4th ed. Alexandria, VA: American Diabetes Association.
> This comprehensive resource for women with gestational diabetes includes detailed information about the condition, tests, diagnosis, management, monitoring glucose, insulin therapy, exercise, physical activity, and healthy eating habits. The book also includes background information on a healthy pregnancy, labor and delivery, and the importance of follow-up after pregnancy. This resource concludes with a gestational diabetes glossary of terms.

> American Diabetes Association. 2011. *American Diabetes Association Complete Guide to Diabetes*. 5th ed. Alexandria, VA: American Diabetes Association.
> This book provides basic information about the different types of diabetes, as well as information about diagnosis, symptoms, testing, management, insulin, glucose monitoring, healthy eating, exercise, complications, and coping.

> Beaser, Richard. 2005. *The Joslin Guide to Diabetes: A Program for Managing Your Treatment*. New York: Simon and Schuster.
> In a section titled "Special Challenges of Diabetes," this book includes a short chapter about diabetes and pregnancy. There is also an overview of the metabolic changes that occur during pregnancy and how gestational diabetes may result. The chapter also provides an overview of gestational diabetes, risk factors, testing, and treatment.

➤ Collazo-Clavell, Maria. 2009. *Mayo Clinic: The Essential Diabetes Book: How to Prevent, Control, and Live Well with Diabetes*. Rochester, MN: Mayo Clinic.
Providing an overview of the different types of diabetes, this book explains how gestational diabetes is different from type 1 or type 2 diabetes. This resource also includes discussion on risk factors, a screening and diagnosis overview, treatments, and a list of complications from uncontrolled blood glucose.

➤ Eisenstat, Stephanie. 2007. *Every Woman's Guide to Diabetes: What You Need to Know to Lower Your Risk and Beat the Odds*. Cambridge, MA: Harvard University Press.
This resource provides a short overview of gestational diabetes, risk factors, and information about diagnostic testing and treatments. The book also includes information on managing diabetes, with sections on eating well and a sample grocery list.

➤ Platt, Elizabeth S. 2009. *100 Questions and Answers about Your High-Risk Pregnancy*. Sudbury, MA: Jones and Bartlett.
The gestational diabetes section in this resource stresses the importance of stabilizing blood glucose levels to prevent complications from occurring during pregnancy. The gestational diabetes section provides women with information on monitoring blood glucose levels and treating gestational diabetes through healthy eating and physical activity.

➤ Walker, W. Allen. 2006. *Harvard Medical School Guide to Healthy Eating During Pregnancy*. New York: McGraw-Hill.
For women with gestational diabetes seeking a more detailed guide about eating properly, this resource provides a special section about diet and gestational diabetes. The book provides women with tips on what foods they should incorporate into a healthy diet and what should be avoided. Other sections of the book cover important topics such as managing weight, meal planning, and staying active.

Selected Web Resources

➤ Agency for Healthcare Research and Quality—"Gestational Diabetes: A Guide for Pregnant Women," http://effectivehealthcare.ahrq.gov/ehc/products/107/162/2009_0804GDM_Cons_singlpgs.pdf
Written in easy-to-understand language, this 16-page online brochure explains gestational diabetes in more detail than most online resources. It presents the information in three parts: overview of gestational diabetes, how it is treated and managed, and follow-up after pregnancy.

➤ American Diabetes Association—"Diabetes Basics: Gestational Diabetes," http://www.diabetes.org/diabetes-basics/gestational/
The gestational diabetes section of this website provides links to two articles about the condition. The first section, "What Is Gestational Diabetes?," provides

information on the background and health consequences of gestational diabetes followed by a video clip and a link to a podcast. The second section, on treating gestational diabetes, explains how proper health care and disease management can lower the risk for medical complications during pregnancy.

➤ California Department of Public Health—"California Diabetes and Pregnancy Program," http://www.cdph.ca.gov/programs/CDAPP/Pages/default.aspx
The purpose of this state-sponsored program and website, under the auspices of the California Department of Public Health, is to educate both medical personnel and community liaisons about the dangers of gestational diabetes and how to prevent and manage the disease. It provides links to many consumer-oriented educational resources that concentrate on gestational diabetes, including overviews, healthy eating, exercise, and prevention.

➤ Cleveland Clinic—"Diseases and Conditions: Gestational Diabetes," http://my .clevelandclinic.org/disorders/diabetes_gestational/hic_gestational_diabetes.aspx
Along with a variety of information about diabetes, the Cleveland Clinic website provides a succinct overview of gestational diabetes concepts. Patients can learn more about causes, diagnosis, glucose monitoring, diet, exercise, insulin, and complications related to gestational diabetes.

➤ dLife—"Gestational Diabetes," http://www.dlife.com/diabetes/gestational
This general diabetes website contains useful information about gestational diabetes. The site provides information explaining the condition, its causes, diagnosis, treatment, and associated complications. Although there is no certain way to prevent developing gestational diabetes, the site contains some strategies for women to reduce their risk of developing this condition.

➤ Eunice Kennedy Shriver National Institute of Child Health and Human Development—"Am I at Risk for Gestational Diabetes?," http://www.nichd.nih.gov/ publications/pubs/upload/gest_diabetes_risk_2005.pdf
This two-page informational pamphlet published by NICHHD provides a succinct summary of the origin of and risks associated with gestational diabetes. It includes a general summary of the disease, its complications for both mother and baby, testing information, and a short risk-assessment questionnaire.

➤ Eunice Kennedy Shriver National Institute of Child Health and Human Development—"Gestational Diabetes," http://www.nichd.nih.gov/health/topics/ Gestational_Diabetes.cfm
This website sponsored by NICHHD provides more in-depth information about the disease, its manifestations, risk factors, and complications. The site includes links to related gestational diabetes clinical trials, news releases, relevant publications and materials, as well as links to useful websites regarding the disease and pregnancy.

➤ Eunice Kennedy Shriver National Institute of Child Health and Human Development—"Managing Gestational Diabetes: A Patient's Guide to a Healthy Pregnancy," http://www.nichd.nih.gov/publications/pubs/upload/Managing_Gestational_ Diabetes_rev.pdf
This is a comprehensive website, sponsored by NICHHD, that addresses multiple informational needs regarding pregnancy and gestational diabetes, including what is the disease, which women are at risk for developing it, what are possible health complications for mother and baby both before and after delivery, how does prevention and management work, and what are some other online resources about related health concerns.

➤ Eunice Kennedy Shriver National Institute of Child Health and Human Development—"What Should I Do After My Baby Is Born?," http://www.nichd.nih .gov/publications/pubs/gest_diabetes/sub11.cfm
The NICHHD website is a resource for those women diagnosed with gestational diabetes who need detailed information on what their next steps should be once the baby arrives. The site provides a specific, step-by-step medical process that is outlined for the first six weeks after delivery, which addresses the three main categories of mothers: normal, impaired glucose tolerance, and those with diabetes. Frequently Asked Questions include breastfeeding when being diagnosed with gestational diabetes and whether the mother is at risk of developing diabetes in the future.

➤ The Hormone Health Network—"Gestational Diabetes," http://www.hormone .org/Resources/Patient_Guides/upload/FS_DIA_Gestational_Diabetes_EN-6- 12.pdf
This short PDF provided by the Hormone Health Network provides an overview of gestational diabetes. Beginning with a brief explanation of gestational diabetes, the handout covers risks, diagnosis, symptoms, and treatment. A list of additional informational resources is included.

➤ Mayo Clinic—"Gestational Diabetes," http://www.mayoclinic.com/health/gestational diabetes/DS00316
Following a brief overview of gestational diabetes, the site provides basic information on the symptoms, risk factors, complications, diagnosis, and treatment of the condition. A coping and support section presents ways to appropriately deal with the stress of being pregnant and managing gestational diabetes.

➤ WomensHealth.gov—"Diabetes," http://www.womenshealth.gov/faq/diabetes .pdf
This handout provides information about the different types of diabetes as they affect women. The handout discusses gestational diabetes and how women can take care of themselves and their baby during their pregnancy.

Selected Audiovisual Resources

➤ Agency for Healthcare Research and Quality—"Gestational Diabetes: A Guide for Pregnant Women," http://www.effectivehealthcare.ahrq.gov/index.cfm/search-for-guides-reviews-and-reports/?pageaction=displayproduct&productID=162
This site provided by AHRQ provides a fifteen-minute audio file of the site's gestational diabetes consumer guide. The guide covers basics such as an overview of gestational diabetes, how the condition is treated, and the importance of follow-up with a physician.

➤ American Association of Diabetes Educators. 2009. *Gestational Diabetes*. 2nd ed. Hunt Valley, MD: Milner-Fenwick.
This comprehensive 45-minute DVD provides women with a detailed overview of gestational diabetes and how the condition develops. A diabetes educator explains the risk factors of gestational diabetes and how women are screened for the condition, how it is diagnosed, complications, risks, blood glucose levels, physical activity, and healthy food choices. Interspersed throughout the video, women who have had gestational diabetes discuss their experiences. The video also covers separate sections about blood glucose monitoring, injecting insulin, and hypoglycemia.

➤ American Diabetes Association—"Diabetes During Pregnancy: What Is Gestational Diabetes?," http://www.diabetes.org/diabetes-basics/gestational/what-is-gestationaldiabetes.html
Narrated by Laura Bustanante along with Lynn Dowdell, this short video explains how gestational diabetes develops. The narrator discusses possible complications from the disease and ways pregnant women can manage the disease effectively to ensure the health of the baby.

➤ Centers for Disease Control and Prevention—"Gestational Diabetes and Women," http://www2c.cdc.gov/podcasts/index.asp
This podcast provided by the CDC features speaker Lucy England of the CDC's Division of Reproductive Health. Dr. England discusses how gestational diabetes can cause health risks for both mother and baby and provides advice on how to manage the disease. She also explains that because women with gestational diabetes are at an increased risk of developing type 2 diabetes, women should work to reduce this risk through lifestyle changes.

➤ Livestrong.com—"Healthy Food Choices for Gestational Diabetes," http://www.livestrong.com/video/2347-healthy-food-choices-gestational-diabetes/
Mary Hondros, who holds a bachelor of science in dietetics, provides women with gestational diabetes a brief overview of eating healthy eating habits. She gives women tips such as eating small meals, including a protein source with meals, and counting carbohydrates throughout the day. Hondros also provides

suggestions about what foods to eat and avoid for women who are experiencing morning sickness.

➤ March of Dimes—"Gestational Diabetes," http://www.marchofdimes.com/pregnancy/complications_gestationaldiabetes.html
This four-minute video provided by the March of Dimes features Siobhan Dolan from the Montefiore Medical Center. Dolan discusses with one of her patients what to do to prevent and manage gestational diabetes and how high glucose can have serious health consequences for both the baby and mother. She emphasizes that gestational diabetes usually goes away after pregnancy, and about half of all women with gestational diabetes will develop type 2 diabetes later in life.

References

American Diabetes Association. 2010. "Revised Standards of Care Call for Changing How Gestational Diabetes Should Be Diagnosed." American Diabetes Association. December 29. http://www.diabetes.org/for-media/2010/revised-standards-of-care-2011.html.

———. 2011a. *American Diabetes Association Complete Guide to Diabetes*. 5th ed. Alexandria, VA: American Diabetes Association.

———. 2011b. "Executive Summary: Standards of Medical Care in Diabetes—2011." *Diabetes Care* 34 (Suppl. 1): S4–S10. http://care.diabetesjournals.org/content/34/Supplement_1/S4.full.

Davis, E. 2009. "Effective Health Care Program: Gestational Diabetes: A Guide for Pregnant Women." Agency for Healthcare Research and Quality. August 5. http://www.effectivehealthcare.ahrq.gov/index.cfm/search-for-guides-reviews-and-reports/?pageaction=displayproduct&productid=162.

dLife. 2010a. "About Gestational Diabetes." LifeMed Media. Last modified August 27. http://www.dlife.com/diabetes/gestational/about.

———. 2010b. "Gestational Complications for Baby." LifeMed Media. Last modified November 9. http://www.dlife.com/diabetes/gestational/baby.

———. 2010c. "Gestational Maternal Complications." LifeMed Media. Last modified November 9. http://www.dlife.com/diabetes/gestational/prevention/pregnancy-complications.

Eunice Kennedy Shriver National Institute of Child Health and Human Development. 2012. "Managing Gestational Diabetes: A Patient's Guide to a Healthy Pregnancy." National Institutes of Health. Last updated January 6. http://www.nichd.nih.gov/publications/pubs/gest_diabetes/.

National Diabetes Information Clearinghouse. 2011. "What I Need to Know about Gestational Diabetes." National Institute of Diabetes and Digestive and Kidney Diseases, National Institutes of Health. Last updated December 6. http://diabetes.niddk.nih.gov/dm/pubs/gestational/.

Chapter 6

Children and Diabetes

Introduction

Type 1 diabetes, formerly referred to as juvenile-onset diabetes, develops when the immune system mistakenly attacks pancreatic beta cells, the insulin-producing cells in the pancreas, resulting in a deficiency of insulin. Without an adequate amount of insulin, the body is unable to metabolize glucose properly, which then builds up in the bloodstream and is excreted in the urine, resulting in the symptoms of diabetes. Although this chapter focuses mainly on type 1 diabetes in children, it is important to know that children can also be diagnosed with type 2 diabetes.

Type 1 and Type 2 Diabetes in Children

More than 13,000 children are diagnosed with type 1 diabetes each year, and now type 2 diabetes is also becoming pervasive in teens and children (KidsHealth.org, 2012). A diagnosis of diabetes presents many challenges for the child and the entire family. The diagnosis may evoke many emotional reactions in the family, including anger, sadness, and guilt. Parents may feel helpless and anxious about managing a chronic disease in a young child. Working with the health care team, educating the entire family about diabetes, and properly managing the disease can ameliorate the challenges and emotions of dealing with a chronic illness. It is important for families to remember that children can achieve a high quality of life while living with diabetes. Over time, the child can learn to manage many aspects of the disease (JDRF, 2012).

Symptoms

The major symptoms of type 1 diabetes include frequent urination, unusual thirst, extreme hunger, unusual weight loss, and extreme fatigue. Some patients may experience irritability, blurred vision, dry and itchy skin, or tingling in the hands and feet. Children with diabetes complain frequently of being thirsty and tired. Often they also show an increased appetite yet will continue to lose weight. The parents of children experiencing such symptoms should consult a physician to obtain an accurate diagnosis so proper management of the disease can begin. Type 1 diabetes can occur at any age; however, the peak ages for type 1 onset are between ages five and six and then again between eleven and thirteen. Symptom onset may be sudden with type 1 diabetes, but with type 2 diabetes there may be no symptoms or symptoms may develop insidiously, leading to a delay in diagnosis. Some children may require hospitalization if diagnosis is not made early (HealthyChildren.org, 2011).

Therapy

There is no cure for type 1 diabetes; however, the disease can be treated and controlled with lifelong insulin therapy. By properly managing the disease, children with diabetes can lead a normal life and avoid health complications. The goals of treatment are to keep insulin levels as close to normal as possible and to treat or prevent diabetic ketoacidosis (DKA). Insulin may be given as an injection under the skin using a syringe, administered through an insulin pen, or injected through an insulin pump. The three types often used are rapid-acting, long-acting, and intermediate-acting insulin (Mayo Clinic, 2012). Children with type 2 diabetes may or may not be prescribed insulin, but they will likely be on medications to keep glucose levels within normal range. Either the parent or the child, if able, will need to monitor and record the child's blood glucose levels regularly (*see* CHAPTER 7, DRUG THERAPY).

Parents will need to remind children and teens that proper management of the disease does not end at insulin injections. Children and teens need to lead a healthy lifestyle that includes a balanced and nutritious diet along with daily physical activity. The child will also need regular visits to health care providers to ensure proper disease management and avoid health complications. The doctor will measure the child's glycated hemoglobin (A1C) levels during visits to monitor the effectiveness of the treatment plan. A1C is a blood test that measures the average blood glucose over the past two to three months. If the A1C level is elevated, the doctor may change the insulin regimen or adjust the child's diet.

Even with diligent care and management, complications can develop that need immediate attention. Patients on insulin must be aware of hypoglycemia, also known as low blood sugar. Insulin may cause the child's blood glucose level to drop below normal. Skipping meals or physical exertion can cause glucose levels to fall. Symptoms of hypoglycemia include sweating, shakiness, hunger, dizziness, nausea, rapid heart rate, fatigue, difficulty concentrating, and headaches (Mayo Clinic, 2012).

Babies, Toddlers, and Preschoolers

Providing care for a young child with diabetes may seem like a daunting task for parents. When a child receives the diagnosis of a chronic condition like diabetes, parents experience many emotions and often feel overwhelmed. Preparation for coping with condition begins by developing a diabetes care plan and distributing responsibilities among family members. The management plan should include insulin therapy, blood glucose testing, and meal planning (Siminerio and Betschart, 2000). Parents should inform siblings that their brother or sister has diabetes and, depending on the siblings' ages or maturity levels, parents may ask them to contribute to the diabetes care plan. Physicians strive for normal growth and development in infants with diabetes; however, diabetes and diabetes management may have an impact on some developmental steps (Betschart, 1999). Some issues parents of babies with diabetes need to be aware and plan for include the following:

- Babies may need to eat and drink even when not hungry or thirsty.
- Parents may need to know when to treat diabetic children for hypoglycemia because babies or young children may not be able to vocalize when they are not feeling well.
- Parents should get used to the idea of performing frequent insulin injections and pricking fingers for blood glucose monitoring tests.
- Some children experience developmental regression after diagnosis.

School Age

Parents will need to make school personnel and teachers aware of their child's condition. Also, teachers will need to learn to recognize the symptoms of low blood sugar. A school nurse can assist children who are not able to check their own glucose levels or self-inject insulin (*see* CHAPTER 15, LIFE OUTSIDE THE HOME, for more on life with diabetes outside of the home). Children should participate as much as possible in their own care. As they grow older and become more responsible, they can begin to take an even more active role in the management of their diabetes.

Teens

In addition to dealing with the day-to-day challenges of trying to fit in among peers, teens with diabetes must also manage their diabetes—injecting insulin, monitoring glucose, and frequently snacking on a daily basis. For teens, the added responsibility of managing their diabetes can be physically and emotionally overwhelming. As teens mature, though, parents should begin to turn over to them the responsibility for managing diabetes. Teens can begin by performing the following diabetes responsibilities (Betschart-Roemer, 2002):

- Regularly monitoring and recording their blood glucose levels
- Monitoring patterns of high or low glucose levels and informing parents
- Discussing methods of improving diabetes management with their parents and health care team
- Visiting their health care provider on a regular basis and communicating effectively with their health care team
- Assessing diabetic supplies and ordering before running out
- Taking steps to ensure safety while driving
- Providing diabetes awareness and education to friends

Summary

Parents, children, and teens must make diabetes care and management a priority. Parents should be involved in the daily care of children with diabetes and should teach them about proper diabetes management as well as how they can advocate for themselves. Increasingly, over time, older children and teens will be able to take on the responsibilities of diabetes management and be able to advocate for themselves when away from home.

Information Sources

Selected Print Resources

For Parents

➤ Betschart, Jean. 1999. *Diabetes Care for Babies, Toddlers, and Preschoolers.* Minneapolis, MN: Chronimed.

  Betschart provides parents with practical advice about how to deal with providing care for a young child with diabetes. The author covers special issues such as injecting insulin, feeding finicky eaters, and dealing with holidays and special occasions.

➤ Hanas, Ragnar. 2005. *Type 1 Diabetes: A Guide for Children, Adolescents, Young Adults—and Their Caregivers.* New York: Marlowe.

  This resource provides an excellent source of information for families with a child diagnosed with type 1 diabetes. The book contains a wealth of information, from the basics to social issues, to pregnancy, travel tips, research, and handling stress.

➤ Mallano, Irene. 2010. *Mommy, What Is Type 1 Diabetes?* Bloomington, IN: AuthorHouse.

  This book is useful for explaining type 1 diabetes to young children through storytelling. There is also a section for parents containing tips on dealing with diabetes in children.

➤ Platt, Elizabeth. 2011. *100 Questions and Answers about Your Child's Type 1 Diabetes.* Sudbury, MA: Jones and Bartlett Publishing.

  In question-and-answer format, this resource provides information to assist parents in managing their child's type 1 diabetes.

➤ Siminerio, Linda, and Jean Betschart. 2000. *American Diabetes Association Guide to Raising a Child with Diabetes.* 2nd ed. Alexandria, VA: American Diabetes Association.

  Though somewhat dated, this resource provides a succinct overview of how to care for a child with diabetes. The book covers an overview of diabetes topics such as caring for a child with diabetes, insulin therapy, glucose monitoring, meal planning, sports safety, and living with diabetes.

➤ Wysocki, Tim. 1997. *The Ten Keys to Helping Your Child Grow Up with Diabetes.* Alexandria, VA: American Diabetes Association.
This resource provides the basics for parents to get started in managing their child's diabetes. The book covers diabetes basics, coping, communication, stress, treatment, social skills, school adjustment, and working with health professionals.

For Teens

➤ Betschart-Roemer, Jean. 2002. *Type 2 Diabetes in Teens: Secrets for Success.* New York: Wiley.
Written for teens, this resource describes type 2 diabetes and how to effectively manage the condition. The book covers issues such as dating, sexuality, self-esteem, safe driving, and managing diabetes at school.

➤ Hanas, Ragnar. 2005. *Type 1 Diabetes: A Guide for Children, Adolescents, Young Adults—and Their Caregivers.* New York: Marlowe.
This resource provides an excellent source of information for teens diagnosed with type 1 diabetes. The book contains a wealth of information, from the basics to social issues, to pregnancy, travel tips, research, and handling stress. Hanas provides very detailed information, most of which focuses on helping older teens and young adults.

➤ Hood, Korey. 2010. *Type 1 Teens: A Guide to Managing Your Life with Diabetes.* Washington, DC: Magination.
The author provides tips for teens on how to deal with diabetes through improving support, setting priorities, fighting diabetes burnout, and being a self-advocate.

➤ Loy, Spike, and Bo Loy. 2007. *Getting a Grip on Diabetes: Quick Tips and Techniques for Kids and Teens.* Alexandria, VA: American Diabetes Association.
Written by brothers who both have type 1 diabetes, teens with diabetes will learn from the many tips presented about how to live a productive life with diabetes. The book is written in an engaging style for young people.

For Children

➤ Gosselin, Kim. 1998. *Rufus Comes Home: Rufus, the Bear with Diabetes.* Plainview, NY: JayJo Books.
In this book, a little boy named Brian gets sick and has to go to the hospital where he learns he has diabetes. Brian wishes for someone with whom he can share his feelings, so his mother surprises Brian with a cuddly, stuffed teddy bear—who also has diabetes.

➤ Gosselin, Kim. 2004. *Taking Diabetes to School.* Plainview, New York: JayJo Books.
This illustrated book is aimed at school-aged children with diabetes. The main character, Jason, describes his life with diabetes—eating healthy meals, going to school, taking insulin, and playing sports.

➤ Loy, Spike, and Boy Loy. 2004. *487 Really Cool Tips for Kids with Diabetes.* Alexandria, VA: American Diabetes Association.
  Written by brothers with type 1 diabetes, this book is a useful resource for both parents and children. Kids with diabetes can use this book as a resource to learn more about living with diabetes, as well as dealing with sports, holidays, eating out, camping, travel, school, and college.

➤ Pirner, Connie. 2011. *Even Little Kids Get Diabetes.* Darby, PA: Diane Publishing.
  Young children with diabetes are the intended audience for this picture book. The main character in the book is a little girl with diabetes. The story covers information about her symptoms and diagnosis and how she and her family cope with diabetes.

Selected Web Resources

For Parents

➤ Canadian Diabetes Association—"Children and Type 1 Diabetes," http://www.diabetes.ca/diabetes-and-you/youth/type1/
  This webpage presents information to allow parents to learn more about type 1 diabetes in children, the parent's role, and how to properly manage their child's condition. Parents will also learn tips about talking to their child and their child's caregivers about diabetes. The site's articles encourage children to take on a larger part of managing their own diabetes issues as they mature into adolescence.

➤ Canadian Diabetes Association—"Children and Type 2 Diabetes," http://www.diabetes.ca/diabetes-and-you/youth/type2/
  This page contains statistics about type 2 diabetes in children. The site provides parents with an overview of type 2 diabetes in children, including risk factors, information about prevention, and resources for finding additional information. The site contains links to information about eating well and engaging in physical activity.

➤ Canadian Diabetes Association—"Dealing with Your Child's Diagnosis of Diabetes," http://www.diabetes.ca/diabetes-and-you/youth/diagnosis/
  The Canadian Diabetes Association website provides a range of information about diabetes and includes sections about childhood diabetes. This page presents a succinct list of tips for parents who are adjusting to their child's new diabetes diagnosis. There is information for parents that discusses caring for children and teens with the condition. The site covers other important areas such as healthy eating for school-age children and dealing with diabetes during special occasions, holidays, and parties.

➤ Diabetes Research Institute—"Diabetes and Kids," http://www.diabetesresearch.org/document.doc?id=274

This two-page brochure, "Diabetes and Kids," provides a useful way of explaining diabetes to children. The brochure discusses what diabetes is and the differences between type 1 and type 2 diabetes; it also includes information on the symptoms of the condition, along with a description about treatment and management. The second part of the brochure includes a crossword puzzle and word find, emphasizing important diabetes terms.

➤ dLife—"Children and Teens," http://www.dlife.com/diabetes/lifestyle/diabetes-children
This site provides information for parents about their child's type 1 or type 2 diabetes. There are general guidelines for helping children and teens manage their diabetes, and parents will find tips on when to turn over some control of diabetes management to the growing child. Parents can also learn about caring for a baby with diabetes. This resource also tackles dealing with the challenges of diabetes at school, such as back-to-school tips, shoe shopping, individualized education programs, and college life.

➤ HealthyChildren.org, http://www.healthychildren.org/
Sponsored by the American Academy of Pediatrics, HealthyChildren.org provides a variety of pediatric health information. Users of the site can find information about type 1 or type 2 diabetes by typing "diabetes" in the search box. The site contains a basic overview of diabetes in children and covers information such as signs and symptoms, disease management, diagnostic tests, insulin therapy, healthful diet, physical activity, and self-care responsibilities for children. The site also explains how to find a pediatric endocrinologist. There is also a one-minute audio file explaining type 1 diabetes to children.

➤ The Hormone Health Network—"Hormones and You: Type 2 Diabetes in Children," http://www.hormone.org/Resources/upload/THF-T2DiabetesChild-5-5v2.pdf
This brochure provides parents a basic overview of understanding type 2 diabetes and information about their role in managing the disease and working with their child. The brochure begins with an explanation of the differences between type 1 and type 2 diabetes, followed by an explanation of risk factors, symptoms, treatment, and management of the condition. The site also includes a Spanish language version of the brochure, along with links to additional information about type 2 diabetes.

➤ JDRF, http://www.jdf.org/
A nonprofit organization promoting type 1 diabetes research, the site offers information for patients and their family members about type 1 diabetes. A section titled "Life with Diabetes" contains information for the newly diagnosed, kids, teens, and adults, as well as information about school, college, and travel. Another section provides links to publications, including the site's online magazine.

➤ Joslin Diabetes Center—"Childhood Diabetes," http://www.joslin.org/info/childhood_diabetes.html
The "Childhood Diabetes" section contains a wealth of information about type 1 and type 2 diabetes in children. There are a number of additional diabetes-related topics in this section, including dealing with diabetes at school, daily life with diabetes, attending summer camp, going to college, and managing the emotional impact of the disease.

➤ KidsHealth.org—"Diabetes Center," http://www.kidshealth.org/parent/centers/diabetes_center.html
This site contains information for parents, teens, and children on many health topics. In the "Parents Home" section, parents can find a wealth of information about childhood diabetes including basics, monitoring, medications, diet, and living with diabetes. There are also links to further investigate diabetes prevention, glucose monitoring, facts and myths, dealing with feelings, hypoglycemia, complications, metabolism, and obesity.

➤ Mayo Clinic—"Type 1 Diabetes in Children," http://www.mayoclinic.com/health/type-1-diabetes-in-children/DS00931
The Mayo Clinic site provides parents with information about what they need to know to manage their child's type 1 diabetes. The site covers basics, symptoms, causes, risk factors, complications, tests, treatment, and support information. By clicking on the "In-Depth" tab, parents can learn more regarding information about symptoms, hyperglycemia, A1C tests, diagnosis, complications, treatments, medications, and lifestyle changes.

➤ Mayo Clinic—"Type 2 Diabetes in Children," http://www.mayoclinic.com/health/type-2-diabetes-in-children/DS00946
This section provides parents with information about effectively managing their child's type 2 diabetes. The site provides information about symptoms, causes, risk factors, complications, diagnosis, tests, treatments, coping, and support. There is also a link to in-depth information about the condition that includes additional information on symptoms, hyperglycemia, A1C tests, complications, treatment, medication, and lifestyle changes.

➤ National Diabetes Education Program—"Overview of Diabetes in Children and Adolescents," http://ndep.nih.gov/media/youth_factsheet.pdf
This lengthy fact sheet has a moderately high reading level but does cover information about hybrid or mixed diabetes and maturity-onset diabetes of the young (MODY), in addition to type 1 and type 2 diabetes in youth. The fact sheet also presents a comparison of type 1 and type 2 diabetes, symptoms, risk factors, and management. A list of additional resources is also included.

➤ National Dissemination Center for Children with Disabilities, http://www.nichcy.org/

The site provides information for parents about a variety of disabilities, including diabetes. Categories of information include type of disability, age group, disability and education laws, and research. The area titled "Other Health Impairment" contains a discussion of diabetes, which is a disability category that may qualify a child for special education.

➤ USDA Food and Nutrition Services—"Eat Smart. Play Hard. Healthy Lifestyle: Introduction," http://www.fns.usda.gov/eatsmartplayhardhealthylifestyle/
Here parents will find information about leading a healthy lifestyle and encouraging their children to make healthy food choices and to be active. The site includes links to getting started with creating a healthier lifestyle, information about making smart choices, meal ideas and recipes for quick and healthy meals, and tips on how to increase physical activity. There is also a link where parents can use a tracking card to get a better picture of the foods and drinks the child consumes during the day, along with the amount of time the child spends in daily physical activity.

For Teens

➤ American Association of Diabetes Educators—"Tips for Teens with Diabetes Series," http://www.diabeteseducator.org/DiabetesEducation/Patient_Resources/AADE_NDEP_Resources.html
This series provides several brochures that contain tips for teens dealing with diabetes. Topics include information about diabetes basics and diabetes management, and tips for being active, dealing with emotions, losing weight, and making healthy food choices. The brochures contain information aimed at teens and provide a list of resources for finding additional information. There are links to color and black-and-white brochures on these topics.

➤ Center for Young Women's Health—"Diabetes," http://www.youngwomenshealth.org/diabetes.html
Aimed at teen and preteen girls, this webpage provides an explanation of diabetes, symptoms, diagnosis, management, and therapy. It describes both type 1 and type 2 diabetes. In addition, there is information about insulin, how it works, and how it is used. The site contains information about disposable syringes, insulin pens, and insulin pumps. Articles also explain glucose monitoring and using a glucometer. Teens can also find out more about leading a healthy lifestyle by eating properly and being physically active. The site contains links to additional resources.

➤ Diabetes UK—"My Life—For Young People with Diabetes," http://www.diabetes.org.uk/Guide-to-diabetes/My-life/
The My Life section for teens provides information that is pertinent for teens dealing with diabetes.

➤ GirlsHealth.gov—"Diabetes," http://www.girlshealth.gov/disability/types/list .cfm#diabetes
In addition to basic health information for girls, the site provides information about diabetes, tips for healthy eating, and coping with diabetes. A variety of PDFs are available, covering topics describing diabetes and providing tips for living with the condition. The site includes links to other sites that contain information about diabetes.

➤ KidsHealth.org, "Diabetes Center," http://www.kidshealth.org/teen/centers/ diabetes_center.html
On this central webpage, this teen-focused website contains information about diabetes basics, treatment, prevention, diagnostic tests, nutrition, and dealing with emotions. There are also links to stories of teens with diabetes, health tips, and information about eating healthy. The site also contains a glossary of important diabetes terms.

➤ National Diabetes Education Program—"Teens: What Is Diabetes?," http://ndep .nih.gov/teens/index.aspx?redirect=true
The site contains a wealth of information for teens who have diabetes, including diabetes basics, being active, nutrition, and dealing with emotions. The site also provides a diabetes quiz, additional publications, and links to additional resources.

‰ Young Men's Health—"Diabetes," http://www.youngmenshealthsite.org/diabetes .html
The Young Men's Health website, aimed at teen boys with diabetes, contains basic information for teens about type 1 and type 2 diabetes. It describes diabetes and the differences between type 1 and type 2 diabetes. The site provides information about the symptoms, diagnosis, treatment, and the importance of lifestyle changes such as diet and physical activity. Additional resources are available through the site.

For Children

➤ Diabetes UK—"My Life—For Young People with Diabetes," http://www.diabetes .org.uk/Guide-to-diabetes/My-life/
The My Life section explains diabetes in a way children can understand and provides interactive activities and games for kids.

➤ GirlsHealth.gov, http://www.girlshealth.gov/disability/types/list.cfm#diabetes
In addition to basic health information for girls, the site provides information about diabetes, tips for healthy eating, and coping with diabetes.

➤ JDRF—"Kids Online," http://www.kids.jdrf.org/
The Kids Online site contains information written for older children with diabetes and teaches them about managing their condition.

➤ KidsHealth.org—"Diabetes Center," http://kidshealth.org/kid/centers/diabetes_
center.html
The Kids Health Diabetes Center explains diabetes to children in a way they can
understand. The site contains information about diabetes basics, monitoring,
treatment, and coping.

➤ Let's Move, http://www.letsmove.gov/
This government-sponsored website encourages children to be healthy by
promoting exercise and eating nutritious foods. This is a great website for those
who are trying to prevent type 2 diabetes and for those with diabetes trying to
manage their disease through a healthy lifestyle.

Selected Audiovisual Resources

➤ dLife—"Kids/Teens," http://www.dlife.com/dlifetv/video/playlist/kids_and_teens
The Kids/Teens link contains several short videos pertaining to diabetes in
children. Videos cover topics such as support groups for children, college life,
insulin therapy, summer camps, dealing with diabetes, and many others.

➤ KidsHealth.org—"How Insulin Is Made and Works," http://kidshealth.org/
parent/diabetes_center/diabetes_basics/diabetes_movie.html?tracking=79996_B
This is a short video that contains information about how insulin is produced
and how it works in the body. It then provides information on how the insulin
production and use process is different in someone with type 1 diabetes and in
someone with type 2 diabetes.

References

Betschart, J. 1999. *Diabetes Care for Babies, Toddlers, and Preschoolers: A Reassuring
Guide.* Minneapolis, MN: Chronimed.

Betschart-Roemer, J. 2002. *Type 2 Diabetes in Teens: Secrets for Success.* New York:
Wiley.

HealthyChildren.org. 2011. "Health Issues: Diabetes." American Academy of Pediatrics. Last updated May 25. http://www.healthychildren.org/English/health-
issues/conditions/chronic/pages/Diabetes.aspx.

JDRF. 2012. "Newly Diagnosed." JDRF. Accessed August 8. http://www.jdrf.org/
index.cfm?page_id=103432.

KidsHealth.org. 2012. "Diabetes Center." The Nemours Foundation. Accessed
August 8. http://www.kidshealth.org/parent/centers/diabetes_center.html.

Mayo Clinic. 2012. "Type 1 Diabetes." Mayo Foundation for Medical Education and
Research. January 25. http://www.mayoclinic.com/health/type-1-diabetes/DS00329.

Siminerio, L., and J. Betschart. 2000. *American Diabetes Association Guide to Raising
a Child with Diabetes.* 2nd ed. Alexandria, VA: American Diabetes Association.

Part II

Diabetes Management Resources

Chapter 7

Drug Therapy

Introduction

Drug therapy is an essential component of most diabetes management programs. Those individuals with type 1 diabetes must take insulin to live. When type 2 diabetes patients are unable to manage their condition through lifestyle changes, taking oral medications and eventually insulin may become necessary. This chapter describes the drugs used to treat type 1, type 2, and gestational diabetes. Understanding the benefits of oral and injectable medications and diabetes treatments will help patients be more adherent in following their prescribed drug regimen. In addition, this chapter covers information about insulin delivery devices, such as insulin pens and insulin pumps. This chapter also provides an overview of glucose control and management tools used in checking glucose levels. The chapter concludes with an annotated list of drug therapy and glucose measurement resources.

Type 1 Diabetes

Although type 1 diabetes has no cure, patients can treat and control the disease with lifelong insulin therapy. The two main goals of this treatment are to keep blood glucose levels as close to normal as possible and to prevent diabetic ketoacidosis (DKA). Dosing with insulin occurs either as an injection under the skin using a syringe or an insulin pen or through an insulin pump. Types include rapid-acting, short-acting, intermediate, and long-acting insulin. The patient's health care provider may prescribe other medications, such as aspirin therapy, high blood pressure medications, or cholesterol-lowering medications, in addition to insulin (Mayo Clinic, 2012).

Effective diabetes management includes insulin therapy in conjunction with lifestyle components such as eating healthy, staying active, and coping with stress. Patients need to take an active role in managing their diabetes, which includes taking insulin as recommended and frequently monitoring glucose levels. Newly diagnosed patients should learn about insulin, how it works, when to take it, and the proper method of injection. In addition, for those taking insulin, it is critical to learn how to monitor glucose levels by using a glucose meter. (For more information about type 1 diabetes, *see* CHAPTER 2, TYPE 1 DIABETES.)

Insulin

In patients with type 1 diabetes, the immune system mistakenly attacks and destroys beta cells, the insulin-producing cells in the pancreas, which results in a complete deficiency of insulin. Because the body needs insulin to survive, patients use insulin to replace and replicate the insulin levels of a normally functioning pancreas. It is important to understand how insulin therapy works to manage blood glucose levels effectively (Diabetes Education Online, 2012b).

In an individual without diabetes, the pancreas releases insulin as needed and keeps glucose levels within a narrow, normal range. At the low end, normal blood glucose levels range from 60 to 100mg/dL overnight and between meals. After meals and snacks, when insulin is higher, the normal range is less than 140 mg/dL (Diabetes Education Online, 2012a).

In a nondiabetic person, the pancreas releases very low levels of insulin overnight, between meals, and if the person is fasting. When a person eats a meal or a snack, there is a large, continuous release of insulin into the bloodstream. Even when the person smells food and takes the first taste, the body is beginning to prepare to receive sugar from the food. When the person ingests food, glucose levels rise, which triggers a release of insulin known as bolus insulin release. Insulin levels climb and then peak about forty-five minutes to an hour after a meal. After peaking, insulin levels fall back to the normal level, which is known as the background or basal insulin level (Diabetes Education Online, 2012a). In nondiabetic individuals, mechanisms are in place to balance this release of insulin. When the body needs more insulin to allow glucose to leave the bloodstream and enter the cells, the pancreas releases more insulin; and when there is less glucose in the bloodstream, the pancreas produces less insulin.

People with type 1 diabetes make no insulin. They must receive insulin replacement therapy to lower blood glucose levels and to duplicate the action of a nondiabetic person's naturally produced insulin. Insulin replacement must be able to mimic both background or basal insulin levels and bolus insulin levels (Diabetes Education Online, 2012a).

Background or basal insulin represents approximately 50 percent of the body's daily insulin need and provides a very low, continuous level of insulin in the body. Basal insulin controls glucose overnight, between meals, and when fasting, and it also counteracts glucose produced by the liver. Long-acting insulin that is injected once or twice each day can maintain basal replacement levels, as can rapid-acting insulin that is continuously infused with an insulin pump (Diabetes Education Online, 2012a).

Bolus insulin replacement duplicates the insulin needed after meals and snacks. In addition, bolus replacement provides the extra insulin needed to correct glucose levels that rise too high, as achieved through use of rapid-acting insulin or regular insulin (Diabetes Education Online, 2012a).

It is also important to understand the action times of the different kinds of insulin by understanding the onset, peak, and duration of each type. Onset refers to the period from when the insulin injection occurs until it begins to affect blood glucose levels. Peak time refers to the period from when the insulin injection occurs until it works to its maximum effect. The duration is how long the insulin actively affects blood glucose levels (Joslin Diabetes Center, 2012).

- Rapid-acting insulin: Onset is about five to fifteen minutes; duration is for three to five hours.
- Short-acting insulin: Onset is thirty to sixty minutes; duration is for five to eight hours.
- Intermediate-acting insulin: Onset is one to three hours; duration is twelve to sixteen hours.
- Long-acting insulin: Onset is one hour; duration is twenty to twenty-six hours.
- Premixed insulin: Premixed insulin is a combination of two different types of insulin. (FamilyDoctor.org, 2012)

Injection

Administration of insulin can occur by one of two methods: injection or infusion. Most type 1 diabetes patients need to take multiple injections each day. Insulin injections use a hypodermic needle and syringe or an insulin pen. Injection sites include the back of the upper arms, the upper buttocks or hips, and the outer side of the thighs. The most common site is the abdomen, at least two inches away from the belly button (FamilyDoctor.org, 2012). Patients should rotate their injection sites in order to avoid having their skin thicken with a buildup of fat under the skin, which can affect how well the insulin absorbs into their system.

Needle and Syringe

A hypodermic needle and syringe is the most common insulin delivery method. The syringes are plastic and disposable, holding up to 30, 50, or 100 units of insulin. A 100-unit syringe holds 1 cubic centimeter (cc) of insulin. The needles are small and range in length from 3/16 inch for infants to 1/2 inch or larger for use in adults (Diabetes Education Online, 2012b). Insulin injection should aim just under the skin at the fat layer, also called subcutaneous tissue.

Insulin Pens

Some patients prefer to use an insulin pen to inject insulin. Insulin pens are easier to use than using a needle and syringe as an insulin delivery device. Insulin pens contain a cartridge, needle, and a dial. The cartridge contains a reservoir of insulin. The dial allows the patient to select the proper amount of insulin to deliver. The needle punctures the skin and delivers the insulin when the patient pushes the plunger. In some devices, both the cartridge and needle are disposable components of the device; in other models, the pens themselves are disposable after each use. Insulin delivery is slower with pens than with needles, so most insulin pens must be held in place for five to ten seconds after the patient pushes in the plunger completely.

Insulin Pumps

Increasingly more popular as an insulin delivery device, insulin pumps allow more control over insulin flow and eliminate the need for multiple injection sites. An insulin pump is a small, computerized device that delivers insulin subcutaneously (under the skin). The system pumps insulin from the device, through a thin tube, and into a catheter that is placed under the skin (dLife, 2012b).

The insulin pump consists of three parts: pump, infusion set, and tubing. The pump itself is small, about the size of a cell phone, and can attach to a belt or hidden in a pocket, bra, garter belt, sock, or underwear. The infusion set attaches to the skin with an adhesive and lets insulin flow from the pump into the skin. The insulin flows through the tubing from the pump to the infusion set (Diabetes Education Online, 2012b).

Patients program the pump to deliver insulin based upon their personal basal and bolus rates. Upon programming, for basal levels the pump can release one unit of insulin per half hour or per hour. The health care team will calculate the dosages a patient needs by determining the average total units of insulin used per day for several days. Based on the total dosage, the health care team can then calculate the basal and bolus dosages (American Diabetes Association, 2012a). The pump will deliver the programmed basal insulin automatically until the rate changes by reprogramming. Patients can also program into the unit their bolus infusion rates to cover the carbohydrates in each meal or snack. Unlike basal insulin, patients must instruct the pump when to deliver the bolus, program in how many grams of carbohydrates they plan to eat, and input their current blood glucose level (Diabetes Education Online, 2012b).

Patients must weigh the advantages and disadvantages of hypodermic injections versus an insulin pump. The pump does offer some advantages over the traditional injection method of delivery. In addition to allowing more precise dosing, the pump offers increased convenience and a more flexible lifestyle, because patients no longer need to worry about insulin injections. The insulin pump also offers increased blood glucose control. In general, insulin pump users maintain glucose levels closer to the normal range and have a decreased risk of experiencing hypoglycemia (dLife, 2012b).

While the pump offers many advantages, it also has disadvantages. Although insurance companies are increasingly covering the costs associated with pump use, an infusion pump and necessary supplies, such as infusion sets, cartridges, and batteries, can be expensive. Before pursuing insulin pump use, patients may want to check with their insurance company to see whether insulin pumps and supplies are covered medical expenses. Learning to use the pump may take time, and there may be technical difficulties associated with its usage. While the pump is generally convenient, it may become inconvenient in certain situations, such as when playing sports. Medical problems, such as skin reactions and infections, may result from pump use, and diabetic ketosis may result if the catheter comes out or gets kinked, which may result in insulin levels dropping too low and glucose levels rising too high (dLife, 2012b).

Hypoglycemia

Low blood glucose, also known as hypoglycemia or insulin reaction, occurs when blood glucose levels fall too low, specifically when blood glucose levels drop below 70 mg/dL. Hypoglycemia happens occasionally to everyone who has diabetes, even to those who diligently manage their disease. Hypoglycemia has four common causes: too much insulin, too much diabetes medication, too little food or a delayed meal, or too much physical activity (Joslin Diabetes Center, 2012). Hypoglycemia is dangerous, and everyone with diabetes—particularly those who take insulin—should learn about hypoglycemia, its symptoms, and how to treat it.

Usually hypoglycemia is mild and presents with such common physical symptoms as shaking, sweating, dizziness, hunger, headache, pallor, behavior change, confusion, and heart pounding. Those with diabetes should learn to recognize the symptoms and, at the first sign of hypoglycemia, check their blood glucose level and ingest a source of food containing 15 to 20 grams of carbohydrates. After fifteen minutes, blood glucose should be checked again (American Diabetes Association, 2012b). Left untreated, a person with hypoglycemia could lose consciousness, resulting in the need for immediate medical attention.

Some patients, particularly those who have had diabetes for a long time or who have neuropathy, may have a condition known as hypoglycemia unawareness. People who have hypoglycemia unawareness may not have any of the symptoms of hypoglycemia and may lose consciousness without warning (American Diabetes Association, 2012b).

Glucose Measurement

To properly monitor blood glucose, patients should regularly use a glucose meter to check for highs and lows throughout the day. Regularly monitoring blood glucose also helps patients learn about the impact of certain foods and activity levels on their blood glucose levels. These regular glucose checks also help patients verify whether their treatment plan is working. Though the frequency and timing of blood glucose monitoring is patient specific, typically patients should develop a schedule of monitoring their levels before and after each meal, when feeling symptoms of hypoglycemia, and when feeling sick (Diabetes Education Online, 2012b). Patients should keep a record of their blood glucose values using a log sheet.

Glucometers are devices used to test blood glucose levels. These meters use a drop of blood obtained from a fingertip to determine blood glucose level. Some meters now allow for testing at alternate sites, such as the forearm, thigh, or hand. A patient begins the process of checking personal glucose level by first thoroughly washing his or her hands and then inserting a test strip into the glucose meter (if the meter does not come with a drum or cartridge of preloaded strips). A lance device pricks the side of the fingertip to obtain a small drop of blood. The patient then squeezes or massages the fingertip until a drop forms and then touches and holds the test strip edge to the blood drop. The meter pulls in the drop to measure blood glucose and then displays the blood glucose level (American Diabetes Association, 2012b).

Type 2 Diabetes

Some patients with type 2 diabetes can lower their blood glucose to within normal limits through diet and exercise. Those who are unable to lower their blood glucose to within the normal range through diet and exercise will need medication to keep levels in the normal range and to prevent complications. Only those with type 2 diabetes are able to use oral medications or noninsulin injectable agents to manage their diabetes; those with type 1 must use insulin. In addition, type 2 patients may also require insulin to manage their blood glucose levels. The goals of treatment are twofold: immediately lowering high blood glucose levels and preventing complications from occurring. Oral medications may not work for everyone, particularly those patients who have had diabetes for more than ten years. Also, diabetes medications may stop controlling blood glucose in some patients who have been taking the medication for a while. When this occurs, a different combination of medications may be beneficial, and occasionally insulin may be needed (American Diabetes Association, 2012a).

As noted, if a patient on oral medications continues to have poorly controlled diabetes, the doctor may prescribe insulin (see previous information about insulin therapy in this chapter). Because patients with type 2 diabetes are at increased risk of developing other health complications, additional medications such as angiotensin-converting enzyme (ACE) inhibitors, statin drugs, and aspirin are recommended to prevent heart and kidney disease. Patients should continue to eat a healthy diet and participate in regular physical activity if they are on medications. Maintaining a proper weight is important, and some patients find that as they lose weight, or become closer to their ideal body weight, they may no longer need medications to control their blood glucose level. Those who must take oral medications to control their glucose levels should become familiar with the particular medication or medications prescribed by their doctor. (For more information about type 2 diabetes, *see* CHAPTER 3, TYPE 2 DIABETES.)

Medication Classes

As noted, in conjunction with healthy eating and regular physical activity, many patients with type 2 diabetes take oral medications that are not insulin to achieve blood glucose control. These medications are grouped into different classes of drugs depending on how they work. Some of these medications work in the patient by increasing insulin sensitivity, decreasing glucose, slowing carbohydrate absorption, or by stimulating the pancreas to increase insulin production (dLife, 2012a). The table (see p. 88) summarizes the classes of medications used for type 2 diabetes.

Gestational Diabetes

Gestational diabetes is a type of diabetes that is first recognized during pregnancy. Although the body makes more insulin during pregnancy, hormones secreted by the placenta block insulin action, and the attendant weight gain makes it difficult for the body to meet its insulin need. The lack of insulin causes glucose to build up in the bloodstream, so the body does not derive the energy it requires from food. Controlling blood sugar during pregnancy is extremely important to prevent difficult complications and to keep the baby and mother healthy, so management of gestational diabetes should be initiated immediately (American Diabetes Association, 2005).

To manage the condition, pregnant women should stay active during their pregnancy through nonimpact exercises, such as walking or swimming. Women should collaborate with their health care team to develop an appropriate physical activity plan. Overall, healthy eating and physical activity will usually help women control weight gain, which will then control gestational diabetes. If healthy eating and physical activity do not ameliorate glucose levels in the bloodstream, further management through insulin will then become necessary to manage gestational diabetes and prevent complications. Women with gestational diabetes need to monitor their blood glucose levels regularly using a blood glucose meter. Women taking insulin also need to be aware of the potential to develop hypoglycemia (American Diabetes Association, 2012a). (For more information about gestational diabetes, *see* CHAPTER 5, GESTATIONAL DIABETES.)

Summary

Along with healthy living, drug therapy is an essential component of managing diabetes. Because those with type 1 diabetes need insulin to survive, they need to

Type 2 Diabetes Medications

Medication Class	Description of Effect
Alpha-Glucosidase Inhibitors	The medications in this class work by keeping blood glucose from rising too high by slowing the digestion of carbohydrates.
Amylinomimetics	This type of medication works by slowing the movement of food through the stomach and keeping the liver from releasing glucose into the bloodstream.
Biguanides	Biguanides work by lowering the amount of glucose produced by the liver. They also work by helping cells be more sensitive to insulin, thus using insulin more effectively to lower blood glucose.
Dipeptidyl Peptidase-4 (DPP-4) Inhibitors	DPP-4 inhibitors help the pancreas make additional insulin when it is needed and prevents the liver from releasing glucose into the bloodstream. The medications in this class work only when glucose levels are high.
Glucagon-Like Peptide-1 (GLP-1) Receptor Agonists	Medications in this class help the pancreas release the correct amount of insulin. This class of medications also slows the absorption of carbohydrates and decreases the pancreas's production of glucagon, which decreases the liver's release of glucose. GLP-1 receptor agonists cause a feeling of early fullness when eating.
Meglitinide	The meglitinide class of medication aids the pancreas in producing more insulin after meals.
Sulfonylureas	This class of oral diabetes medications lowers blood glucose levels by causing the pancreas to produce more insulin and helps the body effectively use insulin.
Thiazolidinedione	Thiazolidinediones help the body use insulin better by improving the cells' response to insulin. These drugs also decrease the release of glucose from the liver. This class of drugs is used for people with insulin resistance.
Combination Oral Medications	Sometimes two medications are used in combination to control blood glucose levels. Patients taking these medications receive the benefit of both drugs but need to take only one pill. Sometimes the combination medication gives patients improved blood glucose control with a lower dosage when compared to taking just one medication.

Source: Compiled from https://patienteducation.osumc.edu/Documents/oral-meds.pdf and http://www.dlife.com/.

learn how insulin works and how to use it properly. Likewise, type 2 diabetes patients should also learn about diabetes medications and insulin when necessary. This chapter described many of the drugs used to treat type 1, type 2, and gestational diabetes so that patients can become more familiar with their use. Understanding medications (oral and injectable) and treatments will not only help patients become more adherent in following their prescribed drug regimen but will also help avoid complications.

Information Sources

Selected Print Resources

> American Diabetes Association. 2009. *Type 2 Diabetes: Your Healthy Living Guide: Tips, Techniques, and Practical Advice for Living Well with Diabetes.* 4th ed. Alexandria, VA: American Diabetes Association.
> This book includes a chapter on type 2 diabetes medication. The chapter contains an overview of type 2 oral medications and insulin. In addition, it describes insulin injection, storage, safety, and disposal. There is also a section on blood glucose monitoring and blood glucose meters.

> American Diabetes Association. 2011. *American Diabetes Association Complete Guide to Diabetes.* 5th ed. Alexandria, VA: American Diabetes Association.
> This resource contains a chapter that details the use of insulin. The chapter covers insulin types, action times, premixed insulin, buying and storing insulin, using insulin, and injection devices. Additional chapters include information about glucose monitoring and blood glucose meters.

> Beaser, Richard. 2005. *The Joslin Guide to Diabetes: A Program for Managing Your Treatment.* New York: Fireside.
> Containing a large section with several chapters devoted to diabetes treatment, this resource contains information about monitoring glucose, taking oral medications, and using insulin. The glucose monitoring chapter explains why, when, and how patients should check their glucose. A chapter on oral medications provides information on how diabetes pills work and the types of pills available for patients. The insulin chapter provides information about the history of insulin, insulin therapy, types of insulin, and injections. Adding to its usefulness, the chapter provides useful illustrations showing how to inject insulin.

> Collazo-Clavell, Maria. 2009. *Mayo Clinic The Essential Diabetes Book: How to Prevent, Control, and Live Well with Diabetes.* Rochester, MN: Mayo Clinic.
> This book contains several chapters devoted to diabetes treatment and glucose monitoring. The chapter on glucose monitoring includes information about when to test and the tools needed to test, recording results, factors affecting

blood glucose, and recognizing problems. The chapters covering treatment include information about insulin types, therapy, injection, pumps, and oral diabetes drugs.

➤ Mertig, Rita Girouard. 2011. *What Nurses Know...Diabetes.* New York: Demos Health.
This resource provides a chapter explaining oral diabetic medications and injectable medications. It begins with a section describing how medications help people with diabetes. Following are sections on oral medications and injectable medications, including insulin. The oral medication section describes the different classes of oral medications and describes each type and how it works. The section on insulin describes how insulin works and its different types. It also details how to measure and inject insulin.

➤ Perrin, Rosemarie. 2007. *Living with Diabetes: Everything You Need to Know to Safeguard Your Health and Take Control of Your Life.* New York: Sterling.
In addition to information about insulin therapy and type 2 diabetes medications, this resource also includes useful information about monitoring blood sugar. The chapter on blood sugar monitoring contains information about how to properly monitor it and the types of meters and lancets. The chapters on treatment contain information on insulin, injecting insulin, insulin storage, and oral medications. There are helpful illustrations in each of the chapters.

Selected Web Resources

General Resources

➤ National Diabetes Information Clearinghouse—"What I Need to Know about Diabetes Medicines," http://diabetes.niddk.nih.gov/dm/pubs/medicines_ez/index .aspx
This comprehensive resource provides an overview of diabetes medications. The range of topics includes information on target glucose levels and how medications affect glucose levels in people with diabetes, as well as information about medications for type 1, type 2, and gestational diabetes. An overview of insulin provides information on types of insulin, taking injections, using an insulin pump, and using an insulin jet injector. For those on oral medications, there is information about the types of pills available and side effects of these medications.

Oral Medications

➤ Diabetes Education Online—"Medication and Therapies," http://dtc.ucsf.edu/ types-of-diabetes/type2/treatment-of-type-2-diabetes/medications-and-therapies/
This webpage starts with a list of steps for treating type 2 diabetes and provides another list with the goals of treatment. In addition, it describes each of the

classes of oral diabetes medications for type 1 diabetes patients. This page also provides information about insulin therapy used in type 2 diabetes patients.

➤ dLife—"Diabetes Medications," http://www.dlife.com/diabetes/oral_medications
This resource provides patients an excellent overview of the different classes of oral medications available, including information on alpha-glucosidase inhibitors, biguanides, D-phenylalanine (DPA), DPP-4 inhibitors, meglitinides, combination oral medications, sulfonylureas, thiazolidinediones, GLP-1 agonists, and amylinomimetics. For each, the page provides information about how that class of medication works, along with how often the medication should be taken and possible side effects. Users of the site can also click on a link to a list of specific medications.

➤ FamilyDoctor.org—"Diabetes: Oral Medicines for Diabetes," http://familydoctor .org/online/famdocen/home/common/diabetes/treatment/388.html
This article provides background information about diabetes, its treatment, and the different classes of oral medications. There is a link to an available audio version of the text.

➤ Ohio State University Wexner Medical Center—"Oral Diabetes Medicines," https://patienteducation.osumc.edu/Documents/oral-meds.pdf
This four-page PDF describes the oral medications prescribed to many people with type 2 diabetes. The handout describes the classes of oral medications, including sulfonylureas, biguanides, thiazolidinediones, meglitinides, phenylalanine, alpha-glucosidase inhibitors, DPP-4 inhibitors, and combination medications.

Insulin

➤ Agency for Healthcare Research and Quality—"Effective Health Care Program: Premixed Insulin for Type 2 Diabetes: A Guide for Adults," http://effectivehealth care.ahrq.gov/index.cfm/search-for-guides-reviews-and-reports/?pageaction= displayproduct&productID=125
The Agency for Healthcare Research and Quality has an in-depth website that provides beneficial information for patients with type 2 diabetes, including this page that discusses the use of premixed insulin. The site includes an overview of type 2 diabetes and why patients with type 2 diabetes may need insulin. There is information about blood sugar and what insulin is, and a section includes a comparison of different medications and a list of questions that patients can ask their health care provider.

➤ Diabetes Education Online—"Medications and Therapies: Type 1 Diabetes," http://dtc.ucsf.edu/types-of-diabetes/type1/treatment-of-type-1-diabetes/ medications-and-therapies/
This source covers information about insulin therapy for type 1 diabetes patients. The page includes links to the goals of insulin treatment and charts providing

target glucose range before and after meals. The associated site also explains insulin basics, types of insulin, insulin administration, medication goals, insulin dosage calculation, and insulin treatment tips.

➤ dLife—"Insulin," http://www.dlife.com/diabetes/insulin
Beginning with an overview of how insulin works, this site provides links to information about injecting insulin, insulin pumps, and storing insulin. An insulin chart on the site details information about the effectiveness of each type of insulin. Readers can also learn more about the different types of insulin delivery devices, including needle and syringe, insulin pens, injection aids, external insulin pumps, and disposable infusion sets.

➤ FamilyDoctor.org—"Diabetes: Insulin Therapy," http://familydoctor.org/online/famdocen/home/common/diabetes/treatment/354.html
This brief site describes the basics about insulin and how it works. The page lists the types of insulin and provides the patient with pertinent information about the best places on the body to inject insulin and a step-by-step guide on how to inject insulin. In addition, rapid-acting insulin users are provided with information to successfully manage taking this type of insulin. The site contains information about when to take rapid-acting insulin, how it works, mixing with other types, preparing a correct dose, where to inject, recognizing and dealing with an insulin reaction, and how to keep blood sugar levels from getting too high or too low. The page also links to an audio version of the text.

➤ The Hormone Health Network—"Diabetes and New Insulins," http://www.hormone.org/Resources/Patient_Guides/upload/FS_DIA_Diabetes_Insulin_EN-web.pdf
This one-page handout contains a brief section about diabetes treatments. The page mainly covers information about the types of insulin and defines insulin-related terms, such as *bolus*, *rapid-acting*, *short-acting*, and *basal insulin*. The article also provides information on the new type of insulin, insulin analogues or designer insulin, which is genetically engineered insulin.

➤ Joslin Diabetes Center—"How to Improve the Insulin Injection Experience," http://www.joslin.org/info/how_to_improve_the_insulin_injection_experience html
Getting used to injecting insulin may be difficult for many. This resource offers new insulin injection users information to make injecting insulin easier. The resource covers such topics as deciding where to inject, proper injection technique, storing insulin, and discarding syringes and needles.

➤ Joslin Diabetes Center—"Insulin Action," http://www.joslin.org/info/insulin_action.html
This resource describes how insulin works and explains the different types of insulin. The page provides a chart of the action times of rapid-acting, short-acting,

intermediate-acting, and long-acting insulin, showing when patients should take it, its onset, its peak, and its duration.

Insulin Pumps and Delivery Devices

➤ American Diabetes Association—"Diabetes Forecast: Consumer Guide Charts," http://forecast.diabetes.org/consumerguide/charts
This page contains a consumer guide chart comparing diabetes-related devices. It includes blood glucose meters, continuous glucose monitors, insulin pumps, insulin pens, aids for insulin sets, and infusion sets.

➤ American Diabetes Association—"Diabetes Forecast: 2011 Insulin Pumps," http://forecast.diabetes.org/magazine/features/2011-insulin-pumps&utm_source=WWW&utm_medium=ContentPage&utm_content=ConsumerGuide-howinsulin&utm_campaign=DF
This article explains how insulin pumps work and describes some of the advantages of using a pump over insulin injections.

➤ American Diabetes Association—"Living with Diabetes: How Do Insulin Pumps Work?," http://www.diabetes.org/living-with-diabetes/treatment-and-care/medication/ insulin/insulin-pumps-how-do-insulin.html
This overview of how insulin pumps work includes substantive information for anyone considering using an insulin pump or getting ready to start using a pump. This resource provides an overview of basal and bolus insulin. In addition, the resource covers information about how to manage the pump when sleeping, showering, or bathing.

➤ dLife—"Insulin Pumps," http://www.dlife.com/diabetes/insulin/insulin_pumps
Readers of this site can learn more about the insulin pump, an alternative to insulin injection. Information on this page includes the benefits of an insulin pump, insulin pump cost, and information about how an insulin pump works. An article covers information on how new patients can be successful using the pump, providing information to consider before pumping, training how to pump, and detailing information about being hooked up to the pump. The article also has a link to pump training locations.

➤ Joslin Diabetes Center—"Insulin Injections versus Insulin Pump," http://www.joslin.org/info/insulin_injections_vs_insulin_pump.html
Stacy O'Donnell and Andrea Penney, nurses and certified diabetes educators at the Joslin Diabetes Center, provide patients considering switching to an insulin pump with a list of pros and cons of each method. This short information page provides patients a succinct listing they can read to make an informed decision about making the switch from insulin injections to insulin pumps.

➤ National Diabetes Information Clearinghouse—"Alternative Devices for Taking Insulin," http://diabetes.niddk.nih.gov/dm/pubs/insulin/index.aspx

This page explains some alternatives to using a needle and syringe to inject insulin. Devices such as insulin pens, external insulin pumps, injection ports, injection aids, and insulin jet injectors are described. There are illustrations provided of the injection devices to demonstrate how these devices work. The site also includes information about the prospects for an artificial pancreas.

Glucose Measurement and Testing Devices

➤ The Hormone Health Network—"Self-Monitoring of Blood Glucose," http://www.hormone.org/Resources/Patient_Guides/upload/self-monitoring-of-blood-glucose-bilingual-071309.pdf
This one-page handout explains the importance of monitoring glucose levels. A chart provides details for each type of diabetes and medication the patient is using how many times the patient should check glucose, the timing of the checks, and the recommended target ranges. The handout provides information on how to check blood glucose levels and when it will be necessary to call in a health care provider. The second page of this handout contains the information in Spanish.

➤ National Diabetes Information Clearinghouse—"Daily Diabetes Record," http://diabetes.niddk.nih.gov/dm/pubs/complications_control/diabetes_record.htm
This website address links to a log sheet that diabetes patients can print copies of to record daily their glucose at breakfast, lunch, dinner, bedtime, and after medications. The record also contains a space for keeping notes on sick days, events, and exercise.

➤ U.S. Food and Drug Administration—"Blood Glucose Monitoring Devices," http://www.fda.gov/MedicalDevices/ProductsandMedicalProcedures/InVitro Diagnostics/GlucoseTestingDevices/default.htm
This site explains what glucose testing devices do and why patients should test regularly. The site provides information about how to select a device and how the device is used.

Hypoglycemia

➤ American Diabetes Association—"Living with Diabetes: Hypoglycemia (Low Blood Glucose)," http://www.diabetes.org/living-with-diabetes/treatment-and-care/blood-glucose-control/hypoglycemia-low-blood.html
This resource contains an overview of hypoglycemia. It provides a list of symptoms of the condition and emphasizes the need to check glucose often. This webpage also provides information on how to treat hypoglycemia and lists what can happen if it goes untreated. There is also an audio version of the text available, as well as a short video.

➤ Mayo Clinic—"Hypoglycemia," http://www.mayoclinic.com/health/hypoglycemia/ DS00198

This page contains an excellent overview of hypoglycemia. It begins with a definition of the condition followed by a link to a page listing common symptoms. The page also links to explanations of the causes of developing hypoglycemia and a list of complications that can develop if hypoglycemia goes untreated.

➤ National Diabetes Information Clearinghouse—"Hypoglycemia," http://diabetes .niddk.nih.gov/dm/pubs/hypoglycemia/index.aspx
This resource provides an excellent overview of hypoglycemia. It includes an overview of the condition followed by symptoms, causes, prevention, and treatment.

Selected Audiovisual Resources

➤ Agency for Healthcare Research and Quality—"Effective Health Care Program: Premixed Insulin for Type 2 Diabetes: A Guide for Adults," http://effectivehealth care.ahrq.gov/index.cfm/search-for-guides-reviews-and-reports/?pageaction= displayproduct&productID=125
From this page there is a link to the audio version. This in-depth site provides beneficial information for patients with type 2 diabetes using premixed insulin. The site provides an overview of type 2 diabetes and why patients with type 2 diabetes may need insulin. The discussion also covers information on blood sugar and what insulin is. The page contains a chart and accompanying text that compare different medications and list questions that patients can ask their health care provider.

➤ American Diabetes Association—"Living with Diabetes: Hypoglycemia (Low Blood Glucose)," http://www.diabetes.org/living-with-diabetes/treatment-and-care/blood-glucose-control/hypoglycemia-low-blood.html
This short video by the American Diabetes Association provides information about the difference between hypoglycemia and hyperglycemia and the need to recognize the two conditions.

➤ dLife—"About Hypoglycemia," http://www.dlife.com/dlifetv/video/about-hypoglycemia
This three-minute video teaches diabetes patients how to recognize the symptoms and treat hypoglycemia.

➤ dLife—"Insulin Pump Users," http://www.dlife.com/dlifetv/video/to-pump-or-not-to-pump
This five-minute video explains the pros and cons of pumping, examines different types of pumps, and provides patients with information to make a decision about whether a pump is the right choice for their lifestyle.

➤ dLife—"Testing Blood Sugar," http://www.dlife.com/dlifetv/video/testing-blood-sugar
This three-minute video teaches the basics on testing blood glucose and explains what each step in the process means.

➤ The Hormone Health Network—"Living Your Best Life: Diabetes and Insulin," http://www.hormone.org/bestlife/insulin.cfm
This video clip profiles four patients using insulin and how using it affects their lives. A certified diabetes educator narrates the video and explains what insulin is and how it is used. The video debunks myths about using insulin, provides information on testing blood glucose levels, describes how to properly store and administer insulin, and how to live a good life.

References

American Diabetes Association. 2005. *Gestational Diabetes: What to Expect: Your Guide to a Healthy Pregnancy and a Happy, Healthy Baby*. 5th ed. Alexandria, VA: American Diabetes Association.

———. 2012a. "Can Diabetes Pills Help Me?" American Diabetes Association. Accessed July 3. http://www.diabetes.org/living-with-diabetes/treatment-and-care/medication/oral-medications/can-diabetes-pills-help-me.html.

———. 2012b. "Getting Started with an Insulin Pump." American Diabetes Association. Accessed July 3. http://www.diabetes.org/living-with-diabetes/treatment-and-care/medication/insulin/getting-started.html.

Diabetes Education Online. 2012a. "Insulin Basics." University of California, San Francisco. Accessed August 9. http://dtc.ucsf.edu/types-of-diabetes/type1/treatment-of-type-1-diabetes/medications-and-therapies/type-1-insulin-therapy/insulin-basics/.

———. 2012b. "Type 1 Insulin Therapy." University of California, San Francisco. Accessed August 9. http://dtc.ucsf.edu/types-of-diabetes/type1/treatment-of-type-1-diabetes/medications-and-therapies/type-1-insulin-therapy/.

dLife. 2012a. "Diabetes Medications." LifeMed Media. Accessed July 3. http://www.dlife.com/diabetes/oral_medications.

———. 2012b. "Insulin Devices." LifeMed Media. Accessed July 3. http://www.dlife.com/diabetes/insulin/about_insulin/insulin-devices.

FamilyDoctor.org. 2012. "Diabetes: Insulin Therapy." American Academy of Family Physicians. Accessed July 5. http://familydoctor.org/familydoctor/en/diseases-conditions/diabetes/treatment/insulin-therapy.html.

Joslin Diabetes Center. 2012. "Insulin Action." Joslin Diabetes Center. Accessed August 8. http://www.joslin.org/info/insulin_action.html.

Mayo Clinic. 2012. "Type 1 Diabetes." Mayo Foundation for Medical Education and Research. January 25. http://www.mayoclinic.com/health/type-1-diabetes/DS00329/.

Chapter 8

Healthy Diet and Meal Planning

Introduction

After a diagnosis of diabetes, patients may feel confusion about lifestyle changes and want to know more about diet and meal planning, specifically foods they should or should not eat. Many myths and misconceptions exist about diabetes and diet, so this chapter gives an overview of healthy eating and alerts the librarian and patient to some of the food misconceptions associated with the disease. This chapter details information about diet, food, nutrients, alcohol, meal planning, food labels, food shopping, and dining out. An annotated list of reliable print, audiovisual, and web resources for finding information on healthy eating, meal planning, recipes, and eating out closes the chapter.

Diabetes and Diet

Contrary to common belief, there is no "diabetic diet"; people with diabetes have the same nutritional needs as those without the condition. They should, however, eat a well-balanced diet with correct portions. Those with diabetes do not need to give up sweets and favorite foods, although they should eat certain foods in moderation. Because foods have an impact on blood glucose, those with diabetes should learn the nutritional facts about carbohydrates and fats, how to read food labels, which foods are the healthiest to eat, and how to determine appropriate portion sizes. Those with diabetes should also learn how to plan meals and shop for foods that are appropriate. People with diabetes do not have to give up dining out; rather, they should learn how to make the best food choices when eating out (American Diabetes Association, 2012c).

The human body digests food and changes it into glucose. Insulin acts as a key to allow glucose to enter the body's cells to be used as energy. People with type 1 diabetes do not make insulin, and people with type 2 diabetes do not use insulin properly and may not make enough insulin. In people with either type 1 or type 2 diabetes, glucose is unable to enter the cells and as a consequence builds up in the bloodstream. A well-balanced, nutritious diet is particularly important for people with diabetes because food intake can be directly related to the amount of glucose that accumulates in the blood. High levels of blood glucose cause serious health complications, such as heart, kidney, digestive, eye, nerve, and sexual problems. Making proper food choices will help patients control their level of blood glucose and can prevent patients from developing serious health complications (FamilyDoctor .org, 2010).

Foods supply the body with calories and nutrients, and the body needs calories from foods to supply energy to the body. The major sources of calories in foods come from carbohydrates, proteins, and fats. Carbohydrates should comprise 45 to 65 percent of the daily calorie intake for both those with diabetes and those without it, protein should comprise 10 to 35 percent, and fat 25 to 35 percent (Diabetes Education Online, 2012c). Understanding proper nutrition will help people with diabetes make better food choices and encourage them to eat a well-balanced, healthy diet.

Carbohydrates

Because carbohydrates are a main source of nutrition, are the most important energy source, and have the greatest impact on blood glucose levels, patients should learn about appropriate inclusion of carbohydrates in the diet. Carbohydrates should not be avoided, but people with diabetes should learn to choose more healthy carbohydrates and limit or avoid less nutritious sources of carbohydrates (Harvard School of Public Health, 2012).

Some foods are rich in complex or "good" carbohydrates, including fruits, vegetables, legumes, milk, yogurt, and foods rich in whole grains, such as whole wheat bread, brown rice, whole grain pasta, whole oats, and bulgur. These foods are healthy and provide the body with needed vitamins, minerals, and fiber.

Easily digested carbohydrates, or simple carbohydrates, are in many foods too, including white bread, white rice, pastries, sugar-sweetened beverages, and processed foods. People with diabetes should avoid or at least severely limit simple carbohydrates. These foods lead to weight gain and can make weight loss difficult (Centers for Disease Control and Prevention, 2011).

As noted, patients with diabetes should limit white bread or breads with refined grains and flours. Instead, they should select whole-grain and high-fiber breads. These breads contain whole wheat, oats, oatmeal, whole rye, whole grain corn, or buckwheat. The same is true when selecting rice or pasta. People with diabetes should avoid white rice or white pasta in favor of brown rice or whole wheat pasta. When purchasing breads, patients should read the food labels and choose foods that contain whole grains as the first item in the ingredient list (American Heart Association, 2010a). In addition, it is best to avoid bagels, doughnuts, and cakes.

Protein

Like carbohydrates, protein should be included in a well-balanced, healthy diet, and people with diabetes should learn to select healthy sources of protein. There are animal proteins and vegetable proteins. Animal proteins and vegetable proteins themselves affect the body in the same way; however, animal proteins can contain more saturated fat. Animal proteins include fish, poultry, red meats, pork, and wild game. Patients should select lean animal proteins such as fish, poultry, and wild game because these contain less saturated fat than other types of animal protein. The American Diabetes Association (2012c) recommends eating fish or shellfish two to three times per week. Vegetable proteins include legumes, nuts, and whole grains. These are healthier sources of protein because they also contain fiber, vitamins, and minerals the body needs (Harvard School of Public Health, 2012).

The Harvard School of Public Health recommends eating a variety of proteins, suggesting that diabetics include more legumes, fish, and poultry in the diet. They also advise avoiding meats that contain a lot of fat and to avoid red meat or eat it only occasionally. When selecting meat cuts, purchase meats that are lean and contain less fat, usually labeled as loin or round meats. When purchasing poultry, the leaner poultry is the lighter meat. Either purchase the skinless poultry or remove the skin at home before cooking. If eating red meat, select only lean cuts and eat small to moderate portions. Also, patients should balance proteins and carbohydrates, reduce the amount of highly processed carbohydrates, and slightly increase protein foods in their diet (Harvard School of Public Health, 2012). The American Heart Association recommends using meat substitutes, such as dried beans, peas, lentils, and tofu, when making typical meat entrees (American Heart Association, 2010a).

Fats and Oils

Because too much fat can be harmful to health, patients should know about fats and know how much to include in their diet. People with diabetes need to limit fats and oils to no more than 35 percent of total calorie intake per day (Diabetes Education Online, 2012b). Patients should be aware that fats and oils contain more calories than proteins and carbohydrates. Fats contain nine calories per gram where both carbohydrates and proteins each contain only four calories per gram (Diabetes Education Online, 2012b). In addition, patients should learn to choose healthier fats for the heart.

Diabetics should use oils sparingly. For patients with diabetes, learning to select healthier types of oils that are low in saturated fat, trans fats, and cholesterol is important. Canola oil, corn oil, olive oil, safflower oil, sesame oil, soybean oil, and sunflower oil, contain healthy fats and are fine in small amounts when cooking. Palm oil, palm kernel oil, coconut oil, and cocoa butter are high in saturated fats, so patients should avoid them. When possible, use nonstick olive oil or canola oil spray. When selecting salad dressings, look for reduced-fat, low-fat, or fat-free types (American Heart Association, 2010b). Vinaigrettes can be a great choice for salad dressing.

Saturated Fats

There are different types of fats, often referred to as "bad" fats and "good" fats. Examples of bad fats include saturated, hydrogenated, and trans fats. Patients should avoid or limit bad fats because they can cause an increase in cholesterol, which can cause heart and blood vessel complications. Over time, these fats can cause a condition called atherosclerosis, which is clogging of blood vessels. If the vessels to the heart become fully blocked, a heart attack may result; if blood vessels in the brain become blocked, it may result in a stroke (Diabetes Education Online, 2012b).

Saturated fats include fats derived from animal and dairy sources and also tropical oils, such as coconut and palm oils. Saturated fats are typically solid at room temperature and include lard, butter, milk fat, marbling in meat, skin from meat, ice cream, and cheese (Diabetes Education Online, 2012b). The American Heart Association recommends limiting saturated fats in the diet to no more than 7 percent of the daily caloric intake (American Heart Association, 2010b).

Trans Fats and Partially Hydrogenated Oils

Trans fats, also known as partially hydrogenated oils, are also considered bad fat. Trans fats are not naturally occurring in foods like many saturated fats but instead are created in a process that adds hydrogen to liquid vegetable oils. This process makes the foods more solid (American Heart Association, 2010b).

Trans fats are in many foods, and patients should look for the inclusion of trans fats on food labels and ingredient lists to avoid eating them. Trans fats are in many packaged snacks or baked goods, stick margarines, processed foods, and fried foods. Patients should be aware of the addition of trans fats in such foods as french fries, doughnuts, pastries, pie crusts, biscuits, pizza dough, cookies, and crackers (American Heart Association, 2010b).

Trans fats are dangerous because this type of fat not only increases low-density lipoproteins (LDL), or bad cholesterol, but also lowers high-density lipoproteins (HDL), or good cholesterol levels. Increased LDL and decreased HDL increases the chances of both heart disease and stroke (American Heart Association, 2010b). The American Heart Association recommends severely limiting the amount of trans fats, suggesting that patients eat no more than 1 percent of total daily calories as trans fats (American Heart Association, 2010b).

Monounsaturated Fats

Monounsaturated and polyunsaturated fats are the good fats in common usage. Although they are known as healthier fats, moderation is the key with good fats as well (Diabetes Education Online, 2012b). Monounsaturated fats are liquid at room temperature; however, they begin to turn into a solid when cooled. Foods containing monounsaturated fats include olive oil, canola oil, peanut oil, sunflower oil, sesame oil, avocados, peanut butter, nuts, and seeds (American Heart Association, 2010b).

Monounsaturated fats, when eaten in moderation and used to replace saturated and trans fats, may have a positive effect on health. These fats, unlike bad fats, actually work to reduce the amount of LDL cholesterol in the blood, thus reducing the risk of heart disease and stroke. Monounsaturated fats also contain healthy nutrients, and some sources contain vitamin E.

Polyunsaturated Fats

Polyunsaturated fats remain liquid at room temperature and when cooled. Soybean oil, corn oil, safflower oil, salmon, mackerel, herring, trout, walnuts, and sunflower seeds are high in polyunsaturated fat. Like monounsaturated fats, eating polyunsaturated fats in moderation and using them to replace saturated and trans fats can have a positive health effect. Polyunsaturated fats can decrease the risk of heart disease by working to lower cholesterol levels. The American Heart Association recommends eating no more than 25 to 35 percent of daily calories as monounsaturated or polyunsaturated fat (American Heart Association, 2010b).

Patients should know about healthy sources of fats and that foods can contain a combination of good and bad fats. Monounsaturated and polyunsaturated fats when eaten in moderation can replace bad fats in the diet. Patients should scrutinize food labels to see what types of fats the food contains before decide whether to consume it.

Sugar and Sweeteners

One of the myths about diabetes is that sugar causes the condition and that patients should avoid it. Research has shown that sugar does not cause diabetes and does not need to be eliminated from the diet. It is important for people to understand the impact of sugar on diabetes and its sources. Patients can eat sugar in moderation as a part of a well-balanced diet. There are different types of sugars: naturally occurring, added, and artificial.

Naturally Occurring Sugar

Naturally occurring sugar is the type of sugar that is naturally present in foods such as fruits, vegetables, and dairy products. Fructose is the natural sugar found in fruits, and lactose is the natural sugar found in dairy products. Patients can use natural sweeteners as sugar substitutes. One example is stevia, which is a naturally occurring sweetener that comes from stevia plant leaves. It does not contain any calories but does provide a small amount of fiber. Some manufacturers of stevia add sugar alcohols in processing it, so patients should use stevia that is unprocessed. Agave nectar is also a naturally occurring sugar. Some companies add fillers to agave nectar that make it similar to corn or sugar syrup, so it is best to use agave nectar that is unprocessed and organic.

Added Sugar

Added sugars are sugars or sweeteners that do not naturally occur in a food and are instead added during preparation to sweeten the food. This type of sugar includes white sugar, brown sugar, corn syrup, evaporated cane juice, honey, molasses, and chemically manufactured caloric sweeteners, such as high fructose corn syrup (American Heart Association, 2012). High amounts of added sugar are found in soda, cake, candy, punch, cookies, pies, and many other commonly eaten sweets (American Heart Association, 2012). Learning to read food labels will help patients identify added sugars in foods. Added sugar contains no nutritional benefit but adds many additional calories. Patients with diabetes need to take the caloric content of the foods into consideration—as well as the additional sugar, which can elevate glucose levels.

Artificial Sweeteners

Artificial sweeteners, also called sugar substitutes, are nonnutritive sweeteners. They do not provide calories or energy to the diet, but they offer the sweetness of sugar. In most people, they also do not affect blood glucose. Artificial sweeteners include saccharin (Sweet'N Low), aspartame (NutraSweet and Equal Classic), acesulfame potassium (Sunett), and sucralose (Splenda). These sweeteners are considered safe. Although they do not contain calories or affect blood glucose, the other ingredients in foods that contain sweeteners may, so patients should use them in moderation as part of a healthy diet (Canadian Diabetes Association, 2012).

Fruits and Vegetables

Patients should incorporate fresh fruits and vegetables into their diet. If fresh is not available, frozen or canned are also options; however, when choosing frozen or canned vegetables, try to buy those that have no salt added and eat them with no additional salt. When purchasing frozen or canned fruits, it is important to select fruits that do not contain added sugar (American Diabetes Association, 2012c).

It is recommended that most people consume nine servings (four and a half cups) of fruits and vegetables in their diet each day (Harvard School of Public Health, 2012). In addition, those with diabetes should eat more nonstarchy vegetables because they contain the lowest amounts of calories and carbohydrates (American Diabetes Association, 2012c). Color and variety are important when eating fruits and vegetables, so diabetics should try to incorporate dark green, rich yellow, orange, purple, blue, and red fruits and vegetables into their diet to ensure the consumption of a variety of vitamins and minerals. Patients should include fruits and vegetables that are high in fiber, such as beans, peas, oranges, bananas, strawberries, and apples. Raw carrots, celery, broccoli, tomatoes, and cauliflower are also good choices. Patients should avoid or at least limit fruit juice in their diet. Fruit juice does not contain much fiber and is high in calories and sugar (American Heart Association, 2010a). While fruits and vegetables are healthy and contain few calories, patients should not eat them in unlimited quantities because the calories continue to add up throughout the day and diabetics need to consider the amounts of natural sugar and carbohydrates included in them.

Dairy

Fat-free skim milk, low-fat 1 percent milk, and soy milk are good choices for patients. Rice and almond milk that do not have added sugar can be good choices. In addition, flavored milk, such as chocolate or strawberry milk, should be limited due to the added sugar and calories. Some cheeses are high in saturated fat and calories, so diabetics should select low-fat or reduced-fat cheese. Nondairy cheese made from tofu is also a good choice. Because egg yolks contain cholesterol, patients may select egg substitute or use egg whites as a healthier choice. Two egg whites can replace each egg a recipe requires. Butter, cream, and ice cream are high in saturated fat, so patients should consume them only in moderation. Soft margarines that have zero grams of trans fat should be used instead of regular butter (American Heart Association, 2010b).

Sodium

People in general should limit sodium in their diet; however, it is particularly important for people with diabetes to do so. High amounts of sodium can elevate blood pressure and increase the risk of kidney disease, heart disease, and stroke. The body requires sodium to maintain a fluid balance within the cells, transmit nerve impulses, and contract and relax muscles. While the body requires salt, most people consume much more than the body needs. On average, Americans consume 3,400 mg of salt per day (Harvard School of Public Health, 2012). Those with diabetes should limit salt intake to no more than 1,500 mg per day—and preferably much less.

Sometimes foods that do not taste salty may still contain a high level of sodium. Reading food labels can help identify the amount of sodium contained in foods. In addition, knowing the most common sources of sodium can help make food choices easier. Sodium is found in processed and prepared foods, natural sources, and added into recipes and at the table.

Processed and prepared foods are very high in sodium and are the source of the majority of sodium in the American diet (Mayo Clinic, 2011). Processed foods include many frozen and canned foods. Breads, prepared dishes, pizzas, cold cuts, bacon, cheese, soup, and fast food all contain a high amount of sodium.

In addition to processed foods, many foods naturally contain sodium. Naturally occurring sodium is found in all vegetables. In addition, dairy products, meat, and shellfish contain small amounts of sodium. Although they contain only small amounts, it adds up throughout the day. When counting the amount of sodium intake for the day, it is important to include the amounts of naturally occurring sodium consumed (Mayo Clinic, 2011).

Salt is also added during home preparation of recipes, and many people add sodium to foods directly from the salt shaker or by using condiments, such as ketchup or soy sauce. Soy sauce contains 1,000 mg of sodium in one tablespoon (Mayo Clinic, 2011). Because many natural foods and most processed foods contain sodium, patients should avoid adding salt to recipes and to foods at the table. Also, condiments such as ketchup, soy sauce, dips, mustards, and relish should be avoided or limited in favor of condiments with little or no sodium.

The Mayo Clinic recommends reducing sodium in the diet by opting to eat more fresh foods. In addition, it recommends reading the nutrition labels of processed foods to identify low-sodium products. When making recipes at home, diabetics should try to prepare dishes without adding salt, which can be just as tasty. Those preparing foods at home can also substitute herbs and spices for salt as a flavor enhancer. The Mayo Clinic also cautions about using salt substitutes and states that many substitutes contain a mixture of table salt with other ingredients (Mayo Clinic, 2011).

Alcohol

Because alcohol may interfere with some medications or complicate medical conditions, such as neuropathy, retinopathy, and high blood triglycerides, people with diabetes should consult with a physician before consuming alcohol. In addition to the possibility of interfering with medications and complicating conditions, people with diabetes must consider the effect of alcohol on blood glucose (Diabetes Education Online, 2012a). Drinking alcohol can result in severe hypoglycemia (low blood glucose) shortly after alcohol consumption and for eight to twelve hours after drinking (American Diabetes Association, 2012a).

Low blood glucose results because the liver, which releases glucose into the bloodstream as part of its regular process, must instead work to break down alcohol, so it does not release glucose into the bloodstream. The result can be worse when drinking alcohol on an empty stomach because the body is not receiving any glucose from foods, which can lead to very low blood glucose levels. Patients who drink alcohol should be aware of the symptoms of low blood glucose and test their blood glucose frequently; however, it is important to realize the symptoms of hypoglycemia and excessive alcohol intake are similar. Patients drinking alcohol should wear an identification bracelet (e.g., a MedicAlert bracelet) stating they are diabetic so they can receive appropriate treatment if hypoglycemia occurs. In addition, because exercise also reduces blood glucose, alcohol should be avoided during exercise to prevent hypoglycemia (Diabetes Education Online, 2012a).

Patients who have consulted their physician and received permission to drink alcohol should drink it only in moderation. In general, the recommendation is that women should consume no more than one serving of alcohol per day and men should consume no more than two servings per day. One serving of alcohol is the equivalent of 12 ounces of beer, 5 ounces of wine, or 1.5 ounces of liquor (UCSF Children's Hospital, 2006).

Meal Planning

For people with diabetes, meal planning is important, as is learning to select proper foods and read nutrition labels when shopping. Making healthy, well-balanced meals at home is simple when there are nutritious ingredients on hand. The keys to meal planning for patients are thinking ahead, controlling portions, and avoiding excess carbohydrate intake.

While not every meal can be eaten at home, patients can use many of the same tips for meal planning at restaurants, such as being aware of portion sizes and choosing a variety of healthy foods to create a well-balanced meal. Dining out at restaurants or at a party at a friend's house does not have to be worrisome. With proper planning, patients can enjoy dining out knowing they can eat well-balanced and healthy meals wherever they are.

Food Labels

Most packaged foods in grocery stores have nutrition labels. Some exceptions may include foods prepared in store, foods contained in very small packages, fresh fruits and vegetables, and foods made by small manufacturers (American Diabetes Association, 2012d). These labels can help people compare foods and make healthy food choices. It is important to know how to read and understand food labels. The nutrition facts on the label display the serving size, amount of calories, nutrients, total fat, saturated fat, cholesterol, sodium, carbohydrates, and fiber in the food (American Diabetes Association, 2012d).

One very important element on the label is serving size, which is where patients should begin when reading a food label. The serving size is listed under Nutrition Facts at the top of the label. The label includes serving size, noted most often as cup, half cup, number of pieces, or weight in grams. It also lists how many servings are in the whole container. The nutrients on the label give values for one serving size. If a person consumes more than one serving, the amount of calories, fat, and sodium increases proportionately (Mayo Clinic, 2012). For example, a typical serving size of ice cream is a half cup, and the amount of calories per serving is 300. If a person eats a whole cup of ice cream, then the amount of calories ingested from that one cup of ice cream is 600. In addition to doubling the calories, the other nutrients, including fat and cholesterol, are also doubled.

Below the serving size information is a section listing total calories per serving and calories from fat per serving. Following this are lines for the amount of total fat, saturated fat, trans fat, cholesterol, sodium, and total carbohydrate, which are all nutrients that patients should strive to limit in their diet. Beneath that are the nutrients: dietary fiber, protein, vitamins, and minerals, which are the nutrients that patients should strive to consume in adequate amounts during the day. The total amounts of nutrients are shown in grams (g) or milligrams (mg). Again, these amounts are per serving. If a patient consumes more than one serving, the numbers increase accordingly.

Next to each of the nutrient values is a percentage that shows the daily value contained in one serving of food compared to a person's total needs. This is labeled as the %DV (percent daily value). The bottom of the label contains information stating that the %DV is based on a 2,000-calorie-per-day diet. If there is enough space, the label will include adjusted amounts based on a 2,500-calorie diet. Calories needed per day vary from person to person, and the 2,000-calories-per-day percentages listed should be used only as a reference point (Mayo Clinic, 2012).

In addition, the ingredients are listed in descending order by weight. This is important to note, because the first items listed make up the largest proportion of the food in each serving. Patients should be sure to check the label for ingredients they intend to avoid, such as trans fats and added sugars. The ingredient list can also be useful to check for healthy ingredients, such as whole grains, and can be beneficial in comparing two products in order to select the most healthful product (American Diabetes Association, 2012d).

Shopping

Preparing foods at home is often healthier than dining out. Patients with diabetes who prepare food at home have more control over the entire menu, ingredients included in each dish, and portions served. Food preparation begins with buying groceries, and those seeking to eat a well-balanced, healthy diet should learn how to shop to select healthy foods. While shopping, patients should read and compare food labels to select foods with the least calories, saturated fats, trans fats, cholesterol, and sodium. Shoppers should also remember to check serving sizes when comparing food labels.

Shoppers should plan ahead and make a list of meal ideas for the week. Then, while shopping, they should purchase only the foods that are on the list prepared beforehand. In addition, shoppers should eat a healthy meal or snack before shopping to avoid being hungry in the grocery store, which may lead to unhealthy food choices. It is important to avoid purchasing high-calorie or tempting processed foods such as cookies, cakes, potato chips, and ice cream. By not having these tempting foods in the home, patients will find it is easier to avoid eating them (National Diabetes Education Program, 2006).

Dining Out

Dining away from home, whether at a restaurant or at a holiday party, provides opportunities for social interaction and entertainment on occasion. Dining out can be quick and convenient, and it is sometimes necessary, particularly when traveling. People with diabetes need to eat on a regular schedule and learn how to order diabetes-compatible meals when dining out to maintain a healthy diet.

Eating on Time

Patients who use insulin or diabetic medications need to eat on schedule to avoid complications of high or low blood glucose. Dining out, either at a restaurant or at a party, can pose problems for those trying to stay on a regular dining schedule. The American Diabetes Association suggests planning ahead by coordinating with others to eat at a specific time and making reservations in advance so that waiting time will be limited. If dinner is planned for later than the normal mealtime, patients can prepare for the delay by eating a snack before the dinner and then eating a regular meal later. In addition, patients may need to adjust insulin injections accordingly to avoid low blood glucose (American Diabetes Association, 2012b).

Ordering

When dining out, patients should try to select a restaurant that includes a menu with a large variety of menu items and many healthy choices. It may be helpful to call ahead or review the menu before going to the restaurant to identify foods that fit into the diet plan. Many restaurants, particularly chain restaurants, include the nutritional information of their menu items online.

When ordering, patients should try to eat the same size meal as normal and ask the server about portion sizes. If portions are large, it is a good idea to eat half the meal at the restaurant and then ask for a to-go box to take home the leftover portion. Another way to ensure portion control is to order an appetizer instead of a full meal and accompany it with a leafy green salad. Some people prefer to order from the children's menu instead of ordering a regular entrée. If another person in the patient's party also keeps track of portion sizes, the two individuals may decide to share an entrée. Patients should remember that appetizers, entrees, and desserts can be shared with others at the table to help reduce portions (American Diabetes Association, 2012c).

In addition, when ordering, patients should select foods that are baked, broiled, grilled, or boiled while avoiding fried or breaded foods. Another good practice is for the patient to ask the server to provide any sauces, gravies, or salad dressings on the side instead of poured over the food. Similarly, if vegetables come topped with added butter or other high-calorie addition, patients can ask the server to hold that topping or ask for a small amount of butter on the side instead. An easy way to experience the flavor of a high-calorie topping while minimizing calorie intake is to dip the fork in the topping and then spear the bite of food. Also, patients should substitute regular salad dressings with low-calorie salad dressings or vinaigrettes (American Diabetes Association, 2012c).

Another way to improve meal nutrition is to ask to substitute a vegetable or a fruit for french fries or other fried options. When ordering a baked potato, patients should ask for it to be served plain, without salt, butter, or sour cream. If the bread basket selection is appealing, patients should limit bread to one serving. Patients may also need to avoid or limit alcoholic drinks, depending on their blood glucose levels (Joslin Diabetes Center, 2012).

Fast Food

Fast food, while cheap, efficient, and convenient, presents unique challenges for people with diabetes. However, with proper planning before ordering this type of food, patients can make healthy choices. Often, a typical fast-food order contains an entire day's worth of fat, salt, and calories (American Diabetes Association, 2012c). Many fast-food chains provide nutritional information online, allowing patients to review menu choices beforehand to find the healthiest items. Patients who eat a fast-food meal during the day should make sure the other meals that day are healthy (American Diabetes Association, 2012c).

Good food selection and moderation are key elements to successful eating at fast-food restaurants. Fried foods should be avoided and replaced with grilled or broiled choices of lean meats, such as chicken breast, turkey, or fish. Sandwich buns, breads, and English muffins should be selected, instead of croissants and biscuits, when eating breakfast at fast-food restaurants to cut back on fat content (American Diabetes Association, 2012c).

Portion control is very important. Supersized meals should be avoided. If possible, patients should order children's portions instead of regular meals. They should always avoid double burgers or double meat in favor of regular-sized sandwiches. When eating pizza, patients should select a thin crust instead of regular or pan crusts and choose vegetables instead of meat toppings, which are usually highly processed pork and beef products (American Diabetes Association, 2012c).

Summary

People with diabetes need to be aware that the foods they eat may impact their blood glucose. While there is no diabetic diet, patients with the condition should strive to eat well-balanced meals and snacks and eat only appropriate portion sizes. Because of this, patients should be aware of the nutritional content of the foods they consume by understanding the various food groups and learning to read food labels. Those with the condition should also learn how to shop for the most nutritious foods at the grocery store and choose appropriate menu items when dining out. Healthy eating is an important element in diabetes management.

Information Sources

Selected Print Resources

General

> Geil, Patti, and Lea Ann Holzmeister. 2006. *101 Tips on Nutrition for People with Diabetes*. Alexandria, VA: American Diabetes Association.
> In question-and-answer format, this book covers information about nutrition, managing medications, sweets, weight, and fitness. It also covers information for parents dealing with the challenges of the nutritional needs of a child with diabetes.

> Higgins, Jaynie. 2009. *Ultimate Diabetes Meal Planner: A Complete System for Eating Healthy with Diabetes*. Alexandria, VA: American Diabetes Association.
> This resource contains weekly diabetes-healthy breakfast, lunch, dinner, and snack plans along with recipes. Users can base their daily plan on 1,500, 1,800, 2,000, 2,200, or 2,500 calories, depending on their needs.

> Holzmeister, Lee Ann. 2010. *Diabetes Carbohydrate and Fat Gram Guide*. Alexandria, VA: American Diabetes Association.
> For those counting carbohydrates or tracking calories, this book lists the amount of calories, carbohydrates, fat, saturated fat, cholesterol, sodium, fiber, and protein found in many commonly eaten foods. The book begins with information about healthy eating and details the American Diabetes Association nutrient recommendations. Foods are broken down by category and alphabetically within each category.

> Powers, Margaret. 2003. *American Dietetic Association Guide to Eating Right When You Have Diabetes*. New York: Wiley.
> This resource helps patients understand diabetes and nutrition so they can plan healthy meals. It covers information on understanding carbohydrates, protein, fats, vitamins, minerals, and dietary supplements. It also lists tips for understanding food labels and selecting healthy foods when dining at home or away.

> Warshaw, Hope. 2009. *Guide to Healthy Fast-Food Eating*. 2nd ed. Alexandria, VA: American Diabetes Association.
> This guide can help those with diabetes learn to make healthy choices when eating at fast-food restaurants. It discusses the many pitfalls of eating fast food, provides strategies to overcome them, and includes tips to eat healthier. It provides information on foods from many well-known fast-food restaurants, including McDonald's, Burger King, Pizza Hut, Dunkin' Donuts, Starbucks, Wendy's, and others.

➤ Warshaw, Hope. 2009. *Guide to Healthy Restaurant Eating: What to Eat in America's Most Popular Chain Restaurants*. 4th ed. Alexandria, VA: American Diabetes Association.

This book helps diabetic patients make healthy decisions when eating at restaurants. It provides nutrition information on menu items from over sixty popular chain restaurants.

Cookbooks

➤ American Dietetic Association Staff. 2007. *The New Family Cookbook for People with Diabetes*. New York: Simon and Schuster.

This cookbook contains more than 370 recipes, most very easy to prepare. There are a variety of different types of recipes, including baked orange French toast, curried chicken salad, baked potato skins, rum-baked black beans, New York cheesecake, apple raspberry crisp, and raisin rice pudding.

➤ Hughes, Nancy. 2007. *The 4-Ingredient Diabetes Cookbook: Simple, Quick, and Delicious Recipes Using Just Four Ingredients or Less*. Alexandria, VA: American Diabetes Association.

Those with diabetes who want to cook healthy meals but do not want to follow complicated recipes will find this a useful cookbook. Each meal is quick and easy to prepare and uses no more than four ingredients. The cookbook contains recipes for breakfast, lunch, and dinner.

➤ Hughes, Nancy. 2010. *15 Minute Diabetic Meals*. Alexandria, VA: American Diabetes Association.

This cookbook is an excellent resource for diabetes patients who want to prepare quick, diabetes-appropriate meals.

➤ Mills, Jackie. 2007. *The Big Book of Diabetic Desserts*. Alexandria, VA: American Diabetes Association.

This cookbook provides 150 dessert recipes for people with diabetes. The recipes do not use sugar substitutions but show how to bake using artificial sweeteners. The recipes are easy to make and low calorie.

➤ Riolo, Amy. 2010. *The Mediterranean Diabetes Cookbook*. Alexandra, VA: American Diabetes Association.

This cookbook contains recipes for Mediterranean-style recipes for people with diabetes. It provides recipes for first courses, main dishes, sides, salads, drinks, and breads.

➤ Spitler, Sue. 2007. *1001 Delicious Recipes for People with Diabetes*. Evanston, IL: Surrey.

This cookbook contains a variety of recipes for individuals with diabetes. There is also a chapter containing vegetarian and vegan recipes.

➤ Stanley, Kathleen, and Connie Crawley. 2007. *Quick and Easy Diabetic Recipes for One: Tips and Recipes for Healthy Eating on Your Own*. Alexandria, VA: American Diabetes Association.

Beginning with an overview of healthy eating for people with diabetes, this cookbook contains a variety of quick and easy recipes that serve one person.

➤ Warshaw, Hope. 2010. *Diabetes Meal Planning Made Easy*. 4th ed. Alexandria, VA: American Diabetes Association.

Now in its fourth edition, this resource helps patients learn to plan healthy meals. It also provides information on how to make favorite recipes healthier and strategies for food shopping and preparation.

Selected Web Resources

General

➤ Academy of Nutrition and Dietetics—"Home: For the Public," http://www .eatright.org/Public/

This website provides a range of information to help both adults and children eat a healthy diet. Information includes healthy weight loss, nutrition for various age groups, and making healthy choices when grocery shopping and dining out. There is also a link to disease management through diet. This page contains an overview of diabetes, followed by information on how to create a healthy meal plan.

➤ American Association of Diabetes Educators—"Healthy Eating," http://www .diabetesselfcare.org/self-care-behaviors/healthy-eating/

This webpage provides resources to help patients learn to make healthy eating choices. It describes what foods should be part of a healthy diet and includes tips for identifying healthy foods and controlling portion sizes.

➤ American Diabetes Association—"Food and Fitness—Planning Meals," http:// www.diabetes.org/food-and-fitness/food/planning-meals/

This resource provided by the American Diabetes Association provides links to information people with diabetes can use to plan healthy meals. It provides information on creating meal plans, counting carbohydrates, understanding the glycemic index (GI), and following special diets.

➤ Canadian Diabetes Association—"Nutrition: Just the Basics," http://www.diabetes .ca/diabetes-and-you/nutrition/just-basics/

This section provides links to many useful resources for eating healthy with diabetes. There are links to information about meal planning, a portion guide, fats, and fiber. It also contains a link to diabetes-friendly recipes.

➤ Centers for Disease Control and Prevention—"Diabetes Public Health Resource: Eat Right," http://www.cdc.gov/diabetes/consumer/eatright.htm

This resource stresses making healthy food choices and provides tips on how to accomplish eating healthier. The resource provides examples of foods to incorporate into the diet and foods that should be eaten less often. There are also links to additional resources for learning to eat healthier.

➤ Diabetes Education Online—"Diet and Nutrition," http://dtc.ucsf.edu/living-with-diabetes/diet-and-nutrition/
This resource provides links to several healthy-eating resources for patients with diabetes. Topics include carbohydrates, fats, protein, alcohol, and how to choose a healthy diet.

➤ Diabetes UK—"Food and Recipes," http://www.diabetes.org.uk/Guide-to-diabetes/Food_and_recipes/
In addition to general information about diabetes, this resource contains information to help diabetic patients make healthy food choices. The page provides links to information for type 1 and type 2 diabetes patients on how to make healthy food decisions. It contains information about the glycemic index, counting carbohydrates, shopping for food, and dealing with holidays and dining out. The site also contains a database of more than 250 diabetes-friendly recipes.

➤ dLife—"What Can I Eat?," http://www.dlife.com/diabetes-food-and-fitness/what_do_i_eat
This webpage provides patients information on foods to eat and foods to avoid. It provides links to additional information about carbohydrate management, sugar and sweeteners, dining out, menu planning, and fats.

➤ FamilyDoctor.org—"Diabetes: Diabetes and Nutrition," http://familydoctor.org/familydoctor/en/diseases-conditions/diabetes/treatment/diabetes-and-nutrition.html
This general resource explains the importance of patients eating a healthy diet. It explains what types of food those with diabetes should eat and provides a sample food exchange list.

➤ Harvard School of Public Health—"The Nutrition Source," http://www.hsph.harvard.edu/nutritionsource/index.html
This website, though not aimed specifically at diabetes patients, provides information beneficial to anyone wanting to learn how to eat healthy. The site contains information about carbohydrates, proteins, fruits, vegetables, and fats. There is information on reaching and maintaining a healthy weight by eating healthy and staying active. The site includes information about reducing sodium intake and choosing healthy drinks, as well as links to more than 100 healthy recipes.

➤ Joslin Diabetes Center—"Diet and Nutrition," http://www.joslin.org/info/Diet_and_Nutrition.html

The webpage provides links to articles about diet and nutrition for patients with diabetes. Included are topics such as successful eating, alcohol intake, carbohydrate counting, low-carbohydrate foods, fats, vitamins and supplements, cooking, meal planning, shopping, sugar-free foods, sugar, fiber, and vegetarian diets.

➤ National Diabetes Information Clearinghouse—"What I Need to Know about Eating and Diabetes," http://diabetes.niddk.nih.gov/dm/pubs/eating_ez/
This easy-to-read webpage reproduces the content of a brochure that is also available for download on this page. The section contains information about diabetes and nutrition, making healthy food choices to keep blood glucose levels controlled, and managing eating with diabetes medications. It also contains a physical activity plan and a diabetes food pyramid with examples of foods and serving sizes.

Recipes

➤ American Diabetes Association—"MyFoodAdvisor," http://tracker.diabetes.org/
This interactive website allows users to learn the nutritional contents of foods and create a meal plan. It also includes a recipe database searchable by main ingredient, type, or nutrition criteria. Users can store recipes in an online recipe box for future use.

➤ Defeat Diabetes Foundation—"Self-Management: Nutrition," http://www.defeat diabetes.org/self_management/text.asp?id=Nutrition_Basics
Beginning with an explanation of the importance of healthy eating with diabetes, this webpage contains articles about incorporating fruits, vegetables, whole grains, and fiber into the diet. The site also provides articles teaching users how to read a food label, buy fresh foods, and store fresh vegetables. There is a link to hundreds of diabetes-friendly recipes arranged by category—appetizers and snacks, beverages, breads, breakfast dishes, desserts, entrées, lunch, salads, sauces and marinades, side dishes, soups and stews, and vegetables.

➤ Diabetes Monitor—"Diabetes Diet and Nutritional Guidance," http://www .diabetesmonitor.com/healthy-living/diet/
This site provides links to many articles of use to patients seeking to learn more about diabetes and nutrition. Topics include carbohydrates, fad diets, meal planning, glycemic index, nutrition guidelines, artificial sweeteners, healthy foods, holiday eating, food portions, chocolate, alcohol, food labels, weight control, cooking, fats, and recipes, among others.

➤ Diabetes UK—"Recipes," http://www.diabetes.org.uk/Guide-to-diabetes/Food_ and_recipes/Recipes/
The site contains a searchable database of more than 250 diabetes-friendly recipes. Users can type in a search term or search by food category or special diet. Dairy-free, gluten-free, and vegetarian recipes are some of the search

options. Each recipe includes nutritional information, and many recipes provide a color picture of the prepared dish. This is a U.K. website, so some of the foods may sound unfamiliar; measurements are in metrics, so unit conversion would be necessary for most U.S. users.

> *Diabetic Gourmet Magazine,* http://diabeticgourmet.com/
> In addition to articles about healthy living with diabetes, this online magazine provides a database for searching for diabetes-friendly recipes. Users can search for appetizers, breads, breakfasts, desserts, main courses, salads, sandwiches, side dishes, and soups. Each recipe includes nutritional information per serving. Recipes have ratings, and user reviews are available for some recipes.

> dLife—"Find Recipes," http://www.dlife.com/diabetes/diabetic-recipes/
> Patients can search for diabetes-friendly recipes on this webpage, narrowing the results by keyword or ingredient. Users can also browse recipes by category. Categories include main ingredient, course, and dietary limitations, such as low-calorie or low-sodium recipes.

> National Diabetes Education Program—"Tasty Recipes for People with Diabetes and Their Families," http://ndep.nih.gov/publications/PublicationDetail.aspx?PubId=131&redirect=true
> This online booklet begins with an overview of diabetes and making healthy food choices, followed by recipes for breakfast, lunch, and dinner.

Selected Audiovisual Resources

> Academy of Nutrition and Dietetics—"Eat Right," http://www.eatright.org/Public/Videos.aspx
> This page on the Eat Right public webpage provides links to short video clips on healthy eating topics. Some of the topics include reducing salt, eating healthy, living with diabetes, and planning healthy breakfasts and snacks.

> MedlinePlus—"Diabetes and Meal Planning," http://www.nlm.nih.gov/medlineplus/tutorials/diabetesmealplanning/htm/index.htm
> This webpage provides an audiovisual tutorial explaining diabetes and meal planning. It emphasizes a healthy and balanced diet and explains the food groups. This resource explains what foods make up a healthy diet and provides guidelines for incorporating healthy foods and eating a healthy diet. A text summary of the tutorial is also available.

References

American Diabetes Association. 2012a. "Food and Fitness: Alcohol." American Diabetes Association. Accessed July 5. http://www.diabetes.org/food-and-fitness/food/what-can-i-eat/alcohol.html.

————. 2012b. "Food and Fitness: Food." American Diabetes Association. Accessed July 5. http://www.diabetes.org/food-and-fitness/food/.

————. 2012c. "Food and Fitness: The Best Food Choices." American Diabetes Association. Accessed July 5. http://www.diabetes.org/food-and-fitness/fitness/weight-loss/food-choices/the-best-food-choices/.

————. 2012d. "Reading Food Labels." American Diabetes Association. Accessed July 5. http://www.diabetesarchive.net/food-nutrition-lifestyle/nutrition/meal-planning/reading-food-labels.jsp.

American Heart Association. 2010a. "Grocery Shopping." American Heart Association. Updated June 11. http://www.heart.org/HEARTORG/GettingHealthy/Nutrition Center/HeartSmartShopping/Grocery-Shopping_UCM_001884_Article.jsp.

————. 2010b. "Saturated Fats." American Heart Association. Updated October 29. http://www.heart.org/HEARTORG/GettingHealthy/FatsAndOils/Fats101/Saturated-Fats_UCM_301110_Article.jsp.

————. 2012. "Sugars 101." American Heart Association. Updated January 20. http://www.heart.org/HEARTORG/GettingHealthy/Nutrition Center/Sugars-101_UCM_306024_Article.jsp.

Canadian Diabetes Association. 2012. "Sweeteners." Canadian Diabetes Association. Accessed July 5. http://www.diabetes.ca/diabetes-and-you/nutrition/sweeteners/.

Centers for Disease Control and Prevention. 2011. "Nutrition for Everyone: Carbohydrates." Centers for Disease Control and Prevention. Last updated October 4. http://www.cdc.gov/nutrition/everyone/basics/carbs.html.

Diabetes Education Online. 2012a. "Diabetes and Alcohol." University of California, San Francisco. Accessed November 27. http://dtc.ucsf.edu/living-with-diabetes/diet-and-nutrition/ diabetes-alcohol/.

————. 2012b. "Understanding Fats and Oils." University of California, San Francisco. Accessed November 27. http://dtc.ucsf.edu/living-with-diabetes/diet-and-nutrition/understanding-fats-oils/.

————. 2012c. "Understanding Food." University of California, San Francisco. Accessed November 27. http://dtc.ucsf.edu/living-with-diabetes/diet-and-nutrition/understanding-food/.

FamilyDoctor.org. 2010. "Diabetes: Diabetes and Nutrition." American Academy of Family Physicians. Updated October. http://familydoctor.org/online/famdocen/home/common/diabetes/living/349.html.

Harvard School of Public Health. 2012. "The Nutrition Source: Carbohydrates: Good Carbs Guide the Way." Harvard University. Accessed July 5. http://www.hsph.harvard.edu/nutritionsource/what-should-you-eat/carbohydrates-full-story/index.html.

Joslin Diabetes Center. 2012. "Dining Out with Diabetes." Joslin Diabetes Center. Accessed July 5. http://www.joslin.org/info/dining_out_with_diabetes.html.

Mayo Clinic. 2011. "Nutrition and Healthy Eating: Sodium: How to Tame Your Salt Habit Now." Mayo Foundation for Medical Education and Research. March 31. http://www.mayoclinic.com/health/sodium/NU00284.

———. 2012. "Nutrition and Healthy Eating: Nutrition Facts: An Interactive Guide to Food Labels." Mayo Foundation for Medical Education and Research. July 26. http://www.mayoclinic.com/health/nutrition-facts/NU00293.

National Diabetes Education Program. 2006. "Small Steps. Big Rewards. Your Game Plan to Prevent Type 2 Diabetes: Information for Patients." National Institutes of Health and Centers for Disease Control and Prevention. http://ndep.nih.gov/media/GP_Booklet.pdf.

UCSF Children's Hospital. 2006. "Alcohol and Diabetes . . . Know the Risks." University of California, San Francisco. http://www.diabetes.ucsf.edu/sites/default/files/PEDS%20Alcohol%20and%20Diabetes.pdf.

Chapter 9

Physical Activity

Introduction

Studies show that physical activity plays an important role in improving overall health in people with diabetes. Exercise increases energy levels, aids in weight loss, and improves the body's ability to use insulin. This chapter provides an overview of the benefits of physical activity for people with diabetes and the types of exercises recommended for them. Following the overview is an annotated list of resources for finding additional information about the importance of physical activity and exercise in the management of diabetes.

Health Benefits of Physical Activity

Engaging in physical activity, from light to moderate exercise to participation in high-endurance sports, is possible for patients with type 1 and type 2 diabetes, as well as those with gestational diabetes; and being physically active is highly recommended by health care providers. Many patients, however, assume their condition necessarily prevents them from being able to participate in physical activities that nondiabetics are able to perform with ease. By increasing physical activity and exercise levels, there is a direct beneficial correlation to being able to manage diabetes more effectively.

Physical activity is also critical in helping provide emotional balance and in reducing the stress related to having a chronic condition. For those people who are diagnosed with prediabetes, increasing physical activity may actually stave off diabetes permanently. Because the rate of diabetes is increasing worldwide, the cost of managing the disease and its attendant complications is also increasing, for both individuals and health management systems. Exercise is one solution for either preventing the condition from occurring or managing it more effectively, thus reducing the number of people who need treatment for the disease.

According to the National Diabetes Information Clearinghouse (2011), individuals who follow a regular exercise and physical activity regimen may accrue the following health benefits:

- Lower blood glucose
- Lower blood pressure
- Lower bad cholesterol and raise good cholesterol

- Improve the body's ability to use insulin
- Lower the risk for heart disease and stroke
- Keep heart and bones strong
- Improve the body's immune system
- Keep joints flexible
- Lower risk of falling
- Help to lose weight
- Reduce body fat
- Provide more energy
- Reduce stress level

To achieve these benefits, a person needs to engage in physical activity on a regular basis. According to the National Institutes of Health guidelines, revised in 2009, individuals must work out an average of at least five days a week doing moderate-level exercise, resulting in at least 2,000 to 3,000 calories burned each week (equivalent to 250 to 300 minutes per week), to both achieve and sustain these health advantages.

Because diabetes is a chronic condition, it is important to become physically fit to ward off any other conditions from developing that, combined with diabetes, could ultimately become debilitating. By working hard to become physically fit, patients can take a proactive role in managing their condition, which puts them in control of the disease—not the other way around.

Types of Exercise

There are many different types of exercise and physical activity, all of which can provide immediate health benefits. Depending upon a person's interests, there is a wide variety of activities from which to choose. Patients with diabetes should not be dissuaded from engaging in any level of activity once they are cleared by a physician or certified diabetes educator to do so. According to Song (2007), a study published in the *Annals of Internal Medicine* found that a combination of both aerobic and weight-training types of exercises was more beneficial for controlling blood sugar than either activity was alone.

As people age, they naturally begin to lose muscle mass. For instance, after age thirty, it is estimated that men and women lose at least 10 percent of muscle and bone tissue (Defeat Diabetes Foundation, 2011). To combat this natural phenomenon, it is important for those with diabetes to commit to an exercise and fitness program so they can increase muscle mass as well as improve their endurance.

The American Diabetes Association (2012) recommends that patients incorporate at least three different types of exercise into a weekly routine to achieve the best health benefits: aerobic activities, including walking, biking, or swimming; weight and strength training; and stretching to increase flexibility. A brief summary of some of the appropriate types of physical activity follows.

Aerobic and Cardiovascular Exercise

Aerobic and cardiovascular exercises are low in terms of intensity; however, they are performed at longer intervals. These exercises increase the heart rate and oxygen intake, which helps condition the body. Patients can do these exercises in a fitness club or at home, using a treadmill, stationary bicycle, elliptical trainer, or swimming pool, or outside by biking, walking, jogging, cross-country skiing, or running. The key aspect of this type of combination exercise is to undertake these activities regularly for an extended period, such as thirty minutes to an hour, at least five times a week. Some of these exercises combine aerobic benefits with strength training, such as water aerobics, which helps build muscle strength along with cardiovascular health.

Strength Training and Endurance Sports

While some patients might shy away from sports that require high levels of exertion, such as weight training or running in a marathon, there is no reason they cannot participate. With proper training and guidance, people can manage either type 1 or type 2 diabetes and enjoy being active in sports. By working to build muscle mass, the patient can help lower glucose levels in the body and reduce the need for insulin. This type of anaerobic exercise supports participation in aerobic types of exercise too: by cross-training during the week between the two types of exercises, there will be less stress on the body. For instance, a person could participate in regular walking or cycling activities three days a week, while the other two could be devoted to strength training and conditioning.

Yoga—Mind and Body

Yoga is an ancient form of exercise that originated in India. By practicing various postures and forms, yoga helps encourage relaxation, reduce stress, and increase flexibility and blood flow throughout the body. It also helps control blood glucose levels in patients with diabetes (Joslin Diabetes Center, 2012). Yoga does not require the purchase of any special equipment other than a mat and proper clothing. Yoga classes are available throughout the United States, emphasizing various styles including hatha, ashtanga, and iyengar.

Precautions for Physical Activity and Diabetes

Those with diabetes and prediabetes should seek the guidance of physicians and diabetes educators to obtain clearance before engaging in any type of physical fitness activities. They should also request further guidance on what types of precautions they should take for their particular health status. When contemplating any exercise program, it is important for people to understand what their health status is presently. For instance, is the patient already someone who is engaging in physical activities and would like to switch to a different and more intense exercise regimen? Or is the person someone who has been sedentary for many years and is just beginning to engage in exercise activities? Patients must also take into account whether they have other health complications besides diabetes or if they are recovering from another type of illness before engaging in any type of exercise (Tirrito, 2012).

Those who are experiencing issues with their eyes need to refrain from exercises that put pressure on the blood vessels, such as weight lifting. Further, those who have already experienced nerve damage in their extremities need to be cautious about walking or jogging even when wearing proper socks and footwear, since numbness in the feet may mask an injury or the presence of sores and blisters (National Diabetes Information Clearinghouse, 2011).

It is important to seek guidance from health care providers regarding management and calibration of insulin intake and any other diabetes medications in combination with a physical fitness regimen. Working out moderately can cause blood glucose to fall precipitously; however, patients might not feel the symptoms immediately. Having a snack before an exercise activity or immediately afterward may ameliorate this problem. Extreme exercise can also release stress hormones, which tells the body it needs more glucose, so a patient may also need an injection of insulin immediately after a workout (American Diabetes Association, 2009).

It is recommended that patients be vigilant about staying hydrated during workouts and not ignore any type of pain they experience because it could be a precursor to a significant injury. Working out in water or bicycling can prevent stress injuries to the feet and joints. It is advisable for the patient to wear a medical alert bracelet that details his or her diabetic status or to exercise with a friend who is aware of what to do in case the patient's blood glucose drops too low.

Summary

There are many benefits to engaging in all levels of physical activities for people with prediabetes or diabetes. Besides lowering blood pressure, cholesterol, and weight, it helps the body balance glucose levels and may even allow for a reduction in the amount of medication needed. Stress reduction and increased energy are also benefits to participating in a regular exercise regimen. When exercising alone, people should wear a diabetic medical alert bracelet in case any type of emergency arises related to a drop in blood sugar levels. People should always consult with their health care provider first before beginning any type of fitness program.

Information Sources

Selected Print Resources

➤ Barnes, Darryl. 2004. *Action Plan for Diabetes*. Champaign, IL: Human Kinetics.
Barnes contends that if people with diabetes exercise adequately, they can decrease the need for insulin injections. This book provides an action plan for starting and maintaining an exercise regimen that includes aerobic, flexibility, strength building, and endurance training. The American College of Sports Medicine helped develop the training plan, which is recommended for people with pre-diabetes, type 1 diabetes, and type 2 diabetes. The book also presents dietary suggestions for those who are undertaking a new physical fitness regimen.

➤ Colberg, Sheri. 2005. *The 7 Step Diabetes Fitness Plan: Living Well and Being Fit with Diabetes, No Matter Your Weight*. New York: Marlowe.
This book is for people who have prediabetes or diabetes and want to gain control of their disease and life through physical fitness. There are seven steps in the book, which the author contends can assist in both preventing diabetes and managing the disease properly. The major areas of discussion include the following: (1) how an overall improvement in activity and physical fitness can help control blood glucose; (2) for those who are inactive or face many health problems, tips on how to increase activity in more manageable increments; (3) how to vary an exercise regimen by combining both aerobic and resistance training; (4) how a good diet combined with physical activity can produce optimal health results; (5) how physical exertion can help manage mental health and produce a healthy outlook; (6) how nutritional supplements can help with overall health; and (7) which motivational strategies for physical fitness work best.

➤ Colberg, Sheri. 2008. *Diabetic Athlete's Handbook*. 2nd ed. Champaign, IL: Human Kinetics.
This book is written by a type 1 diabetes patient who did not have the benefit of today's testing equipment when she participated in sports and recreational activities in the late 1960s. After experiencing the benefits of exercise in her youth, the author intends this book to help others achieve the correct balance between self-managing their diabetes while simultaneously participating in many types of exercise. Part 1 of the book focuses on the physiology of diabetes and physical exertion, including balancing medications and monitoring glucose levels. Part 2 provides specific advice on participation in the following types of exercise: general fitness, including aerobic exercise, resistance training, and water aerobics; endurance sports such as marathons, triathlons, running, cycling, and cross-country skiing; endurance-power sports, such as basketball, field hockey, ice hockey, and gymnastics; and power sports, such as bodybuilding, baseball, softball, and volleyball.

➤ Goldberg, Linn, and Diane L. Elliott. 2000. *The Healing Power of Exercise: Your Guide to Preventing and Treating Diabetes, Depression, Heart Disease, High Blood Pressure, Arthritis, and More.* New York: Wiley.

The authors wrote this book to assist people who are experiencing various health challenges, including diabetes. The first part of the book stresses the importance of a regular exercise regimen to improve all areas of health. Chapter 5 specifically addresses diabetes: which exercises can help prevent it as well as treat the condition most effectively. Subsequent chapters address how to exercise to lose weight and lower blood pressure, both of which are important for patients to address to improve their overall health.

➤ Hayes, Charlotte. 2006. *The "I Hate to Exercise" Book for People with Diabetes.* 2nd ed. Alexandria, VA: American Diabetes Association.

The author emphasizes that people with diabetes can control their glucose better if they exercise regularly because it enables the muscle cells to do a better job of storing and using glucose; suppresses the liver from producing an excess of glucose; increases muscle mass, which assists in using glucose more effectively; and helps to maintain a healthy body weight. The book also gives advice on how to customize a physical fitness program, discusses the benefits of being active in everything people do, and provides sample exercises.

Selected Web Resources

➤ American Diabetes Association—"Diabetes and Physical Activity," http://www.princeton.edu/healthier/docs/DiabetesEmail-3.pdf

This one-page PDF outlines the benefits of physical activity, how physical activity affects glucose levels, how much physical activity is appropriate, and what types to engage in, as well as providing exercise guidelines and precautions, ideas on how to incorporate exercise into a workday, and general exercise tips.

➤ American Diabetes Association—"Diabetes Basics: Physical Activity," http://www.diabetes.org/diabetes-basics/prevention/checkup-america/activity.html

This succinct web resource outlines the benefits of physical activity for patients, including maintaining healthy levels of glucose, blood pressure, and cholesterol levels. The webpage provides information on the following types of exercise: general aerobic activities such as walking, swimming, and dancing; strength training including workouts with weights; and flexibility exercises. The page also includes further tips on getting started and keeping a record of progress.

➤ Centers for Disease Control and Prevention—"Physical Activity and Health: The Benefits of Physical Activity," http://www.cdc.gov/physicalactivity/everyone/health/index.html

The webpage outlines the benefits of physical exercise, including controlling weight; reducing the risks of diabetes, cardiovascular disease, and cancers;

strengthening bones and muscles; and improving emotional health. While not specifically for patients with diabetes, the information is useful for anyone seeking motivation to undertake an exercise program to prevent or help treat a chronic disease.

➤ Defeat Diabetes Foundation—"Self-Management: Fitness and Exercise," http://www.defeatdiabetes.org/self_management/text.asp?id=Fitness_and_Exercise
The need to combine being healthy with being physically fit is critical because they can be exclusive states, which is not optimal for the body. Conditioning exercises should focus on both aerobic and anaerobic activities. Various types of activities discussed include jumping rope, bicycling, swimming, walking, water aerobics, martial arts, ice-skating, cross-country skiing, snowshoeing, downhill skiing, and snowboarding. Many of these activities are enjoyable for the entire family, so everyone can participate in helping the person with diabetes become more healthy and fit.

➤ Diabetes Health—"Weight Training and Diabetes," http://www.diabeteshealth.com/read/2005/09/01/4323/weight-training-and-diabetes/
This page is an outline of the basics of weight training, including what the benefits of this type of exercise are for patients. With the admonition that patients should first clear any exercise program with a physician, this resource provides information on how to get started, weight-training facts, and three detailed sample weight-training programs for people with different health goals: one for women concerned about osteoporosis, one for competitive athletes, and one for older men who need strength training. The page presents safety precautions that those undertaking a weight-training regimen should know about, as well as a detailed glossary of weight training terminology.

➤ Diabetic Lifestyle—"Diabetes: Beginning an Exercise Program," http://www.diabeticlifestyle.com/exercise/diabetes-beginning-exercise-plan
This resource provides tips on how to start an exercise program and what to expect in terms of health benefits. For those who have been sedentary most of their lives, it is important to seek medical clearance before starting any program. The page also presents advice on what types of exercise to do, how often, and during what part of the day.

➤ Diabetic Lifestyle—"Exercise Option: Water Aerobics," http://www.diabeticlifestyle.com/exercise/exercise-option-water-aerobics
This webpage is an overview of water aerobics and how performing this activity will benefit a person with diabetes. There are also important safety and medical tips for engaging in this type of exercise, such as staying hydrated, wearing a medical alert bracelet, taking a waterproof form of carbohydrates if needed, and ensuring that the patient participates in a class or with a buddy to ensure safety in case of hypoglycemia.

➤ Gestational Diabetes—"Help Control Gestational Diabetes with Exercise," http://gestationaldiabetes.org/help-control-gestational-diabetes-with-exercise/
Being pregnant and diagnosed with gestational diabetes can be very stressful. This resource helps explain how engaging in light to moderate exercise will help to improve gestational diabetes and alleviate associated complications. This webpage provides information on the benefits of physical activity, how to exercise and when, and the most helpful types of exercises.

➤ Indian Health Service, Division of Diabetes Treatment and Prevention—"Physical Activity and Diabetes Hub," http://www.ihs.gov/medicalprograms/diabetes/index.cfm?module=learn_pa
While this resource focuses on health care practitioners working with American Indians and Alaska Natives, it is useful for anyone with diabetes who wants to learn more about how including exercise as part of their daily health regimen can be beneficial. This webpage has a colorful and intuitive information center, the "Physical Activity and Diabetes Hub," where patients can select from the following categories to learn more: physical fitness "how to videos" which can be downloaded to a mobile device; access to a one-hour course on physical activity and diabetes prevention; an online training module regarding physical fitness and diabetes; physical fitness guide cards, complete with audio, video, and text; a prerecorded WebEx on physical activities and diabetes; access to exercise screening guidelines; and a physical activity podcast, which can be downloaded.

➤ Joslin Diabetes Center—"Diabetes and Yoga," http://www.joslin.org/info/diabetes_and_yoga.html
This page presents a succinct summary that explains the basics of yoga and how it can benefit someone with diabetes. While not a replacement for other types of exercise, there are positive health aspects of combining yoga with a regular exercise regimen, such as improving posture, balance, and emotional outlook. The page lists tips on how to find a yoga class and the right teacher. Patients should consult with a doctor or certified diabetes educator before beginning a yoga regimen because some postures may be harmful to a patient's eyes or certain musculoskeletal areas.

➤ Joslin Diabetes Center—"8 Tips for Running with Diabetes," http://www.joslin.org/info/8_tips_for_running_with_diabetes.html
This page is a tip sheet for those who want to take up running as their primary or secondary exercise. Tips include starting slowly by walking first, obtaining a physician's clearance, wearing recommended running shoes and clothing, setting goals, and managing diabetes with exercise.

➤ Joslin Diabetes Center—"Tips for Increasing Physical Activity," http://www.joslin.org/care/tips_for_increasing_physical_activity.html
This webpage is a summary of helpful suggestions on how to increase physical activity while managing diabetes. Tips include getting off the bus at an earlier stop

and walking the rest of the way to the destination; reducing e-mail traffic by getting up and delivering information to people in person; walking at lunchtime as well as before or after work; and using television time for workout DVDs or related physical fitness training. Increasing physical activities, in turn, will increase fitness levels, which should be the goal for all patients with diabetes. Patients should work toward the capability of exercising moderately for at least thirty minutes per day.

➤ Mayo Clinic—"Diabetes Management: How Lifestyle, Daily Routine Affect Blood Sugar," http://www.mayoclinic.com/health/diabetes-management/DA00005
Integrating healthy habits, such as balanced nutrition intake and incorporating exercise into a daily routine, can produce optimal results. Tips for exercise include obtaining medical clearance from a health care provider to determine whether participating in physical activities is advisable; setting an exercise schedule to coincide with food intake; knowing what blood sugar levels should be, both before and after exercise; staying hydrated; and being prepared with a snack or glucose pill if exercise causes blood sugar to drop precipitously.

➤ University of Michigan Health System—"Type 1 Diabetes: Physical Activity," http://www.med.umich.edu/diabetes/education/physactivityt1.htm
This webpage outlines the benefits of exercise for types 1 and 2 diabetes patients and recommends several safety protocols while doing so, such as wearing a medical alert bracelet, avoiding exercise when ketones are present, wearing proper footwear, making sure to have carbohydrates readily available before and after exercise, and stopping the workout if experiencing any type of pain or breathing difficulties. A list provides of various exercise activities and the amount of calories burned by the hour and minute.

➤ U.S. Department of Health and Human Services, National Diabetes Information Clearinghouse—"What I Need to Know about Physical Activity and Diabetes," http://diabetes.niddk.nih.gov/dm/pubs/physical_ez/
This substantive resource addresses various aspects of managing types 1 and 2 diabetes with a regular exercise and physical fitness regimen. It provides details on how a physically active lifestyle can benefit someone with diabetes and recommends types of exercises. It also notes the types of exercises to avoid, depending upon a person's diabetes complications, along with what time of day is best for physical activities. Before starting any type of regular physical fitness plan, patients should consult with their health care provider first for clearance and additional guidance.

References

American Diabetes Association. 2009. "Diabetes and Physical Activity." American Diabetes Association. http://www.princeton.edu/healthier/docs/DiabetesEmail-3.pdf.

American Diabetes Association. 2012. "Diabetes Basics: Physical Activity," American Diabetes Association. Accessed July 6. http://www.diabetes.org/diabetes-basics/prevention/checkup-america/activity.html.

Defeat Diabetes Foundation. 2012. "Self-Management: Fitness and Exercise." Defeat Diabetes Foundation. Accessed July 6. http://www.defeatdiabetes.org/self_management/text.asp?id=Fitness_and_Exercise.

Joslin Diabetes Center. 2012. "Diabetes and Yoga." Joslin Diabetes Center. Accessed July 6. http://www.joslin.org/info/diabetes_and_yoga.html.

National Diabetes Information Clearinghouse. 2011. "What I Need to Know about Physical Activity and Diabetes." National Institute of Diabetes and Digestive and Kidney Diseases, National Institutes of Health. Last updated December 6. http://diabetes.niddk.nih.gov/dm/pubs/physical_ez/index.aspx.

Song, S. 2007. "Study: The Best Exercise for Diabetes." Time.com. September 17. http://www.time.com/time/health/article/0,8599,1662683,00.html.

Tirrito, S. J. 2012. "Diabetes and Endurance Athletes." Life Time Fitness. Accessed August 8. http://www.lifetimeendurance.com/public/321.cfm.

Chapter 10

Complementary and Alternative Medicine

Introduction

Complementary and alternative medicine (CAM) is not currently recognized as a facet of conventional Western medicine. Individually, complementary medicine is a practice used in conjunction with Western medicine, while alternative medicine is used in place of Western medicine. As more patients with diabetes are becoming interested in using complementary and alternative treatments, it is important that they are able to use reliable resources for finding information about CAM. While some CAM treatments may be beneficial to diabetes patients, other treatments may be ineffective or even harmful. In the same vein, patients should be sure to inform their health care provider if they are now using or are considering using CAM. This chapter provides a basic overview of CAM and its use in diabetes treatment, including links to finding reliable and authoritative print and web resources. Patients need to be able to evaluate effectively any resources used to find information about CAM.

CAM Overview

According to the National Center for Complementary and Alternative Medicine (2011), CAM is defined as "a group of diverse medical and health care systems, practices, and products that are not generally considered to be part of conventional medicine." While some CAM therapies are effective, many can be harmful to patients. Receiving a diagnosis of diabetes, as well as managing this chronic condition, can be stressful. Patients eager to wrest control over their condition often turn to CAM as a way to treat the disease in a more unconventional and perhaps less taxing way.

Patients considering complementary or alternative medicine should first consult with their health care team to find out more information about whether the CAM treatment they are interested in pursuing would be beneficial to their health. In addition, when researching CAM treatments, patients must be able to distinguish credible claims from false ones in advertisements and in legitimate-appearing websites. It would be inadvisable for a patient to commit to a CAM therapy that purports to cure or treat diabetes without conventional medicine; any potential

CAM treatment should be researched and evaluated before use. The three main parts to CAM, according to the National Center for Complementary and Alternative Medicine (2011), include natural products, such as herbs and dietary supplements; mind and body medicine, which focuses on brain, mind, and body interaction; and body manipulation, such as chiropractic or massage work.

Herbs and Dietary Supplements

Natural remedies may be an attractive option because patients believe such treatments are not manufactured pharmaceutical products, which may be expensive or have unwanted side effects, and natural remedies will likely be more beneficial to the body. According to the American Diabetes Association (2012), 22 percent of patients with diabetes use a form of herbal therapy, and 31 percent use dietary supplements. The health interview used to retrieve this information also determined that Hispanics, African Americans, Asians, and Native Americans are more likely to turn to herbs and dietary supplements to treat their diabetes.

However, these natural remedies can be harmful to the patient. For instance, according to Shane-McWhorter (2009) many of the available herbs and dietary supplements may counteract the positive effects of insulin or blood pressure medication. Some may even prevent the normal clotting of blood that should occur, which is dangerous when a patient needs surgery. In addition, the U.S. Food and Drug Administration does not regulate these types of remedies, so it is possible that some supplements contain harmful contaminants or that the dosages are incorrectly labeled (American Diabetes Association, 2012).

These supplements are often in the form of botanicals (herbs), vitamins, minerals, and fatty acids. Most supplements can be purchased online or at pharmacies and grocery stores. According to Shane-McWhorter (2009), some of the more popular herbs and supplements include the following:

- Aloe
- Alpha lipoic acid
- Bitter melon
- Chromium
- Cinnamon
- Fenugreek
- Fish oil
- Garlic
- Ginkgo biloba
- Ginseng
- Iron
- Jambolan
- Magnesium
- Omega-3 plant oils
- Pine bark extract
- St. John's wort
- Vanadium
- Zinc

It is important that patients share information about any herbs or dietary supplements they are currently taking, or are contemplating taking, with their health care provider. Shane-McWhorter (2009) recommends the following discussion tips to ensure patients' safety:

- Make sure to list any supplements or vitamins you are taking in your medical record.
- Explain to your doctor why you are taking the supplement.
- Be proactive in informing your doctor if you are taking supplements or contemplating stopping taking supplements.
- Check to see what the side effects or drug interactions the supplements may have, including with other medical conditions you have.
- Ask how the supplement affects blood glucose, cholesterol, and blood pressure.
- Make a list of the supplements you are taking before the appointment or bring the bottles with you.
- Tell the doctor the dosage level you have been following and for how long you have been taking the supplement.
- Do not stop taking any prescribed medicines because you are also taking herbal or dietary supplements.

Mind and Body Combination

According to the National Center for Complementary and Alternative Medicine (2011), mind-body therapies promote the use of the mind to positively affect the body's functioning and overall health. Examples of this type of therapy include acupuncture, meditation, and yoga. Acupuncture, an ancient Chinese tradition, uses stimulation techniques with the insertion of needles at specific body points to promote healing. Practitioners assert that acupuncture can assist with relieving chronic pain and help with diabetic neuropathy; however, there are no scientific studies proving this claim.

Patients can choose among various forms of meditation. Three of the most popular practices include mindfulness, transcendental, and focused awareness meditation (Nelson, 2006). Mindfulness meditation focuses on breathing, which helps to relax the mind and body. Transcendental meditation includes using a word repeatedly as a method to increase focus while simultaneously promoting relaxation. Focused awareness meditation includes incorporating an object, such as a candle or figurine, into the patient's vision as a way to promote peacefulness. Because diabetes is a stressful condition, meditation can be a way to help lower blood glucose levels and dissuade patients from overeating or engaging in other more harmful activities. In addition, it can help lower blood pressure and slow heart rate (Nelson, 2006).

Yoga incorporates the use of various body postures to promote breathing and relaxation while also building muscle strength. Norton (2011) reports that a recent study demonstrates participation in yoga classes may help decrease weight as well as help control blood sugar levels. The study concludes that incorporating more vigorous forms of exercise into patients' daily lives is necessary to have a meaningful effect on weight loss. Further, the study notes that high levels of oxidative stress, which can promote other diseases and conditions, are lowered by the regular practice of yoga.

Body-Based Practices—Chiropractic and Massage

Using spinal adjustments, a chiropractor can help body functionality by ensuring that nerve pathways are not blocked from transmitting signals to various areas of the body. Some practitioners believe that performing spinal adjustments will help restore nerve function to areas previously injured from the effects of diabetes (Islets of Hope, 2006). However, no scientific literature supports this claim. Insulin is still the main component for managing diabetes. However, if patients are experiencing back problems that are preventing them from exercising regularly, chiropractic care may help improve their mobility issues.

Massage therapy, including Swedish, Rolfing, Trager, and craniosacral techniques, are all designed to enhance the circulatory and lymph node system and promote relaxation. Patients sometimes pursue massage in the belief that it helps insulin intake at injection sites, normalizes glucose levels, and relieves neuropathy. Ezzo, Donner, and Nickols (2001) performed a literature review of the scientific data and concluded that massage may briefly increase insulin intake at injections sites. However, that effect might not always be desirable. Further, she concluded the studies examining massage's effect on normalizing glucose levels were not statistically significant. Ezzo also notes studies have not found that massage helps with diabetic neuropathy symptoms.

Summary

While there have been remarkable advances in modern medicine in the twenty-first century, there is no cure for type 1 or type 2 diabetes. It is tempting for patients to want to circumvent physician-recommended prescription medications, changes to diet, and physical activity regimens with nontraditional therapies because CAM treatments are perceived, often incorrectly, to be more effective than Western approaches. Many of the herbs and dietary supplements that patients use are, in fact, harmful because they reduce insulin intake or interact poorly with other prescribed medications. Mind and body therapy work often has a positive effect because it helps reduce the stress associated with managing the condition, increases circulation, lowers blood pressure, and helps maintain insulin levels. It is crucial that all patients with diabetes contemplating pursuing any type of CAM therapy consult with their health care provider first, and always communicate candidly whether they are already using any CAM treatment options.

Information Sources

Selected Print Resources

➤ Mayo Clinic. 2010. *Mayo Clinic Book of Alternative Medicine*. 2nd ed. New York: Time Home Entertainment.

This book provides a general overview of alternative therapies. There is a section focusing on diabetes and complementary and alternative treatments, and an overview of diabetes, conventional treatment, and then CAM treatment. The discussion of CAM treatment covers some low-risk therapies that may benefit patients with diabetes; it also covers other low-risk therapies such as yoga, Ayurveda, Chinese medicine, and acupuncture.

➤ Perrin, Rosemarie. 2007. *Living with Diabetes: Everything You Need to Know to Safeguard Your Health and Take Control of Your Life*. New York: Sterling.
This books explains the differences between complementary medicine and alternative medicine. It also defines commonly used terms and stresses communicating with a health care provider before using any CAM treatments. There are lists of several dietary supplements that are being studied to determine whether scientific evidence will show they can be beneficial in the treatment of diabetes.

➤ Shane-McWhorter, Laura. 2009. A*merican Diabetes Association Guide to Herbs and Nutritional Supplements: What You Need to Know from Aloe to Zinc*. Alexandria, VA: American Diabetes Association.
The author, a pharmacist, emphasizes that many patients are eager to self-treat their diabetes with what they assume are safe supplements because they are natural botanical herbs, vitamins, fatty acids, minerals, and other dietary supplements. The author emphasizes that patients must be cautious because many supplements can be harmful when taken in certain combinations—and especially when taken in lieu of prescription medicines for controlling glucose levels. Certain supplements, taken in conjunction with prescription diabetes medicines, may cause the prescribed medicine not to work properly. Providing a factual and unbiased examination of forty supplements, this resource includes information about each, its purported benefits, and any adverse effects it may have for a person with diabetes. Whenever patients are interested in adding an herbal or nutritional supplement to their daily regimen, they must first consult with their physician or other health care provider to discuss what effect it might have on their current medical treatment plan. If patients are already using supplements, it is imperative they inform their physician and take the supplements in their original packaging (or information sheets about the supplements) to their appointments.

Selected Web Resources

➤ American Diabetes Association—"Living with Diabetes: Herbs, Supplements, and Alternative Medicines," http://www.diabetes.org/living-with-diabetes/treatment-and-care/medication/herbs-supplements-and-alternative-medicines/
This webpage summarizes some of the key points in Laura Shane-McWhorter's 2009 book, *The American Diabetes Association Guide to Herbs and Nutritional*

Supplements: What You Need to Know from Aloe to Zinc. It provides information on using supplements safely, the different types available, and the potential side effects and drug interactions.

➤ Defeat Diabetes Foundation—"Self-Management: Complementary and Alternative Medical Therapies for Diabetes," http://www.defeatdiabetes.org/self_management/text.asp?id=CompAltMeds_Diabetes

This resource describes various types of CAM therapies that people with diabetes are using. It encourages patients to share with their physician or other health care provider if they are currently incorporating any of these treatments into their daily regimens, or are contemplating doing so, because there can be adverse and harmful side effects. The page provides descriptions for the following therapies: acupuncture, biofeedback, chromium, ginseng, magnesium, and vanadium.

➤ Diabetes.co.uk—"Managing Diabetes: Alternative Treatment," http://www.diabetes.co.uk/alternative-treatment/alternative-treatment.html

This webpage provides links to some of the popular alternative treatments for diabetes with the caveat that not all treatments are beneficial to patients and some can be harmful. There are links to detailed descriptions for the following therapies: traditional Chinese medicine and acupuncture; Ayurveda, an Indian holistic medicine; dietary and herbal supplements; vegetarianism; aromatherapy; relaxation therapy and guided imagery; massage therapy and reflexology; homeopathic treatments; biofeedback; and, art, music, and color therapy.

➤ Islets of Hope—"Diabetes Treatment Option: Alternative and Complementary Therapies for Persons with Diabetes," http://www.isletsofhope.com/diabetes/treatment/alternative/main_1.html

With the disclaimer that this is an informational source only and that patients should discuss alternative and complementary therapies with a physician before trying any of them, this resource provides substantive descriptions of CAM treatments. The page links to the following areas, which are discussed in conjunction with their application to people with diabetes: acupuncture and the combination of Western and Chinese therapies; chiropractic care; benefits of yoga; biofeedback, meditation, and prayer; homeopathic treatments; herbals and natural remedies; vitamins and supplements; and a section on those who purport to "cure" diabetes, followed by a discussion on deceptive advertising.

➤ National Center for Complementary and Alternative Medicine—"Diabetes," http://nccam.nih.gov/health/diabetes/CAM-and-diabetes.htm

A fact sheet on complementary and alternative medical treatments for diabetes, including dietary supplements, this webpage describes several popular supplements and summarizes the scientific research on their effectiveness. There are discussions and links to the following supplements, which are discussed in detail: alpha lipoic acid, chromium, omega-3 fatty acids, polyphenols, garlic, magnesium, coenzyme Q10, ginseng, vanadium, as well as other botanicals. Patients should share their interests in any of these types of supplements with their health care team—and should not replace scientifically proven medical treatments with unproven ones that could be harmful.

➤ National Diabetes Information Clearinghouse—"Complementary and Alternative Medical Therapies for Diabetes," http://diabetes.niddk.nih.gov/dm/pubs/alternative therapies/
This summary provides links to information about CAM therapies and encourages patients to communicate with their health care team before pursuing any of these treatment options. Links are provided to information about CAM and dietary supplements; Ayurvedic interventions; effects of Omega-3 fatty acids on lipids; a consumer advisory on vitamin E supplements; how to select a CAM practitioner; an alphabetical listing of treatments and therapies; and further information on clinical trials taking place for alternative therapies for diabetes.

➤ U.S. National Institutes of Health, Office of Dietary Supplements—"Dietary Supplement Fact Sheets," http://ods.od.nih.gov/factsheets/list-all/
While not focused on diabetes, the webpage provides a comprehensive collection of many dietary supplements in an easy-to-use alphabetical listing. When clicking on the link to each supplement, the reader is directed to a page with substantive information, which describes the supplement, where it is derived, what are its recommended intakes, current issues or controversies surrounding the supplement, health risks, and medication interactions. Additional links on each supplement's page provide further information from reliable sources, such as peer-reviewed journal articles or other government agencies like the National Cancer Institute or the National Center for Complementary and Alternative Medicine.

References

American Diabetes Association. 2012. "Living with Diabetes: Herbs, Supplements, and Alternative Medicines." American Diabetes Association. Accessed July 12. http://www.diabetes.org/living-with-diabetes/treatment-and-care/medication/ herbs-supplements-and-alternative-medicines/.

Ezzo, J., T. Donner, and D. Nickols. 2001. "Is Massage Useful in the Management of Diabetes?" *Diabetes Spectrum* 14, no. 4: 218–224.

Islets of Hope. 2006. "Alternative and Complementary Treatments for Diabetes: Chiropractic Care." Islets of Hope. Last updated April 29. http://www.islets ofhope.com/diabetes/treatment/alternative/chiropractic_care_1.html.

National Center for Complementary and Alternative Medicine. 2011. "What Is Complementary and Alternative Medicine?" National Institutes of Health. Last updated July. http://nccam.nih.gov/health/whatiscam/#intro.

Nelson, J. B. 2006. "Meditation and the Art of Diabetes Management." Diabetes Self-Management. Updated July 24. http://www.diabetesselfmanagement.com/articles/alternative-medicine-complementary-therapies/meditation_and_the_art_of_diabetes_management/1/.

Norton, A. 2011. "Yoga Shows Some Benefits for Diabetes." Reuters Health. September 2. http://www.reuters.com/article/2011/09/02/us-yoga-diabetes-idUSTRE7814 FL20110902.

Shane-McWhorter, L. 2009. *American Diabetes Association Guide to Herbs and Nutritional Supplements: What You Need to Know from Aloe to Zinc.* Alexandria, VA: American Diabetes Association.

Chapter 11

Clinical Trials

Introduction

According to the U.S. Food and Drug Administration (2009), a clinical trial is a research study involving human volunteers that seeks answers to a specific health question. Those in charge of clinical trials, also known as clinical research studies, conduct the trials carefully and safely by following a predetermined protocol. Typically, before human volunteers enter any clinical trial, researchers test the new therapies or procedures on animals first. If any of the therapies and treatments show promise, they may then be tested on human volunteers through clinical trials.

Researchers use different types of clinical trials to answer questions regarding disease prevention, therapy, screening, diagnosis, or improving quality of life (U.S. Food and Drug Administration, 2009). They conduct clinical trials to determine the safety and efficacy of new therapies, procedures, or devices; they may also perform clinical trials to find additional types of care that can improve the quality of life for people with chronic diseases (National Institutes of Health, 2011). Any new therapy must prove safe before the U.S. Food and Drug Administration (FDA) will approve it for use in the United States. Clinical trials allow patients with diabetes access to treatments that have the potential to be of benefit to them before the treatments are available on the market. This chapter provides information about clinical trial protocol, types, and phases; it concludes with a list of resources on clinical trials in general as well as resources for finding diabetes-related clinical trials.

Protocol

Every clinical trial has a carefully designed and outlined plan called a study protocol. The protocol explains the background, objectives, study design, inclusion and exclusion criteria, study procedures, and potential harm that may occur to the volunteer during the trial (Mulay, 2002). The protocol also explains the various tests, procedures, and medications the study will employ and details what information will be gathered during the trial. The protocol helps ensure that the trial maintains the safety of the participants and answers the study questions. The protocol outlines participant eligibility, provides detailed test schedules, describes medications and their dosages, and sets the length of the study (ClinicalTrials .gov, 2007).

Protocol Review

To safeguard clinical trial participants, federal law requires an institutional review board (IRB) to review and approve each clinical trial involving human subjects in the United States. IRB members usually include health care providers, statisticians, people trained in ethics or law, clergy, and community members. The members review the study protocol to ensure that the trial is ethical and that the participants' rights are protected. If the IRB approves the study, the law requires that the review board must then periodically monitor the study (National Institutes of Health, 2011).

Participation

All clinical trials contain guidelines, known as inclusion and exclusion criteria, that dictate participant eligibility. The study protocol outlines these characteristics in detail. Each trial will likely have its own unique eligibility requirements. Inclusion criteria, such as type of disease or condition and ability to comply with study requirements, are factors that must be present to allow a patient to participate in the study. Exclusion factors, such as age, gender, other medical conditions, previous treatments, and lab result parameters, are factors that, if present, may disqualify a patient from participating in the trial. Being specific with eligibility requirements is important: focusing on a narrowly defined group of volunteers helps protect study participants and ensure scientifically reliable study results (American Diabetes Association, 2012).

Informed Consent

Before a person enrolls in a clinical trial, the health care team must discuss with the patient all possible risks and benefits involved in participating in the trial. The patient must also read and sign an informed consent document that includes all procedures and details of the study before participation can occur. The consent form contains information about and explains the purpose of the study as well as procedures involved; potential risks and discomforts; potential benefits; compensation for participation; financial obligation; emergency care and injury compensation; confidentiality, participation, and withdrawal; identification of investigators; and the rights of the research subjects. If new information about the trial therapy arises during the clinical trial, the consent form may have to be revised, incorporating the new finding.

FDA guidelines mandate that consent forms, which can be very lengthy, must be available in the native language of the trial participant. Law also dictates that the forms be written at an eighth-grade reading level (Mulay, 2002). Nurses and doctors can assist those with low literacy in reading consent forms. Patients intending to become participants in a clinical study must be comfortable enough to ask questions to ensure they understand the procedures and expectations of the study. However, the informed consent form is not a contract, so patients can withdraw from clinical trials at any time for any reason.

Clinical Trial Types

Researchers typically use one of several types of clinical trials to answer a particular research question:

- Treatment trials: These trials test a new therapy or a new combination of drugs. The trial may test drugs that have never been commercially used in patients or it may test drugs that already are on the market to find new uses for them. Sometimes treatment trials test a combination of marketed therapies to see if they are more effective than a single drug when used together.
- Prevention trials: Prevention trials are conducted for finding the best methods for preventing a disease or condition. For diabetes, the focus of prevention trials is often on medications or lifestyle changes.
- Diagnostic trials: A diagnostic test looks for the best methods, tests, or procedures for diagnosing a disease. With diabetes, the trials include testing for the best ways to diagnose diabetes or the complications of diabetes.
- Screening trials: These trials are conducted to find the best method for detecting a disease or condition in people.
- Quality-of-life trials: These trials focus on finding ways to improve the quality of life of people with chronic conditions.
- Natural history studies: This type of study follows and records the progression of disease and health for those with a particular illness or condition under study.

Clinical Trial Phases

Clinical trials go through four phases, with each phase serving a different purpose:

- Phase I: Phase I trials are the first time a drug or therapy is available for testing on humans, so Phase I trials contain small numbers of volunteers, typically twenty to eighty people. During Phase I trials, researchers evaluate the therapy's safety, dosage range, and side effects. If the volunteers in Phase one tolerate the therapy well, the therapy will then move into Phase II trials.
- Phase II: Testing opens up to a larger group of volunteers for Phase II, but numbers are still fairly low: usually 100 to 300 people. Phase II trials further evaluate the safety and side effects of the drug and confirm the effectiveness in this group of participants. If this phase warrants it, the trial moves on to Phase III.

- Phase III: In Phase III trials, the treatment is given to a much larger group: usually 1,000 to 3,000 volunteers. In addition to continuing to evaluate the drug's safety and side effects, at this point the new treatment is compared against a standard treatment or placebo (an inactive ingredient) to test its effectiveness. Again, if results are promising from Phase III tests, the drug may go on the market after FDA approval.
- Phase IV: After the drug has FDA approval and is on the market, Phase IV trials may occur. Phase IV trials often attempt to determine alternative uses of the treatment for treating other conditions or diseases as well as continuing to assess effectiveness, safety, and side effects of the drug. (ClinicalTrials.gov, 2007)

Clinical Trial Concepts

Sometimes part of the design of a clinical trial is to compare the new product to a placebo. A placebo is an inactive ingredient that resembles the therapy being tested but has no therapeutic effectiveness (Speid, 2010). The use of a placebo as a comparison is very reliable; however, because the placebo has no medical effectiveness, providing volunteer patients with only a placebo may jeopardize those who need treatment for a serious illness. Instead, the study may compare a new device or medication against an existing product to determine whether the new product works as well as the established therapy. Clinical trial participants receive the drug under test, the placebo, or the approved therapy by chance, not by choice, in a process of assignment called randomization. If a placebo will be one of the potential assignments in a trial, the researchers will tell the potential trial participants in advance of entering the trial that they may receive a placebo (National Institutes of Health, 2011).

To prevent an influence on the results of the study, clinical trials are by design either single-blind or double-blind. In a single-blind study, the research team knows whether the participant is receiving the new therapy, the placebo, or the approved therapy. However, the patient does not know which therapy he or she is receiving. In a double-blind study, neither the patients nor the research team members know which therapy the participants are receiving. If necessary, the research team in the double-blind trial has the ability to determine which therapy the participant is receiving (National Institutes of Health, 2011).

Questions for the Research Team

As in all aspects of diabetes care, communication with the health care team is essential when a patient is considering participating in a clinical trial. While the informed consent document covers many areas, it is important for the patient to be sure that he or she prepares a list of questions that need answers before agreeing to enter the trial. Patients may want to ask some of the following questions regarding clinical trial participation:

- What is the purpose of the clinical trial?
- How long will the trial last?
- What side effects might I experience?
- What are my responsibilities during the trial?
- Will I have to pay for any charges involved?
- How will participation in the trial affect my daily life?
- How often will I need to attend appointments?

In addition to these questions, the National Cancer Institute website contains a detailed checklist of questions for patients to ask, as does the American Diabetes Association website, both of which are included in this chapter's Information Sources.

Summary

Some patients may wish to participate in a clinical trial. Clinical trials are carefully planned research studies that can help identify new therapies, preventive measures, screening processes, or even new ways of improving the quality of life of individuals with a certain disease or condition. The research studies follow a carefully planned protocol to ensure the safety of the participants. The IRB then reviews the protocol to ensure that the rights of every trial participant are protected. Potential participants should become familiar with the terms and concepts involved in clinical trials, such as the clinical trial phases and randomization. In addition, patients should also ask questions of their health care team or the study's research team when considering participating in a trial.

Information Sources

Selected Print Resource

➤ Speid, Lorna. 2010. *Clinical Trials: What Patients and Healthy Volunteers Need to Know*. New York: Oxford University Press.
  While not specific to diabetes clinical trials, this book provides an overview of what patients and healthy volunteers need to know about clinical trials. The book includes information about understanding clinical trials, ethics, risks, and benefits. It also explains the drug development process. The resource also provides information for special groups such as the elderly, children, disabled and vulnerable groups, and those with rare diseases. It concludes with a list of resources about clinical trials and for finding clinical trials.

Selected Web Resources

General

➤ American Diabetes Association—"Clinical Trials," http://www.diabetes.org/news-research/other-research-resources/clinical-trials/
This resource provides a great starting point for people with diabetes who are looking for information about clinical trials. The page provides brief information about clinical trials along with links to additional resources.

➤ National Cancer Institute—"A Guide to Understanding Informed Consent," http://www.cancer.gov/clinicaltrials/conducting/informed-consent-guide
Though written for cancer patients participating in clinical trials, this helpful guide is beneficial to those interested in participating in a clinical trial, as it can help them understand more about the informed consent process. The page also contains a link to a checklist of questions patients should ask the research team.

➤ National Institutes of Health—"NIH Clinical Research Trials and You," http://www.nih.gov/health/clinicaltrials/index.htm
This general resource for clinical trial information provides users of the site a range of information for understanding and finding clinical trials. It contains information about clinical trial basics and provides a list of questions to ask if interested in participating. There are also volunteer stories, links to educational resources, a glossary of terms, and a link to finding clinical trials.

➤ WebMD—"Clinical Trials: A Guide for Patients," http://www.webmd.com/a-to-z-guides/clincial-trial-guide-patients
This section of the WebMD website provides a succinct overview of clinical trials. It begins with background information and explains the different phases of clinical trials. The sections describe the advantages of participating in a clinical trial, outline potential problems, and explain informed consent. There is also a list of important questions to ask before participating in a clinical trial.

Finding Clinical Trials

➤ Clinical Islet Transplantation Consortium, http://www.citisletstudy.org/
The website provides information about a National Institutes of Health–sponsored islet transplantation trial, which may be of interest to type 1 diabetes patients.

➤ ClinicalTrials.gov, http://www.clinicaltrials.gov/
A service of the National Institutes of Health, this website provides a database for finding federally and privately supported clinical trials conducted nationally and internationally. The site is not just limited to diabetes trials; users can search by medical condition and location, and narrow results by gender, age group, phase, funding, and so forth.

➤ Immune Tolerance Network—"Active Clinical Trials," http://www.immunetolerance
.org/public/clinical-trial-info/active-trials
The Immune Tolerance Network is a nonprofit, government-funded consortium
of researchers conducting trials to establish new treatments for immune-related
diseases, including type 1 diabetes.

➤ JDRF—"JDRF Type 1 Diabetes Clinical Trials Connection," https://trials.jdrf
.org/patient/
This webpage by JDRF, formerly known as the Juvenile Diabetes Research Foundation, assists patients in understanding clinical trials and facilitates finding an
appropriate clinical trial.

➤ National Institute of Diabetes and Digestive and Kidney Diseases—"Opportunities
for Patients and Family Members to Participate in Clinical Studies," http://www
.t1diabetes.nih.gov/t1d_ctcr/allstudies.asp
Users of the site can search for type 1 diabetes clinical trials by eligibility, location,
or list all studies.

➤ Type 1 Diabetes TrialNet, http://www.diabetestrialnet.org/
Clinical trials are available in the United States and internationally for people
newly diagnosed with type 1 diabetes and for relatives of people with type 1 diabetes who are at risk for developing the condition.

Selected Audiovisual Resources

➤ MedlinePlus—"Clinical Trials," http://www.nlm.nih.gov/medlineplus/tutorials/
clinicaltrials/htm/index.htm
This webpage provides links to an interactive slide tutorial explaining clinical
trials. It provides information about why the studies are held, who can participate,
how the trials are designed and conducted, the importance of informed consent,
and ethical and legal concerns. There is also a printable transcript available of
the slide show.

➤ National Heart, Lung, and Blood Institute—"Children and Clinical Studies,"
http://www.nhlbi.nih.gov/childrenandclinicalstudies/index.php
This video series is not specific to diabetes clinical trials, but explains the importance of research in children. This set of short videos explains why research is
important, how to get started, and what to do once enrolled in a clinical trial.
The collection also provides information about patient rights and resources for
finding information.

➤ NIH Senior Health—"What Is a Clinical Trial?," http://nihseniorhealth.gov/
breastcancer/planningtreatment/video/bc3_na_intro.html
This link accesses a brief video that describes clinical trials and what patients
participating in them should know. The video covers information about the trial

protocol, informed consent, and potential risks, as well as the randomization process and the four clinical trial phases.

References

American Diabetes Association 2012. "Clinical Trials." American Diabetes Association. Accessed June 8. http://www.diabetes.org/news-research/other-research-resources/clinical-trials/.

ClinicalTrials.gov. 2007. "Understanding Clinical Trials." National Institutes of Health. Last updated September 20. http://clinicaltrials.gov/ct2/info/understand.

Mulay, M. 2002. *Making the Decision: A Cancer Patient's Guide to Clinical Trials.* Boston: Jones and Bartlett.

National Institutes of Health. 2011. "NIH Clinical Research Trials and You: The Basics." National Institutes of Health. Last reviewed January 11. http://www.nih.gov/health/clinicaltrials/basics.htm.

Speid, L. 2010. *Clinical Trials: What Patients and Healthy Volunteers Need to Know.* New York: Oxford University Press.

U.S. Food and Drug Administration. 2009. "Basic Questions and Answers about Clinical Trials." U.S. Department of Health and Human Services. Last updated July 16. http://www.fda.gov/ForConsumers/ByAudience/ForPatientAdvocates/HIVandAIDSActivities/ucm121345.htm.

Part III

Life with Diabetes

Chapter 12

Collaborating with the Health Care Team

Health Care Team Members

Diabetes is a complex disease. To treat it most effectively, patients must participate proactively in their own care. In the preliminary stages of finding a primary care doctor or other specialist, patients should ask how much experience the physician or specialist has working with diabetes patients. The entire spectrum of the disease requires the input of a wide array of health care providers, including doctors with different specialties, nurses, diabetes educators, dieticians, pharmacists, and mental health professionals. Knowing how to communicate effectively with these medical professionals enhances the collaborative effort between patients and their health care team. For those individuals who are at risk for diabetes, working closely with these health care professionals could prevent them from developing the condition.

Patients should visit their diabetes health care team regularly and not skip appointments. Taking an active role in their health care can help patients receive the best possible care and manage their disease. One way for patients to take an active role is to communicate as effectively and efficiently as possible with their health care team. It may be useful for patients to bring a list of written questions with them; because visits to most medical professionals are usually brief, hurried patients may forget to ask something important. For parents of children with diabetes, it is likely that they will have to pose some or all of the health questions to the medical professionals on their children's behalf. Further, it is useful for patients or parents to take notes when speaking with medical and health care professionals or to ask them to provide a written summary so that topics and details covered are memorialized. Also, patients should never be afraid to speak up and ask questions if they do not understand something.

Diabetes puts patients at risk for a number of complications, so the patient's health care team may consist of a variety of health care providers. Specialists, in addition to the regular health care team, can help patients prevent problems or manage them when they occur. A brief description of each of these health care providers follows, along with examples of questions patients can pose to elicit valuable information and what data they should bring to their appointments to keep their entire team current regarding their health status.

Primary Care Physician

The primary care physician is the leader of the health care team and provides guidance to both the patient and the other members. Generally, the physician practices in family medicine or internal medicine and is knowledgeable about the intricacies of the disease process. Patients most likely present to this physician in the initial stages of diabetes when their symptoms prompt them to seek medical attention. Physicians can prescribe medications and give patients referrals to other health care members of the team. Patients should see their primary care physician or endocrinologist on a regular basis (American Diabetes Association, 2012b).

Certified Diabetes Educator

Certified diabetes educators help patients manage their disease effectively through training, medical skills building, and counseling. They help patients to monitor and test their glucose levels, give themselves insulin injections, and use associated medical equipment properly. To become a certified diabetes educator, one must be a health care professional, have two years of diabetes education experience, be currently employed in a diabetes education position, and then pass a rigorous examination. These educators are found in many fields: various medical specialties, mental health professions, social work, nutrition, and public health, among others. If they successfully pass these requirements and the exam, they earn the credential given by the National Certification Board for Diabetes Educators (American Association of Diabetes Educators, 2012).

Dentist

A dentist is an integral member of the health care team, along with dental hygienists and technicians, and is medically trained in both the prevention and treatment of diseases of the mouth and maxillofacial region. Everyone needs routine dental care; however, diabetes can cause certain problems in the mouth requiring extra care, sometimes because excess glucose in the mouth makes it easier for bacteria to grow. The risk of dental problems increases for patients with diabetes because their white blood cells, which normally fight bacterial infections, are often impaired, which can lead to both gingivitis and periodontitis. Further, diabetes can cause blood vessels to expand, which leads to ineffective healing after any type of dental intervention, from deep teeth cleaning to oral surgery (National Diabetes Information Clearinghouse, 2012).

Dietitian

A dietitian, trained in the science of food and nutrition, educates people on how to prepare a well-balanced and healthy diet to support their particular medical goals. For a person who is at risk for prediabetes, eating a nutritionally sound diet can help to prevent the manifestation of the disease (American Diabetes Association, 2012b). Further, by eating a balanced diet, patients can lose excess weight, perform physical exercise more easily, and control their blood sugar more efficiently.

Endocrinologist

An endocrinologist is a physician who specializes in the body's endocrine system, which includes the glands that secrete hormones to support the body's various organs and functions, such as the pancreas. In both type 1 and type 2 diabetics, their ability to secrete or process the insulin hormone is directly affected. An endocrinologist is very knowledgeable about the disease and can work with patients to manage their diabetes properly.

Mental Health Professional

Mental health professionals include psychiatrists, psychologists, social workers, and therapists who are trained to provide counseling assistance to adults and children. For those who are newly diagnosed or who are in a maintenance mode of the disease, various issues can arise at work, school, or home that may cause concern and worry. A trained mental health professional can objectively work with patients with diabetes and their families to overcome obstacles that may be negatively affecting their overall health and well-being (Joslin Diabetes Center, 2012a).

Nephrologist

A nephrologist is a trained internal medicine doctor with a subspecialty in diseases related to the kidney, its functions, and its processes. Diabetic nephropathy, which is a disease of the kidneys, is a direct result of having diabetes. Kidney functions are affected negatively by an excessive amount of blood sugar; the excess glucose weakens and destroys the kidney's ability to pass waste (Mayo Clinic, 2012a). While not all patients with diabetes develop this disease, they are at higher risk. Diabetic nephropathy is one of the leading causes of death for patients, so working with a nephrologist in the early stages of the disease is important to prevent serious health complications (National Kidney and Urologic Diseases Information Clearinghouse, 2010).

Nurse

A nurse's education and training focuses on helping prevent and treat illness and disease, and acting as an advocate for patients with other health care providers. Nurses specializing in the care of patients with diabetes educate patients and families on how to manage the disease, take medications properly, monitor and test blood glucose levels, establish healthy eating habits, and prevent or treat associated medical complications (American Diabetes Association, 2012b).

Ophthalmologist

An ophthalmologist is a medical doctor educated and trained to treat disease of the eyes. Because diabetes can negatively affect blood vessels, it is important for patients to see an eye care professional annually to check for damage or changes. Diabetic retinopathy, which generally occurs in both eyes, is a disease that damages the blood vessels of the retina and can ultimately lead to blindness (National Eye Institute, 2012). During these annual visits, an ophthalmologist can prescribe a course of action to ameliorate or prevent further complications, including cataracts and glaucoma, which can be exacerbated by diabetes.

Pharmacist

A pharmacist is educated and trained to dispense various types of medications. As part of the diabetes health care team, pharmacists can assist with providing screening tests for those at risk for the disease, help those who have diabetes monitor their glucose levels, and provide general health education to help manage the disease (American Diabetes Association, 2012b). Pharmacists work in conjunction with the patients' primary care physicians by making needed referrals to other specialists. They maintain records of all prescription medications patients are taking, which is vital in preventing pharmaceutical complications.

Podiatrist

A doctor of podiatric medicine is educated and trained to treat problems with the feet and lower legs. While podiatrists do not specialize in diabetes, many of them are familiar with complications that arise from poor blood flow and circulation, such as nerve damage that causes numbness and tingling in the feet and toes. What would normally be considered minor foot ailments, such as foot sores, corns, or calluses can become a serious health concern for a patient with diabetes (American Diabetes Association, 2012b). Consulting with a podiatrist on ways to prevent foot and nerve problems associated with the disease and having them treat any ailments is vital because the risk of amputation of the lower extremities for patients with diabetes is high.

Questions to Pose to Health Care Providers and Information to Bring to Appointments

To make each visit with a medical or health professional as productive as possible, it is important for patients or parents of children with diabetes to bring specific questions to pose, so they can elicit pertinent information. It is equally important for these patients to bring data and anecdotal reports regarding their own or their children's health to ensure the health care team is current regarding their medical status. A sample list of the types of questions to pose to medical professionals includes the following (American Diabetes Association, 2012a; Joslin Diabetes Center, 2012b):

- What is my (or my child's) glucose level?
- What should my glucose level be?
- What should I do if my glucose levels are too high or too low?
- What is my cholesterol level?
- What should my cholesterol level be?
- What should I do if my cholesterol level is too high?
- What is my blood pressure?
- What should my blood pressure be?
- What should I do to reduce my blood pressure if it is too high?
- How often should I monitor my glucose?
- Is there a specific time of day I should monitor my glucose?
- What are the different types of insulin?
- What is the best way to take insulin for my circumstances: by pump or by shot?
- When should I take insulin throughout the day?
- How often should I take insulin throughout the day?
- How old should my child be before injecting insulin himself or herself?
- Are there side effects to the medications I am taking?
- What are the symptoms of low blood sugar?
- What are the symptoms of high blood sugar?
- How do I test for ketones?
- How much physical activity is it safe for me to engage in on a daily basis?
- How does exercise affect my insulin intake?
- What type of nutritional guidelines should I follow?
- How does what I eat affect insulin intake?
- How does having diabetes affect other medical issues I may have?
- How often should I visit particular medical specialists, such as the dentist, ophthalmologist, or dietitian?
- When should I schedule my next appointment with a particular medical specialist?
- What are the long-term effects are of type 1 or type 2 diabetes?
- Is my family at risk of developing diabetes?

A sample list of the types of the patient's personal health information to bring to appointments with medical professionals includes the following (Mayo Clinic, 2012b):

- Your (or your child's) recent blood glucose readings
- How often you have experienced high or low blood sugar readings

- How much insulin you are taking daily
- Blood pressure readings, if conducted at home
- A list of any other medications you are taking, including over-the-counter vitamins or supplements
- Any allergies you have to medications
- Any physical symptoms you are experiencing that are causing you concern, such as problems with eyesight, urination, circulation, feet and lower legs, or fatigue
- Any emotional symptoms you are experiencing, such as stress or depression
- A summary of your recent sleep patterns
- A summary of your recent energy levels
- The type of diet and nutritional plan you are following
- How much exercise and physical activity you are engaging in daily or weekly

Summary

Many different medical specialties compose the diabetic health care team, including the primary care physician, certified diabetes educator, dentist, dietician, endocrinologist, mental health professional, nephrologist, nurse, ophthalmologist, pharmacist, and podiatrist. It is crucial that the patient or parent of a child with diabetes communicate openly and candidly with every member of the health care team. If one area of the body suffers impairment, it can have a negative effect on the rest of the body and undermine overall health. Patients or parents should maintain a daily health log that includes the latest test results, such as blood glucose readings, and adhere to a plan to write lists of questions to ask health care team members during appointments.

Information Sources

Selected Print Resources

➤ American Diabetes Association. 2011. *American Diabetes Association Complete Guide to Diabetes.* 5th ed. Alexandria, VA: American Diabetes Association.
In addition to basic information about the different types of diabetes, this book contains a chapter about working with the diabetes health care team. The chapter provides an outline of each type of provider patients with diabetes may expect to see and provides information on how to communicate effectively with the diabetes care team.

➤ Keene, Nancy. 1998. *Working with Your Doctor: Getting the Healthcare You Deserve.* Sebastopol, CA: O'Reilly.
Though a bit dated and not specific to diabetes, this book contains valuable information for patients and encourages them to build a relationship with their

health care team through effective communication. The book contains information on taking charge of health care, finding a doctor, communicating, knowing patient rights and responsibilities, and asking questions.

➤ Perrin, Rosemarie. 2007. *Living with Diabetes: Everything You Need to Know to Safeguard Your Health and Take Control of Your Life*. Toronto: Sterling.
This book contains a section explaining the diabetes health care team by listing each team member title and providing background of how that provider plays a critical role in the care of patients.

➤ Rubin, Richard. 2003. *101 Tips for Coping with Diabetes*. Alexandria, VA: American Diabetes Association.
A section of the book titled "Getting the Best Health Care" provides patients with numerous tips about the roles of the various diabetes specialists and provides tips on communicating well with them and visiting them regularly.

➤ Warshaw, Hope. 2009. *Real-Life Guide to Diabetes: Practical Answers to Your Diabetes Problems*. Alexandra, VA: American Diabetes Association.
This title devotes a chapter to seeking and finding support. The chapter provides patients with information about how to locate diabetes specialists as well as find information about endocrinologists, primary care physicians, certified diabetes educators, pharmacists, and other health care providers.

Selected Web Resources

➤ American Association of Diabetes Educators—"Find a Diabetes Educator," http://www.diabeteseducator.org/DiabetesEducation/Find.html
This webpage accesses a national database of diabetes educators that can be located using an easy search engine with categories of state, zip code, or name. If searching using a broader category, the results list will provide names of diabetes educators in a particular state or zip code. Patients can then click on an educator's name, which then links to a page that provides his or her educational credentials, employer, and contact information.

➤ American Diabetes Association—"Living with Diabetes: Your Health Care Team," http://www.diabetes.org/living-with-diabetes/treatment-and-care/who-is-on-your-healthcare-team/your-health-care-team.html
This page provides practical advice on how to build a health care team that is geographically close to the primary care physician, as well as one that communicates effectively with one another. It lists and briefly defines the key members of the health care team, including primary care physician (often with a subspecialty in endocrinology), nurse educator, registered dietitian, endocrinologist, ophthalmologist, optometrist, social worker or therapist, podiatrist, pharmacist, dentist, and physical fitness trainer.

➤ Cleveland Clinic—"Working with Your Diabetes Health Care Team," http://my.clevelandclinic.org/disorders/Diabetes_Mellitus/hic_Working_with_Your_Diabetes_Health_Care_Team.aspx
This section provides guidance on how to work effectively with all members of the health care team, including doctors, dieticians, diabetes educators, exercise trainers, and pharmacists. In a question-and-answer format, it lists the types of questions one should ask, how often one should see a physician, what pertinent information to provide, and what lab tests should be performed. In addition, there is a section on how to monitor both the development and progression of diabetic complications including various forms of eye disease, kidney disease, and nerve disease.

➤ Joslin Diabetes Center—"Diabetes Education: Why It's So Crucial to Care," http://www.joslin.org/info/diabetes_education_why_its_so_crucial_to_care.html
One of the critical aspects of successful diabetes management is education about the many components of the disease and how they interrelate. Self-management training is stressed by the Joslin Diabetes Center and includes key members of the health care team, including physicians, certified diabetes educators, nutritionists, and exercise physiologists. For those patients who can travel to the Joslin Diabetes Centers, which are located throughout the United States, there is a comprehensive educational plan that includes a tailored sequenced program for individuals. A variety of medical personnel can assist the patient formulate a customized wellness plan.

➤ Joslin Diabetes Center—"9 Questions for Your Diabetes Care Team," http://www.joslin.org/info/9_questions_for_your_diabetes_care_team.html
For a productive dialogue to be established between patients and their health care team, this webpage lists nine questions patients should ask a physician or other specialist regarding their condition and how to improve their health: (1) When was the last time my glycated hemoglobin (A1C) was tested? (2) What were the results of my last lipid profile? (3) How often should I be checking my blood glucose? (4) What kind of dietary guidelines should I be following? (5) How do my feet look? (6) What were the results of my last dilated eye exam by an ophthalmologist? (7) What is my blood pressure? (8) When was my last test for microalbuminuria? (9) What is my kidneys' filling capacity?

➤ KidsHealth.org—"Doctors and Hospitals," http://kidshealth.org/parent/system/index.html#cat173
For parents who are unfamiliar with navigating the health care system on their child's behalf with regard to diabetes, this webpage provides links to information about the key medical personnel with whom they will be in contact, how to communicate effectively with physicians, how to balance academics with diabetes, and how to transition from pediatrics to adult care.

➤ Mayo Clinic—"Type 1 Diabetes: Preparing for Your Appointment," http://www
.mayoclinic.com/health/type-1-diabetes/DS00329/DSECTION=preparing-for-
your-appointment
This webpage provides practical tips on attending medical appointments after a
type 1 diabetes diagnosis to ensure the patient has all the necessary information
to provide to his or her physician. The patient should know the answers to all of
the following for his or her own situation: frequency of blood glucose monitoring; the different types of insulin and what the correct dosages are; insulin
administration, such as shots or an insulin pump; how to recognize the symptoms of both low and high blood sugar and what to do in both situations; how
to test and treat the presence of ketones; diet and how it can affect diabetes both
negatively and positively; how to count carbohydrates; exercise and how it
affects the levels of insulin needed; and how often should the patient see other
health care providers who are part of the team.

➤ MedlinePlus—"Diabetes Foot Care," http://www.nlm.nih.gov/medlineplus/
tutorials/diabetesfootcare/htm/index.htm
This webpage has an interactive tutorial that guides patients with diabetes
through the steps of taking care of their feet properly, preventing problems from
occurring, and selecting the right kinds of shoes. A reference sheet summarizes
the main parts of the tutorial, including how to keep feet healthy and prevent
serious problems before they occur, tips on daily and regular foot care, preventing injuries, nutrition, exercise, and regular checkups by a podiatrist or general
physician.

➤ National Diabetes Education Program—"Five Questions to Ask Your Health
Care Team about Type 2 Diabetes," http://ndep.nih.gov/media/five_questions_
to_ask_your_health_care_team_508.pdf?redirect=true
Written by a diabetes nurse educator, this resource provides five questions that
will elicit pertinent information from a health care provider regarding the
patient's medical testing, scores, monitoring, risk factors, and how often
appointments with physicians should be scheduled.

➤ National Diabetes Information Clearinghouse—"Prevent Diabetes Problems:
Keep Your Mouth Healthy," http://www.diabetes.niddk.nih.gov/dm/pubs/
complications_teeth/
This webpage provides an easy-to-comprehend, step-by-step guide with illustrations for patients to ensure their teeth and gums are maintained properly and
discusses the risks they face because of their disease. In addition to proper dental
care, the resource emphasizes that a patient with diabetes should do the following
on a daily basis: follow a healthy nutritional plan; exercise for at least thirty
minutes; take all medicines as directed; check blood glucose readings and record
them; check feet for any blisters, sores, cuts, swelling, or discolored toenails;

brush and floss teeth; make efforts to reduce blood pressure and cholesterol; and refrain from smoking.

➤ National Eye Institute—"Facts about Diabetic Retinopathy," http://www.nei.nih
.gov/health/diabetic/retinopathy.asp
This webpage provides a description and definition of diabetic retinopathy along with illustrations and a progression time line of the condition. There is an outline of the causes and risk factors for developing the condition, as well as a discussion of who is most at risk to develop diabetic retinopathy. The page presents a list of symptoms, although in the earlier stages of the disease there are usually none. There is discussion on how the condition is confirmed and various treatment options.

➤ National Kidney and Urologic Diseases Information Clearinghouse—"Kidney Disease of Diabetes," http://www.kidney.niddk.nih.gov/kudiseases/pubs/kdd/
Because diabetes is the major cause of kidney disease, patients with diabetes should be aware of the causes, symptoms, and plan for treatment. This resource discusses the general course of kidney disease, diagnosis, its link to high blood pressure, dialysis, transplantation, and what a patient can do to slow down the progression of the disease, as well as what preventive measures to take.

➤ National Patient Safety Foundation—"Ask Me 3™," http://www.npsf.org/for-healthcare-professionals/programs/ask-me-3/
Ask Me 3 is a patient education program designed to provide guidance to patients on how to communicate most effectively with their health care team by asking three pertinent questions: (1) What is my main problem? (2) What do I need to do? (3) Why is it important for me to do this?

➤ TeensHealth—"Your Diabetes Health Care Team," http://kidshealth.org/teen/
diabetes_center/treatment/diabetes_team.html
Written for the teen reader, this webpage describes all the members of the diabetes health care team, including pediatric endocrinologists, certified diabetes educators, dietitians, and mental health professionals. In easy-to-comprehend language, the webpage describes each professional's specialty and how each can specifically address both physical and emotional concerns.

➤ U.S. Department of Health and Human Services—"Working Together to Manage Diabetes: A Guide for Pharmacy, Podiatry, Optometry, and Dental Professionals," http://ndep.nih.gov/media/PPODprimer_color.pdf
While written for the medical professional, this substantive brochure can assist the information professional to learn more about the areas of diabetes addressed by the specialty areas of pharmacy, podiatry, optometry, and dentistry. The section titled "Diabetes Management and Team Care" illustrates the ways in which different health care professionals, including certified diabetes educators and

physicians across various disciplines, can work collaboratively to provide optimal treatment for the patient. Likewise, using this collaborative approach, the patient is empowered to work hard as the most important member of the health care team.

Selected Audiovisual Resources

➤ Health.com—"Ask Your Physician to Refer You to a Diabetes Educator," http://www.health.com/health/condition-video/0,,20192959,00.html
This brief video summarizes why a diabetes educator usually has more time and resources to assist a patient with questions or concerns than a physician might.

➤ Health.com—"I'm Lucky I Found an Endocrinologist," http://www.health.com/health/condition-video/0,,20192958,00.html
In this short video, a type 2 diabetes patient discusses the challenges of finding an endocrinologist.

➤ Health.com—"I'm the Quarterback of My Diabetes Health Care Team," http://www.health.com/health/condition-video/0,,20192932,00.html
This video emphasizes the importance of patients taking the lead in their own health care team and how working cooperatively with all of the members is crucial to the successful management of the disease.

➤ Health.com—"Seeing a Physician Is Key," http://www.health.com/health/condition-video/0,,20192938,00.html
This short video encourages patients who do not have insurance to actively seek other sources, including charities, to pay for visits to a physician to care for their diabetes properly.

References

American Association of Diabetes Educators. 2012. "Find a Diabetes Educator." American Association of Diabetes Educators. Accessed July 12. http://www.diabeteseducator.org/DiabetesEducation/Find.html.

American Diabetes Association. 2012a. "Living with Diabetes: Questions to Ask Your Doctor." American Diabetes Association. Accessed July 12. http://www.diabetes.org/living-with-diabetes/parents-and-kids/everyday-life/questions-to-ask-your-doctor.html.

———. 2012b. "Your Health Care Team." American Diabetes Association. Accessed July 12. http://www.diabetes.org/living-with-diabetes/treatment-and-care/who-is-on-your-healthcare-team/your-health-care-team.html.

Joslin Diabetes Center. 2012a. "Diabetes Education: Why It's So Crucial to Care." Joslin Diabetes Center. Accessed July 12. http://www.joslin.org/info/diabetes_education_why_its_so_crucial_to_care.html.

————. 2012b. "9 Questions for Your Diabetes Care Team." Joslin Diabetes Center. Accessed July 12. http://www.joslin.org/info/9_questions_for_your_diabetes_ care_team.html.

Mayo Clinic. 2012a. "Diabetic Nephropathy." Mayo Foundation for Medical Education and Research. Accessed July 12. http://www.mayoclinic.org/diabetic-nephropathy/ about.html.

————. 2012b. "Type 1 Diabetes: Preparing for Your Appointment." Mayo Foundation for Medical Education and Research. January 25. http://www.mayoclinic.com/ health/type-1-diabetes/DS00329/DSECTION=preparing-for-your-appointment.

National Diabetes Information Clearinghouse. 2012. "Prevent Diabetes Problems: Keep Your Mouth Healthy." National Institute of Diabetes and Digestive and Kidney Diseases, National Institutes of Health. Last updated May 10. http://www .diabetes.niddk.nih.gov/dm/pubs/complications_teeth/.

National Eye Institute. 2012. "Facts about Diabetic Retinopathy." National Eye Institute. Last updated June. http://www.nei.nih.gov/health/diabetic/retinopathy .asp.

National Kidney and Urologic Diseases Information Clearinghouse. 2010. "Kidney Diseases of Diabetes." National Institute of Diabetes and Digestive and Kidney Diseases, National Institutes of Health. Last updated September 2. http://www .kidney.niddk.nih.gov/kudiseases/pubs/kdd/.

Chapter 13

Support

How Support Groups Can Help

Patients with diabetes interact frequently with members of their health care team to discuss various medical issues, receive guidance on treatment programs, and report information. Likewise, these same patients share their feelings and concerns about their diabetes with family members and friends, who offer support. It is also helpful for patients, both adults and children, to connect with other patients who are experiencing similar issues coordinating their medical condition with daily routines and the unique challenges they face.

Making the decision to join a support group is a sign of strength, not weakness. People with chronic illnesses need to explore every area of help, not just those that are solely medical and health related. Being able to cope with the emotional aspects of having diabetes is equally as important as maintaining proper glucose levels, eating nutritiously, and exercising daily. For those facing chronic illness, attending support groups is another avenue to share feelings with people who are empathetic, not just sympathetic, to their issues.

These support groups offer companionship, the opportunity to share success stories and challenges, and to listen to fellow patients' worries and concerns. Meetings can be conducted in person, such as at a community center or someone's private home, virtually through the Internet, or by telephone. When selecting a support group to join, patients should conduct preliminary research on its background and sponsorship. It is important to determine whether there are any commercial affiliations because the underlying intent might be to sell group members diabetes-related products. Likewise, these groups should not offer any type of formal medical opinion or advice, unregulated medical devices or supplies, or any type of pharmaceuticals (Joslin Diabetes Center, 2012). Support groups can be found in person (local groups) and online (e.g., chat groups and social networking).

Support Sources

In-Person Support Groups

There is a wide variety of in-person support groups. Some groups are sponsored by public or private entities, such as hospitals, medical practices, local or municipal government agencies; some groups are formed by private citizens. Depending on the group, meetings may be daily, weekly, or monthly. The range in choice allows patients to identify which groups suit their particular goals and schedule. Some of these support groups are for patients with diabetes only; others offer membership to family members and friends as well.

People who are interested in these groups but cannot locate any in their geographical area may want to start one on their own (eHow, 2012). For juvenile diabetes, there are groups that connect children to other children, as well as their parents to other parents. Health care providers, local hospitals and medical centers, and the web resources noted later in this chapter can help locate these kinds of support groups.

Online Support Groups

For the millennial generation of children and young adults who are already comfortable relating to their peers using e-mail, text messaging, social networking sites, and chat rooms, joining a diabetes support group online is an extension of this type of communication style (Prevention.com, 2012). Older adults who may not have been exposed to these technologies can easily learn to access these types of forums as well. Likewise, adults who do not live near an in-person support group or who have time restraints that prevent them from attending these meetings should consider joining an online support group. It is a good alternative way to stay connected.

When investigating an online support group, patients should look at the host website very carefully and note whether it provides a disclaimer that the support group is not offering specific medical advice or is a substitute for professional medical treatment or diagnosis. If it does have the disclaimer, patients can have more trust in the posted messages as well as their moderation, which may occur in online discussions and chat rooms.

Inclusion of Family and Friends in Support Groups

Family and friends can provide crucial support to a person with diabetes. It is incumbent upon the family member or friend to become as knowledgeable as possible about the disease, its management, and ramifications for long-term health. Many support groups welcome family members, partners, and friends of patients with diabetes. Patients should make sure to inquire whether the particular group they are interested in joining allows additional members of the home health care team.

Summary

Support groups exist in many different formats, such as in person, online, and by telephone. When dealing with the complexities of diabetes or prediabetes, it is important to include the use of a suitable support system, which allows people with diabetes and their family members and friends to be an integral part of their health care regimen.

Information Sources

Selected Print Resources

➤ Becker, Gretchen. 2007. *The First Year: Type 2 Diabetes: An Essential Guide for the Newly Diagnosed*. New York: Marlowe.
  For those newly diagnosed with type 2 diabetes, this book provides a helpful section on networking with others who have the same type of condition. The section includes information on e-mail lists, chat rooms, and in-person support groups.

➤ Garnero, Theresa. 2008. *Your First Year with Diabetes: What to Do Month by Month*. Alexandria, VA: American Diabetes Association.
  This book provides reasons why a person should join a support group and what its offerings should include for participants. The section on support groups is brief in this particular book.

➤ Roszler, Janis. 2004. *The Secrets of Living and Loving with Diabetes: Three Experts Answer Questions You've Always Wanted to Ask*. Chicago: Surrey.
  This books provides tips and advice on how to enlist support from family and friends. It also includes information about support groups, how they can be an important component of managing diabetes, and how to find them.

➤ Warshaw, Hope. 2009. *Real-Life Guide to Diabetes: Practical Answers to Your Diabetes Problems*. Alexandra, VA: American Diabetes Association.
  This title devotes a chapter to seeking and finding support and emphasizes it is important that patients should not feel like they are alone in managing diabetes or its complications. In addition to listing avenues of support, the book provides activities to engage in that provide a sense of community, where patients can gain knowledge through sharing and building relationships.

Selected Web Resources

➤ American Diabetes Association—"Community: Find Support Now," http://community.diabetes.org/?loc=header_connect
  This webpage links to different support communities, including "Adults Living with Type 1 Diabetes," "Adults Living with Type 2 Diabetes," "Recently Diagnosed," and "The Place for Parents." After registering to be part of the online community, patients can do the following:
  • Post messages and reply to other members' posts.
  • Receive an e-mail notice when someone responds to a specific post or topic.

- Exchange private messages with other members.
- Personalize their experience by using the customization settings.
- Post comments on blogs.
- Post ideas, vote on favorite ideas, and comments.

In the "Main Community" section of the message boards, patients can review titles of several major topics to determine whether they want to become part of that particular board discussion and learn more, such as eating right with diabetes, diabetes technology and equipment, exercise and fitness, gestational diabetes, or information for teens and young adults.

➤ Children with Diabetes—"Support Groups," http://www.childrenwithdiabetes .com/support/
This online community supports both children and their parents by sharing resources, information, and support. The support groups section provides a state-by-state detailed listing of many different types of resources available to parents and children who have type 1 diabetes. There are links to all fifty states and various support groups that address the issues of children with diabetes. The support groups connect parents of children with diabetes, so that when the families meet the children can also connect with one another for support. When clicking on a particular state, the support groups and contact information show in list form, some of which provide direct links to the organization.

➤ Defeat Diabetes Foundation—"Self-Management: Diabetes Support Groups and Education Programs," http://www.defeatdiabetes.org/self_management/text.asp? id=diabetes_support_gro
This webpage lists peer support groups for people with diabetes. It includes an exhaustive list of names, addresses, telephone numbers, and contact information, searchable by state, for a wide variety of support groups.

➤ JDRF—"Online Diabetes Support Team," http://www.jdrf.org/index.cfm?page_ id=103451
This resource provides an online diabetes support team sign-up and support group information. Anyone can sign up for this support group, including people with diabetes and friends or family members who want to learn more about the disease and how they can help. By answering basic demographic information about the person with diabetes, the online registration team recommends the most suitable support group.

➤ Joslin Diabetes Center—"Finding the Right Diabetes Support Groups," http:// www.joslin.org/info/finding_the_right_diabetes_support_groups.html
This resource outlines the reasons why patients or people who support them should seek a support group for diabetes—from patients simply being able to feel they are a part of a community that understands their condition, to friends and family who want to provide more substantive help to their loved one who

has diabetes. The Joslin Diabetes Center offers support that addresses specific areas of concern, such as groups for women, men, couples, various ethnic groups, and ones for children with diabetes and their parents. The Joslin Center recommends that patients seeking a support group first determine the credentials of the person who is running it; make a list of goals for being in the group; and make sure to ask specific questions about the purpose of the group to ensure it will be a mutually beneficial fit.

➤ Joslin Diabetes Center—"How Do I Get Support from Family and Friends?," http://www.joslin.org/info/how_do_i_get_support_from_family_and_friends.html
This resource informs on how to communicate with family and friends on providing helpful support for the patient. It emphasizes that patients must first educate their supporters about diabetes, tell them in specific terms what is needed from them in terms of help and support, and teach them exactly how they can do this. This puts the onus on the person with diabetes to seek support and not behave passively with family and friends; those who would be supportive may not otherwise know what type of help the patient needs or how to provide it.

➤ Joslin Diabetes Center—"Message Boards," http://forums.joslin.org/
Through a professionally moderated discussion board about living with the disease, this online message board center is a way for patients throughout the country to stay connected and learn new information. Patients will need to create a username and password to join this site's message boards. Occasionally, Joslin professionals will answer questions posed to the discussion board community; however, they emphasize that this is no substitute for in-person medical advice from a health care provider.

➤ National Diabetes Education Program—"Tips for Providing Support," http://ndep.nih.gov/media/dealing-how-to-support-loved-one.pdf
This PDF lists tips for providing support to a loved one with diabetes including the following: making an effort to understand the complexities of diabetes; helping reduce cholesterol levels and blood pressure; and knowing when to seek professional help to provide more substantive support.

➤ Prevention.com—"Diabetes Support Group," http://www.prevention.com/community/forums/index.jsp?plckForumPage=Forum&plckForumId=Cat%3AHealthForum%3A5121004491
Though offered through *Prevention* magazine, this free support group message board is moderated extensively by a Prevention.com community senior host, so commercial interests or irrelevant posts do not interfere with offering a place for patients with diabetes to discuss issues and concerns online. Once registered, users can search the community for specific topics or discussion threads.

➤ Students with Diabetes, http://studentswithdiabetes.health.usf.edu/
This resource states that its goal is to create a community and connection point for students with diabetes on college campuses. The first chapter of the organization was created at the University of South Florida and provides a community for college students to come together to find creative solutions to the challenges they face while living with diabetes. There are links to college campus groups across the United States with contact information. The resource also provides a link to blogs about a variety of diabetes topics of interest to college students.

References

eHow. 2012. "How to Facilitate a Diabetic Support Group." eHow. Accessed July 12. http://www.ehow.com/how_5535802_facilitate-diabetic-support-group.html.

Joslin Diabetes Center. 2012. "Finding the Right Diabetes Support Groups." Joslin Diabetes Center. Accessed July 12. http://www.joslin.org/info/finding_the_right_diabetes_support_groups.html.

Prevention.com. 2012. "Diabetes Support Group." Rodale. Accessed July 12. http://www.prevention.com/community/forums/index.jsp?plckForumPage=Forum&plckForumId=Cat%3AHealthForum%3A5121004491.

Chapter 14

Legal, Insurance, and Financial Issues

Introduction

Patients who receive the diagnosis of a chronic illness, such as diabetes, are presented with the daunting task of understanding legal, financial, and insurance issues while simultaneously managing the medical aspects of their condition. Discriminatory practices in both workplaces and in schools can mean a loss of income or can undermine the educational experience. Likewise, incurring the expense of health care costs attendant with diabetes is challenging, even with insurance. This chapter provides an overview of the legal, insurance, and financial issues for patients with diabetes. There is an annotated list of helpful print and web resources to guide the patient through this complex process.

Legal Issues

People with diabetes understand that much time, thought, and energy needs to be dedicated to managing the condition in a responsible way on a daily basis. In the workplace environment, some employers and colleagues make improper assumptions about the abilities of diabetics to both manage their disease and simultaneously perform their job functions at a high level. Likewise, in the school setting, many teachers and administrators are unaware of the basics of health care management of children with diabetes and do not provide adequate resources or a schedule for them to address their medical needs.

When people with diabetes travel, attend camps, or make use of a public venue, their health care concerns can be overlooked by various entities, so they are sometimes unable to enjoy the same activities as nondiabetics. Of course, not all people with diabetes are subjected to discrimination in the workplace or other venues, and every individual's health issues and circumstances are unique. However, for those people who do perceive they are being treated unfairly, federal and state laws provide recourse and remedies to protect the adult or child patient from discrimination in the workplace, school, or other setting.

Federal Laws
Americans with Disabilities Act of 1990

Title I of this federal legislation applies to any entity that employs fifteen or more people. It prevents private companies, state and municipal governments, labor unions, and employment agencies from discriminating against otherwise-qualified individuals throughout the entire spectrum of the job process, including hiring, compensation, promotion, training, and termination. While some patients might find they cannot work in particular hazardous or arduous occupations, such as the military, commercial trucking, or firefighting, each individual should be evaluated on a case-by-case basis to determine whether the condition can be accommodated.

Individuals with Disabilities Education Improvement Act of 2004

Part B of this federal legislation covers children and young adults from ages three to twenty-one years old. This law states children identified with a disability that prevents them from learning will be afforded special education or other types of intervention necessary to help them achieve their educational needs.

Some children with diabetes may qualify for these types of services under the health impairment provision of this law. Specifically, the child's condition would have to hinder his or her ability to learn due to addressing health care needs throughout the day. This law provides for an Individualized Education Program (IEP) to be developed between the school and the child's parents so that any necessary medical concerns are built into the school day, such as checking glucose levels, allowing for more frequent bathroom breaks, and accessing trained personnel to assist with any health issue that may arise.

Rehabilitation Act of 1973

Section 504 of the Rehabilitation Act of 1973 prevents discrimination against qualified people with disabilities by any entity that receives federal funding. This law would apply to anyone who could perform the core functions of the job but who also needs suitable arrangements to address health issues in the workplace.

State Laws

Most states have antidiscrimination laws that protect people with diabetes in the workplace or at school. Many of these state employment laws mirror federal legislation and can be found in the individual states' statutory codes or administrative regulations. Likewise, state laws also govern health care practices for children with diabetes in the school system, including who is qualified to assist them in obtaining glucose results and administering insulin. It is useful for parents to check with their physician, school, or local public law library to determine the latest state laws applicable to their child's particular situation.

The decision to seek legal redress, either state or federal, for alleged discrimination is a difficult one because there are many factors to be considered in pursuing this type of remedy, such as workplace or school repercussions, time, and money. If patients or family members feel they have been discriminated against in the workplace, school, or in a public venue, there are options to pursue this course of action.

First, they can contact the American Diabetes Association, which provides free advice and advocacy on their behalf. The organization is dedicated to addressing these concerns through four main areas: education, negotiation, litigation, and legislation. Second, they can perform their own legal research about their particular issue at local public, state, court, and law libraries. The librarians can direct them to pertinent legal resources but cannot provide any legal advice. Finally, patients and family members can obtain legal advice at a reduced rate or for free by contacting their local legal aid center or clinic.

Insurance and Financial Issues

Before 2010, many patients with diabetes were treated unfairly, albeit legally, by health insurance companies due to their medical condition. Many patients, including children, were denied health coverage outright, forced to pay high premiums, or had their insurance rescinded when they became seriously ill. There were large gaps between what a person with diabetes needed for his or her medical condition, including medications and supplies, and what the insurance companies would agree to cover.

In March 2010, U.S. Congress passed the Patient Protection and Affordable Care Act. Some of the reforms in this new law do not go into effect until 2014, so to cover this time span the Patient's Bill of Rights was issued by government agencies, including Health and Human Services, Labor, and Treasury departments in June 2010. These regulations provided further clarification of the new law for health insurance consumers and became enforceable in early fall 2010.

This landmark health care insurance reform legislation, commonly referred to as the Affordable Care Act, affects people with diabetes in several key areas. Children with diabetes under age nineteen will be able to obtain insurance coverage despite having a preexisting condition. As young adults, they will be able to stay on their parents' insurance coverage until they are twenty-six years of age. Likewise, adults with preexisting conditions who heretofore were blocked from receiving insurance can enroll in the Pre-existing Condition Insurance Plan (PCIP). This coverage will last until 2014 when the Affordable Care Act's regulations go into effect, which explicitly prohibits exclusion of adults with preexisting conditions from obtaining health insurance.

These new regulations also provide that insurance companies may no longer set lifetime limits on insurance coverage, nor set restrictions on annual limits of coverage. Patients will be able to select their own primary care doctor from their network for both themselves and their children. Emergency care can occur at an out-of-network hospital without prior approval from an insurance company. In addition, if a person's condition leads to further medical complications, the Affordable Care Act also prohibits insurance companies from arbitrary retroactive rescission of coverage when the patient becomes ill. The law also prohibits insurance companies from charging higher premiums simply because an adult or child has diabetes.

The new law also applies to seniors with diabetes who are covered by Medicare because it provides a rebate of up to $250 on prescription drugs to close what is commonly referred to as the "doughnut hole" in health insurance. Free wellness exams will be available for seniors, which will also include medical course-of-action plans for their prediabetic condition or their diabetes. For both seniors and adults, the new law sets aside $15 billion for type 2 diabetes prevention. The National Diabetes Prevention Program is set up under the new legislation to work in conjunction with local health care programs.

The U.S. Supreme Court ruled on June 28, 2012, to uphold the major tenets of the law in a 5–4 decision (*National Federation of Independent Business v. Sebelius*). Despite this ruling, within the 112th Congress, there is still movement from both the House and Senate to repeal the Affordable Care Act completely or in part. Some members of Congress ran on political platforms in 2010 that included strong opposition to this legislation and vowed to make good on their promise to remove what they considered to be a job-killing bill that also hinders the private sector from determining its own market for health insurance. Further, many people consider the new legislation to be an intrusive government intervention into their individual health care choices. The Republican presidential candidate for the 2012 election, Mitt Romney, focused on repealing this law as a major part of his presidential platform.

Judicial intervention regarding the new health care legislation has also been occurring since the law's passage. In late 2010, U.S. District Judge Henry E. Hudson of Virginia, whose opinion summarized that compelling people to buy health insurance is unconstitutional, struck down part of the new law. In early 2011, U.S. District Judge Roger Vinson of Florida issued an opinion that echoed the Virginia ruling, saying that mandating people to purchase health insurance is unconstitutional and a violation of the Commerce Clause. Judge Vinson also stated that since compelling people to buy health insurance is a major component of the new legislation, the entire foundation of the law is undermined.

It is likely that additional legislation will be introduced throughout the next two years, which could possibly jeopardize this law that helps people with diabetes and those with prediabetes. The American Diabetes Association, among other organizations, is advocating strongly on behalf of the Affordable Care Act because it helps the lives of an estimated 24 million people with diabetes in the United States.

The Family and Medical Leave Act of 1993 is federal legislation that protects adults with diabetes or for those adults caring for children with the condition from losing their job due to missed days of work to attend to their health condition. Individuals may take up to twelve weeks of unpaid leave for this reason in whatever permutation works for their schedule. If the employee has any unused sick or vacation time, the twelve weeks of unpaid leave could first subtract from those hours before moving into unpaid time off, depending on the employer's policy.

To qualify under the tenets of FMLA, a person must be in the employ of a company that has at least fifty employees located within seventy-five miles of one another, and that person must be on the payroll for twelve consecutive months. Further, a physician must complete paperwork stating that the patient or family member's condition reaches the threshold of what is known as a serious condition. Specifically, the condition must require either a hospital stay, surgery, or numerous medical visits to manage the disease. The employer then may either approve or disapprove of FMLA for the employee. Any disputes of an employer's final decision may lead to litigation in court or through a complaint process with the Department of Labor.

The new health care legislation notwithstanding, many people with diabetes or prediabetes are unable to afford visits to the doctor, prescription drugs, medical supplies, or transportation to and from medical clinics. There is help available from nonprofit groups and pharmaceutical companies to provide much-needed medicine and related supplies for free or at low cost. Connecting people with diabetes to these resources can be critical in allowing them to cover the gap between insurance coverage and out-of-pocket expenses (Patient Advocate Foundation, 2012).

Medical supplies including test strips, insulin pumps, and lancets can be costly for both those patients who are covered by insurance and those who are not, although the Affordable Care Act may be able to remedy some of these deficiencies in insurance coverage. It is important for the patients or patients' caregivers to reach out to their physician initially if they cannot afford to pay for prescription medicines or supplies. Many of the pharmaceutical company assistance programs require that a physician apply for help on behalf of the patient (RxHope, 2012).

Many patients also contend with disease complications, such as requiring dialysis. While having a chronic kidney condition automatically qualifies a person for Medicare, other attendant costs, such as transportation to and from a dialysis center, are not covered. The loss of a limb is another diabetic complication that insurance does not always cover, including such costs as the surgery, the prosthetic limb, and postsurgery physical therapy. Complications of the eye, including blindness, can also occur with diabetes, so annual eye exams are essential for overall health management. There are many resources available to help patients with these health management issues.

Summary

Even though federal and state laws protect people with diabetes from discrimination in workplaces, schools, and other settings, it can be an arduous process to exercise these rights while also managing the medical aspects of the condition. Likewise, it is also challenging to understand the intricacies of most health insurance plans and to manage the attendant financial obligations of diabetes. The print and web resources that follow provide assistance and guidance with navigating these complex areas.

Information Sources

Selected Print Resources

Legal

➤ Repa, Barbara. 2010. *Your Rights in the Workplace*. Berkeley, CA: Nolo.
  This book examines general workplace rights, as well as more specific concerns, such as health insurance, the Family and Medical Leave Act, illegal discrimination and federal and states laws, job loss, and Social Security Disability Insurance. There is a chapter on workplace discrimination that covers state and local laws, the Americans with Disabilities Act, and how it affects employers and employees.

➤ Warshaw, Hope S. 2009. *Real Life Guide to Diabetes: Practical Answers to Your Diabetes Problems*. Alexandria, VA: American Diabetes Association.
  This book provides a wide range of information for patients, including information about knowing patient rights and ending discrimination. There is a detailed discussion of the ramifications for patients regarding federal antidiscrimination laws, such as the Americans with Disabilities Act and the Family and Medical Leave Act. Additional sections also discuss patients' rights in places of public accommodation and while attending school.

Insurance and Financial

➤ Dawson, Leslie Y. 2004. *How to Save up to $3000 a Year on Your Diabetes Costs*. Alexandria, VA: American Diabetes Association.
  Patients with diabetes can find a variety of tips on saving money on their diabetes-related expenses in this book. Tips include saving money on healthy foods, drugs, supplies, and insurance; there are also other helpful hints for cost cutting.

➤ Garnero, Theresa. 2008. *Your First Year with Diabetes: What to Do Month by Month*. Alexandria, VA: American Diabetes Association.
  The book, published by the ADA, provides an excellent resource for those newly diagnosed with diabetes. A section includes tips on saving money on health care and information about health insurance, including Medicare and Medicaid.

➤ Guerin, Lisa, and Deborah C. England. 2009. *The Essential Guide to Family and Medical Leave*. 2nd ed. Berkeley, CA: Nolo.
  Written in nontechnical language, this is a good resource to answer many questions for employees contemplating using the Family and Medical Leave Act to address

their own diabetes or a family member's condition. This book includes detailed information about the Family and Medical Leave Act, such as who qualifies for it, how the person can be medically certified, affiliated federal and state laws, and reinstatement of a job.

➤ Northrop, Dorothy E. 2007. *Health Insurance Resources: A Guide for People with Chronic Disease and Disability*. New York: Demos Medical.

While not specifically written for patients with diabetes, this resource provides comprehensive insurance information for anyone with a chronic disease. The book covers topics such as managed care and indemnity plans, Medicare, Medicaid, Social Security Disability Insurance, Supplemental Security Income, grievances and appeals, the Health Insurance Portability and Accountability Act (HIPAA), and state mini-COBRA (Consolidated Omnibus Budget Reconciliation Act) laws.

Selected Web Resources

Legal

➤ American Diabetes Association—"Living with Diabetes: Employment Discrimination," http://www.diabetes.org/living-with-diabetes/know-your-rights/discrimination/employment-discrimination/

Using nontechnical language, this resource summarizes the legal rights a person with diabetes is entitled to during every phase of employment, from the hiring process to salary, promotion, discipline, and termination. Further information addresses taking leave for diabetes-related medical issues.

➤ American Diabetes Association—"Living with Diabetes: Individuals with Disabilities Education Act," http://www.diabetes.org/living-with-diabetes/parents-and-kids/diabetes-care-at-school/legal-protections/individuals-with-disabilities.html

In some children, their diabetic condition impedes their ability to learn. This resource provides general information about the Individuals with Disabilities Education Act (IDEA), a federal law, and what it covers for children with diabetes, their parents' or guardians' rights, and Individualized Education Programs (IEPs).

➤ American Diabetes Association—"Living with Diabetes: Know Your Rights: How to Get Help," http://www.diabetes.org/living-with-diabetes/know-your-rights/how-to-get-help/

For individuals with diabetes who feel that they have been discriminated against in a setting such as work, school, correctional facilities, or public accommodations, this resource provides the pertinent contact information to request assistance. The organization works in four key areas of diabetes discrimination: education, negotiation, litigation, and legislation.

➤ American Diabetes Association—"Living with Diabetes: Public Accommodations and Government Programs," http://www.diabetes.org/living-with-diabetes/know-your-rights/discrimination/public-accommodations/
Legal rights extend to persons with diabetes in a wide variety of venues, including those operated by government or private entities. Federal laws protect patients when traveling by air, attending concerts, or participating in camps (day or longer) or recreational programs. This webpage provides contact information to assist those who have experienced discrimination because of their own or their child's diabetic condition.

➤ American Diabetes Association—"Living with Diabetes: School Discrimination," http://www.diabetes.org/living-with-diabetes/know-your-rights/discrimination/school-discrimination
It is important for parents with children who have diabetes to be aware of the legal rights available to them in the school environment. This resource outlines training resources, special considerations, and tips for parents on how to be effective advocates for their child in the school system.

➤ American Diabetes Association—"Living with Diabetes: State Laws and Policies," http://www.diabetes.org/living-with-diabetes/parents-and-kids/diabetes-care-at-school/legal-protections/state-laws-and-policies.html
A drop-down menu contains links to the most current statutory and regulatory authorities in all the states, as well as policy guidelines regarding children with diabetes in the school system. The American Diabetes Association acts as an advocate for children attending school to ensure their rights are protected. This webpage provides information for parents so they can contact legal advocates who are familiar with diabetes issues to discuss their particular situation.

➤ Cornell University—"Employment Considerations for People Who Have Diabetes," http://www.ilr.cornell.edu/extension/files/download/Diabetes.pdf
This is a four-page concise summary of diabetes in the workplace. It discusses how federal laws can protect employees with diabetes. In addition, it provides information on other workplace implications of the disease, including the different types of jobs that patients are capable of performing, training, promotion, and a discussion of the reasonable accommodations, which should be provided so the condition can be managed properly.

➤ Job Accommodation Network—"Accommodation and Compliance Series: Employees with Diabetes," http://www.askjan.org/media/diabetes.html
While written for the perspective of employers who want to ensure they are complying with Title 1 of the Americans with Disabilities Act, this resource provides clear and easy-to-comprehend legal information regarding workplace accommodations for those employees with diabetes. It provides further information on particular aspects of diabetes, such as how to assist employees when

dealing with hypo- or hyperglycemia, neuropathy, fatigue, weakness, vision impairment, kidney disease, and cognitive or psychological limitations.

➤ U.S. Equal Employment Opportunity Commission—"Questions and Answers about Diabetes in the Workplace and the Americans with Disabilities Act (ADA)," http://www.eeoc.gov/facts/diabetes.html
The EEOC enforces the employment component of the Americans with Disabilities Act. This resource provides background on the federal law and how it applies to the person with diabetes in the entire spectrum of employment, from hiring to loss of job, using a question-and-answer format with workplace examples.

➤ Washburn University School of Law—"State, Court, and County Law Libraries," http://www.washlaw.edu/statecourtcounty/
This resource provides a directory of state, court, and county law libraries by geographic location in the United States. Individuals can find additional information from these libraries about how to obtain free or low-cost legal advice.

Insurance and Financial

➤ American Diabetes Association—"Prescription Assistance," http://www.diabetes .org/living-with-diabetes/treatment-and-care/health-insurance-options/ prescription-assistance.html
This webpage provides a concise listing of pharmaceutical companies that manufacture diabetes drugs and supplies, including the names of their assistance programs and contact information with affiliated websites.

➤ American Diabetes Association—"Questions and Answers about Health Reform and Diabetes," http://www.diabetes.org/living-with-diabetes/treatment-and-care/ health-insurance-options/qa-health-care-reform-01-11.pdf
This resource reviews basic questions and answers about the new health insurance reform legislation signed into public law on March 23, 2010. It examines various ways the new law affects a person with diabetes or a caregiver for someone with diabetes.

➤ Centers for Disease Control and Prevention—"Financial Coverage for Diabetes Expenses," http://www.cdc.gov/diabetes/consumer/financial.htm
This question-and-answer format addresses the two major financial concerns of the patient, including what insurance covers and how to locate free or low-cost health coverage and medical services.

➤ Centers for Medicare and Medicaid Services—"Medicare Helps Cover Diabetes Supplies and Services to Keep You Healthy," http://www.medicare.gov/Publications/Pubs/pdf/11410.pdf
Published by the U.S. Department of Health and Human Services, this concise two-page information sheet outlines which supplies and services Medicare covers and includes a checklist of questions patients can ask their physician.

➤ Centers for Medicare and Medicaid Services—"Medicare Coverage of Diabetes Supplies and Services," http://www.medicare.gov/publications/pubs/pdf/11022 .pdf
  This comprehensive online pamphlet provides details regarding supplies covered under Medicare Parts B and D, including testing equipment, supplies, insulin pumps, therapeutic shoes, and supplies. The pamphlet also discusses the wide range of diabetes medical services that are covered under Medicare, such as screening, self-management training, nutrition therapy services, and foot and eye exams. There is also information for those with limited income and resources.

➤ Defeat Diabetes Foundation—"Self-Management: Financial Help for People with Diabetes," http://www.defeatdiabetes.org/self_management/text.asp?id= Programs_Assistance
  This webpage provides information on federal and state insurance programs, how to locate local health care centers, hospital care, dialysis assistance, financing an organ transplant, prosthetic care, and technological assistance to aid a patient to work from home.

➤ EyeCare America—"ABCs of Diabetes and Eye Health," http://www.eyecare america.org/eyecare/news/abcs-of-diabetes-and-eye-health-nov-2009.cfm
  A program of the Foundation of the American Academy of Ophthalmology, this website provides contact information to assist patients with diabetes age sixty-five or older who have not seen an ophthalmologist in three years and do not belong to a health maintenance organization (HMO) or the Veterans Administration (VA) in receiving an eye exam and access to eye care educational materials. There is an online referral for people of all ages to see if they qualify for a free eye exam provided by volunteer ophthalmologists.

➤ HealthCare.gov—"The Health Care Law and You," http://www.healthcare.gov/ law/index.html
  HealthCare.gov is an official government website that provides a comprehensive overview of the federal law known as the Patient Protection and Affordable Care Act, which was recently upheld by the United States Supreme Court, including key features of the law, timeline, audience-specific resources, and implementation resources.

➤ Health Resources and Services Administration—"Hill-Burton Free and Reduced Cost Health Care," http://www.hrsa.gov/gethealthcare/affordable/hillburton/
  There are more than 200 health care facilities in the United States that provide reduced or free health care costs in return for receiving federal grants for modernization programs. This webpage provides a link to those facilities by individual state; it also delineates the eligibility criteria for patients to receive Hill-Burton care services.

➤ Joslin Diabetes Center—"Money Saving Strategies for Diabetes Care Supplies," http://www.joslin.org/info/money_saving_strategies_for_diabetes_care_supplies .html
This webpage is a brief summary of what a patient can do to save money, including how to contact diabetes supplies companies directly for samples, attending the American Diabetes Association Expo, and taking advantage of available pharmacy rebates and coupons.

➤ National Diabetes Education Program—"The Power to Control Diabetes Is in Your Hands: Information about Diabetes and Related Medicare Benefits," http:// ndep.nih.gov/media/NDEP38_PowertoControl_4c_508.pdf
This online booklet provides basic information about diabetes, its management, and Medicare in an easy-to-understand question-and-answer format. At the end of the booklet, there are targeted questions for patients to ask their health care team, with spaces for writing in the answers they receive.

➤ National Diabetes Information Clearinghouse—"Financial Help for Diabetes Care," http://www.diabetes.niddk.nih.gov/dm/pubs/financialhelp/
This is a comprehensive overview of the various sectors that can provide financial assistance for a diabetes patient, including state and federal insurance programs, health care services, kidney services, prosthetics, prescription drugs, technological assistance, and nutritional information for women with gestational diabetes.

➤ National Eye Institute—"Financial Aid for Eye Care," http://www.nei.nih.gov/ health/financialaid.asp
This webpage has a listing of various organizations and entities that provide financial assistance for a variety of eye care issues, including exams, surgery, prescription glasses, and prescription drugs.

➤ National Kidney and Urologic Diseases Information Clearinghouse—"Financial Help for Treatment of Kidney Failure," http://www.kidney.niddk.nih.gov/ku diseases/pubs/financialhelp/
While not specifically written for the diabetes patient, kidney complications can arise due to the disease. This webpage provides information regarding federal and state insurance plans, patient assistance programs from prescription drug companies, and contact information for numerous kidney programs, foundations, and funds.

➤ Office of Rare Diseases Research—"Patient Travel and Lodging," http://rare diseases.info.nih.gov/Resources/Patient_Travel_Lodging.aspx
This website provides links to reduced and charitable airfares for those patients who are receiving medical assistance far from home. There are also links to lodging and hospitality houses for both patients and families.

➤ Partnership for Prescription Assistance—"Prescription Assistance Programs," http://www.pparx.org/en/prescription_assistance_programs
For those patients without prescription drug coverage, this website provides links for assistance with obtaining drugs for reduced rates or free. The website provides contact information so patients can speak directly with trained specialists to assist them in navigating the application process.

➤ Patient Advocate Foundation—"Diabetes Resources," http://www.copays.org/resources/diabetes.php
For those who are insured but cannot afford the copayments for certain services or supplies, this website provides a link to the Patient Advocate Foundation's financial assistance form. There is also a link that provides information on how to contact a case manager who can provide further assistance with insurance and medical debt.

➤ RxHope—"Medication Search by Patient Assistance Program," http://www.rxhope.com/Patient/ProgramList.aspx
This website provides a comprehensive set of links to prescription assistance programs so that patients can see what drugs are available at low cost or no cost and what the requirements are to participate in each program. Patients then must contact their physician, who can request the drugs on their behalf.

References

Americans with Disabilities Act of 1990. Pub. L. No. 101-336, 108th Cong., 2d Sess. (July 26, 1990).

Family and Medical Leave Act of 1993. Pub. L. No. 103-3, 103d Cong., 1st Sess. (February 5, 1993).

Individuals with Disabilities Education Improvement Act of 2004. Pub. L. No. 101-476, 108th Cong., 2d Sess. (January 20, 2004).

National Federation of Independent Business v. Sebelius, Docket No. 11-393 (11th Cir. 2012).

Patient Advocate Foundation. 2012. "Co-Pay Relief Center: Diabetes Resources." Patent Advocate Foundation. Accessed July 13. http://www.copays.org/resources/diabetes.php.

Patient Protection and Affordable Care Act of 2010. Pub. L. No. 111-148. 111th Cong., 2d Sess. (March 23, 2010).

Rehabilitation Act of 1973. Pub. L. No. 93-112. 93d Cong., 1st Sess. (September 26, 1973).

RxHope. 2012. "Medication Search by Patient Assistance Program." RxHope. Accessed August 8. https://www.rxhope.com/Patient/ProgramList.aspx.

Chapter 15

Life Outside the Home

Introduction

Most people have responsibilities that require being away from the home for several hours a day, whether at a job or at school. While it may be easier to manage diabetes with uninterrupted time at home, many people with diabetes face the challenge of working around their daily responsibilities to monitor glucose, eat as scheduled, inject insulin, and engage in physical activity. Bosses, supervisors, coworkers, teachers, or fellow students might not understand what being a patient with diabetes entails on a daily basis. Communicating openly with these people and sharing facts and information with them can help make the work or school environment more accommodating and comfortable.

School

Schoolchildren with diabetes have certain legal rights to ensure they receive the same education as their peers. Both federal and state laws mandate children with diabetes be provided with the time, means, and assistance to manage their diabetes during the regular school day and when participating in extracurricular activities. Individual student action plans should be developed so that school personnel are aware of their roles in administering medications, identifying when meals or snacks are appropriate, and handling diabetic-related medical emergencies (American Diabetes Association, 2012).

School policies may dictate which personnel are involved in the day-to-day management of the child with diabetes, so parents should read any written communications thoroughly and ask questions for clarification before the school year begins. Further, parents should meet with the school's administration and the child's teacher and teacher's aides to discuss the condition and what procedures to follow for various scenarios. It is helpful to provide school personnel with instructions and contact information.

For children and young adults with diabetes, the management of diabetes usually includes working with an approved health care provider at the school or other aides to assist with insulin injections and coordinating activities around this care. It is imperative that the parents of these children be active partners with the school and its designated nurses, aides, or teachers who will be entrusted with their child's daily care.

Working in conjunction with the school's nurse or other health care provider, the parents of grade-schoolers to older adolescents can decide on the diabetes management plan that is best for their child's particular situation. While teenage children can assume more responsibility for their own care, such as self-administering medications, the school must still have a plan in place to handle situations that are outside the daily school routine, such as field trips or participation in sports.

Extracurricular activities for children and teenagers require thoughtful planning and management. Some activities, such as school outings, attending or participating in sporting events, and overnight trips, can pose challenges. Students might not be able to follow their regular schedules as rigorously as they do during the regular school day, so they may eat snacks and meals at times that are not optimal for maintaining safe blood sugar levels (Betschart-Roemer, 2002). A child with diabetes may require space and time to test blood sugar levels and have someone assist with injecting insulin. Meeting with the school personnel who are supervising any outside activities is important so that any deviation from the child's daily schedule can be discussed in detail.

Work

Many public and private organizations and companies now understand the merits of implementing workplace health programs to assist their employees with maintaining a healthy lifestyle and preventing serious medical conditions, such as diabetes. In certain instances, when employees participate in a program, they can receive discounted insurance premiums or other incentives (DiabetesAtWork.org, 2012).

Federal and state laws protect the ability to manage diabetes properly in the workplace (*see* CHAPTER 14, LEGAL, INSURANCE, AND FINANCIAL ISSUES). Attending to diabetes management should not cause any disruption in the day. Patients can ensure their bosses and supervisors they can self-administer glucose tests and inject insulin seamlessly at their own workstation or in a more private location, if available. Being able to snack or eat lunch at preset times should be accommodated, so that blood sugar levels do not fall precipitously or spike throughout the workday.

Patients should educate work colleagues about their condition so that people are aware of their special medical status should an emergency arise. Further, supervisors and bosses can educate the entire workforce about diabetes with regard to preventing the disease, managing it if an employee already has it, and coordinating workers' schedules to accommodate testing and self-medication.

Summary

Managing diabetes while away from home is something that both children and adults must learn to do effectively if they want to maintain their blood glucose at safe levels. Under the guidance of parents and in conjunction with the school's administrative and health care team, children should be able to manage their diabetes throughout the school day and be allowed appropriate accommodations during the day or while participating in extracurricular activities to both test blood glucose levels and administer insulin as needed. Likewise, for adults in the workplace, employers must provide accommodation to ensure that workers have adequate time and space to self-test their blood glucose levels and administer insulin. Both state and federal laws protect the rights of children and adults to perform these functions.

Information Sources

Selected Print Resources

➤ Betschart, Jean, and Susan Thom. 2001. *In Control: A Guide for Teens with Diabetes.* New York: Wiley.
Written for the teenager with diabetes, this book covers topics in a frank and candid fashion. Topics include a discussion about how marijuana, alcohol, and substance abuse can have a negative impact on a teenager with diabetes; how sexuality is affected by the disease; how to form helpful health care teams; and how to participate as fully as possible in extracurricular activities.

➤ Betschart-Roemer, Jean. 2002. *Type 2 Diabetes in Teens: Secrets for Success.* New York: Wiley.
Although this book is written for teens, it is also beneficial for parents in its detailed section on managing diabetes and medications while at school. The book also contains a sample plan of care for the student with diabetes.

➤ Gaynor, Kate. 2008. *The Bravest Girl in School.* Dublin, Ireland: Special Stories Publishing.
This short book demonstrates to children how important it is to follow their doctor's guidance, eat a healthy diet, and take their insulin every day, even though the injections might hurt.

➤ Gosselin, Kim, and Moss Freedman. 2004. *Taking Diabetes to School.* Plainview, NY: JayJo Books.
This book, written for children ages four through eight, shows a grade-school child with diabetes discussing the disease and its management with his peers at school.

➤ Hanas, Ragnar. 2005. *Type 1 Diabetes: A Guide for Children, Adolescents, Young Adults—and Their Caregivers.* New York: Marlowe.
Parents and their older children will find this book beneficial in learning to deal with diabetes while at school. Topics covered include dealing with hypoglycemia, talking with teachers and classmates, school routines, and exams.

➤ Loy, Bo, and Spike Loy. 2004. *487 Really Cool Tips for Kids with Diabetes.* Alexandria, VA: American Diabetes Association.

The authors, brothers who were both diagnosed with type 1 diabetes early in their lives, have assembled in this book a collection of useful tips and strategies for managing diabetes. The book's topics, which are aimed at children and adolescents, include discussing the disease with classmates, dealing with bullies, playing sports, participating in extracurricular activities like band and field trips, eating well, understanding substance abuse issues, dating, and driving.

➤ Parker, Victoria. 2011. *I Know Someone with Diabetes.* Oxford, England: Raintree. This book, written for children, helps take the mystery out of the disease by discussing it in an easy-to-understand language and demonstrates why it is important to be a good friend to a classmate who has diabetes.

➤ Peurrung, Victoria. 2001. *Living with Juvenile Diabetes: A Practical Guide for Parents and Caregivers.* New York: Hatherleigh. This title provides information for parents whose child with diabetes attends school, including educating teachers, staff, and students about diabetes.

Selected Web Resources

➤ American Diabetes Association—"Living with Diabetes: Safe at School," http:// www.diabetes.org/living-with-diabetes/parents-and-kids/diabetes-care-at-school/?loc=DropDownADV-promo1 As part of the organization's campaign to ensure children's health, safety, and well-being while away at school, this webpage offers information on managing diabetes with the assistance of a health care team during daily school activities, taking tests, participating in extracurricular and sport activities, and traveling on extended field trips. There are also links to additional information on legal protections, resolving conflicts with care provided at school, written care plans, and school staff training.

➤ Children with Diabetes—"Diabetes at School," http://www.childrenwithdiabetes .com/d_0q_000.htm This is a comprehensive website that addresses the needs of children with diabetes at school, including information in several areas: "School Bill of Rights for Children with Diabetes"; links to laws regarding nondiscrimination, including a sample 504 plan; information sheets for teachers and child care providers with an overview of diabetes; detailed instructions on how to formulate a 504 plan; a checklist of what a parent can do before school begins to make the transition seamless; a one-page instruction sheet for teachers that summarizes the child's particular care needs; and information that can be provided to classmates regarding diabetes and hypoglycemia.

➤ DiabetesAtWork.org—"Diabetes at Work," http://diabetesatwork.org/ This website provides the framework for the DiabetesAtWork.org program launched in 2002 by the Centers for Disease Control and Prevention. This website, aimed at employers, provides assistance in the following areas: (1) developing a diabetes prevention or management program; (2) estimating the number of employees in the company who have diabetes; (3) estimating the total cost of diabetes in the company; (4) choosing or designing a health plan for people with diabetes; and (5) obtaining support from company leadership for a diabetes program.

➤ KidsHealth.org—"School and Diabetes," http://kidshealth.org/parent/diabetes_center/living_diabetes/school_diabetes.html#cat20724
This webpage offers guidance for parents who are working with the school system to assist in the management of their child's disease while away from home. The organization provides information on what a child should be able to do at school, such as check blood sugar levels; take insulin or other diabetes medications; eat snacks when necessary; eat lunch at predesignated times; be allowed access to water and frequent restroom breaks; be allowed to participate in both physical activities and field trips; and receive treatment for low blood sugar episodes.

➤ National Diabetes Information Clearinghouse—"Taking Care of Your Diabetes at Special Times," http://diabetes.niddk.nih.gov/dm/pubs/type1and2/special times.aspx
This webpage provides basic tips on how to manage diabetes effectively while away from home, including at school and at work. For instance, it recommends that, no matter where they happen to be, patients should follow their meal plan; take their medicines and check blood glucose normally; tell teachers, friends, or co-workers about the signs of low blood glucose; keep snacks nearby and carry them at all times; and inform the school nurse or company nurse about their condition.

Selected Audiovisual Resources

➤ American Diabetes Association—"Safe at School" video series, http://www.schooltube.com/
SchoolTube is a website that provides free video content for students and teachers. As part of the organization's commitment to ensuring the safety and legal rights of children and teens who are diabetic, the American Diabetes Association created a thirteen-part video series that addresses various aspects of the condition and its management while attending school.
  - "Safe at School: Chapter 1—Diabetes Basics," http://www.schooltube.com/video/3603eb87132455372d2a/Safe-at-School-Chapter-1-Diabetes-Basics
  - "Safe at School: Chapter 2—Diabetes Medical Management Plan," http://www.schooltube.com/video/cfe8a72e7d0d8e06c278/Safe-at-School-Chapter-2-DMMP

- "Safe at School: Chapter 3—Hypoglycemia," http://www.schooltube.com/video/4a2ec684a1e5e932f6c5/Safe-at-School-Chapter-3-Hypoglycemia
- "Safe at School: Chapter 4—Hyperglycemia," http://www.schooltube.com/video/50674ae1e0cd4ba0f9ea/Safe-at-School-Chapter-4-Hyperglycemia
- "Safe at School: Chapter 5—Glucose Monitoring," http://www.schooltube.com/video/fa2cc1c91738c03eed22/Safe-at-School-Chapter-5-Blood-Glucose-Monitoring
- "Safe at School: Chapter 6—Glucagon Administration," http://www.schooltube.com/video/20fc0c44956685dce928/Safe-at-School-Chapter-6-Glucagon-Administration
- "Safe at School: Chapter 7—Insulin Basics," http://www.schooltube.com/video/e852bb71bde2d1c79dda/Safe-at-School-Chapter-7-Insulin-Basics
- "Safe at School: Chapter 8—Insulin by Syringe and Vial," http://www.schooltube.com/video/8f3b78d2e91f4cebc3a2/Safe-at-School-Chapter-8-Insulin-by-Syringe-Vial
- "Safe at School: Chapter 9—Insulin by Pen," http://www.schooltube.com/video/77e6683382437643de55/Safe-at-School-Chapter-9-Insulin-by-Pen
- "Safe at School: Chapter 10—Insulin by Pumps," http://www.schooltube.com/video/77fe9325efd133c7c6e0/Safe-at-School-Chapter-10-Insulin-by-Pumps
- "Safe at School: Chapter 11—Ketones," http://www.schooltube.com/video/dcbea77226baee59fb04/Safe-at-School-Chapter-11-Ketones
- "Safe at School: Chapter 12—Nutrition and Physical Activity," http://www.schooltube.com/video/67574aa2ab812dd3068b/Safe-at-School-Chapter-12-Nutrition-Physical-Activity
- "Safe at School: Chapter 13—Legal Considerations," http://www.schooltube.com/video/38fcff49537dec783c06/Safe-at-School-Chapter-13-Legal-Considerations

➤ dLife—"Diabetes at School," http://www.dlife.com/dlifetv/video/diabetes-at-school
This five-minute video provides tips for dealing with diabetes while in school.

References

American Diabetes Association. 2012. "Living with Diabetes: Safe at School." American Diabetes Association. Accessed July 6. http://www.diabetes.org/living-with-diabetes/parents-and-kids/ diabetes-care-at-school/?loc=DropDownADV-promo1.

Betschart-Roemer, J. 2002. *Type 2 Diabetes in Teens: Secrets for Success.* New York: Wiley.

DiabetesAtWork.org. 2012. "Diabetes at Work." National Institutes of Health, Centers for Disease Control and Prevention. Accessed July 6. http://diabetesatwork.org/.

Chapter 16

Travel Concerns

Introduction

As with workplace and school issues, travel can also present unique challenges to diabetes patients. Being aware of these issues and planning in advance can help patients overcome some of the obstacles involved with travel. Traveling for work or for recreation may mean a patient is away from home for days or weeks at a time; however, a patient should not fear or avoid travel because of his or her diabetic status. With proper planning, patients can enjoy trips by road, rail, ship, or plane without undue concern. This chapter provides an annotated list of helpful resources to aid individuals in making travel arrangements while simultaneously managing their own or their family member's diabetes.

Trip Preparation

It is recommended that adults or children visit with their physician, preferably four to six weeks ahead of time, before embarking on any type of long trip to ensure they are medically cleared to do so. If medically cleared to travel, patients must bring documentation about their condition, allergies, and what medications are being taken in case of a medical emergency while away from home (Klobassa Davidson and Moreland, 2011).

In addition, it is important for patients to have with them a prescription for the diabetes medications they are taking should anything adverse occur to the medicine they are carrying. Patients should double the amount of medications and testing materials they expect to need in case they are delayed in returning home. For travel, it is a good idea to have prescriptions through a pharmacy chain, instead of a local pharmacy, so they can easily be refilled (Stahl, 2012).

Medical alert identification, such as a bracelet or necklace, should be worn at all times to identify the patient's status. In addition, patients should ensure the medical identification they are wearing is written in the language of the country they are visiting so that health care workers can readily identify their status.

If a person with diabetes is visiting a location that has extreme temperatures, either hot or cold, the patient should pack medications in proper insulated packaging or with ice packs. When a person with diabetes is visiting a foreign country and purchases insulin at that location, there should be no problem because most countries use a universal concentration. However, the concentration of the insulin should be verified before using syringes to administer dosages. If flying, patients should contact the airline two or more days before the flight to request a healthy meal, if they know food will be served.

Travel

No matter the method of travel, it is important to know the travel dates, times, and whether there are scheduled intermittent stops or layovers where travelers can avail themselves with food, especially since such amenities are not always offered on certain modes of transportation. Even when knowing the particular travel mode timetable, patients should assume there will be delays or even cancellations and plan to have an adequate amount of medication and food available to provide insulin or needed sustenance. In addition, patients should be aware of the added security that exists for various modes of transportation and carry needed medications and equipment with them instead of checking these items or storing them where they cannot be readily accessed.

When flying, it is important to carry all essential equipment and medication, clearly marked with their original pharmacy labeling, in a carry-on bag, which should be stored in front of the passenger, not in the overhead bin where items can be damaged, dislodged, or misplaced (Joslin Diabetes Center, 2012). Going through security lines in airports is simpler if patients follow Transportation Security Administration protocols for notifying agents about their diabetic status and informing them about medications and equipment stored in their carry-on bags.

Crossing time zones by any mode of transportation means coordinating insulin shots appropriately, such as needing less when traveling east because the day will be shorter but needing more if traveling west because the day will be longer (Chandran and Edelman, 2003). A diabetes care specialist or physician can assist with adjusting insulin shots when traveling in different time zones.

Travelers should assemble a first-aid kit to bring on any road, ship, or rail trip to address any unforeseen medical emergencies. A glucagon emergency kit can help provide glucose quickly should the need arise but should only be brought along if a traveling companion knows how to use it. Some patients pack extra glucose tablets, which do not require anyone else to know how to administer them. It is a good idea to pack additional medication that is kept easily accessible, as well as appropriate snacks, such as fruit, cheese, or juices, to prevent precipitous drops in glucose levels should travel delays occur and food services be unavailable (Kruger, 2006).

There are cruises by ship specifically designed for those with diabetes, where physicians, educators, and personnel from such well-known clinics as the Joslin Diabetes Center are in attendance to provide seminars, host workshops, and also be available for consultations. When visiting towns or cities outside the United States, travelers should avoid drinking tap water, and make sure to take extra precautions when eating the local food because it might have been prepared in unsanitary conditions (American Diabetes Association, 2012). Patients should make use of the onboard ship's medical facility if there are any concerns; however, if they experience any serious issues, patients will most likely be transported to a hospital on shore (Chait, 2009).

When reaching the travel destination, it is recommended the person with diabetes take it easy for the first couple of days to adjust to the new time zone or climate. It is imperative when traveling that patients check glucose levels more often than normal as various elements, such as different types of food intake, exertion level, or temperature, might affect levels adversely. It is natural to want to explore any new geographical surroundings; however, patients must be cautious about taking care of their feet properly and should wear sensible shoes and change their socks if they become wet. In addition, patients with diabetes should never walk barefoot or expose themselves to the possibility of infection or foot injury.

Summary

Before traveling for work or pleasure, there should be substantive planning arrangements, such as obtaining medical clearance for extended trips, ensuring there is an adequate supply of diabetes medications and prescriptions to obtain more if necessary, packing medications in insulated containers, having snacks or other food readily available, and bringing proper footwear and clothing. After traveling, it is helpful for people with diabetes to reflect upon their experience and make adjustments as necessary when preparing for future trips. While those with diabetes should never be discouraged from traveling because of their medical status, it is important to take all aspects of the disease into consideration, so the trip is both enjoyable and safe.

Information Sources

Selected Print Resources

➤ Garcia, Marilyn L. 2005. *Diabetic Travel Tales and Tips: Adventures from around the World*. Pasadena, CA: Mandean.
  A humorous take on a serious issue, the author documents her travel adventures around the globe as a type 1 diabetes patient. She provides useful tips on managing the disease while traversing time zones, purchasing medicine in foreign countries, and dealing with airport security.

➤ Kruger, Davida F. 2006. *The Diabetes Travel Guide*. 2nd ed. Alexandria, VA: American Diabetes Association.
  This book provides a straightforward explanation on how to travel safely with diabetes, including tips and resources for putting together a diabetes survival kit, dealing with medical insurance companies, and preparing for any type of disaster that could befall a traveler with diabetes.

➤ Warshaw, Hope S., and Joy Pape. 2009. *Real-Life Guide to Diabetes: Practical Answers to Your Diabetes Problems*. Alexandria, VA: American Diabetes Association. This book contains a chapter on preparing for travel, including taking care of medical issues, adapting to sudden changes in the travel schedule, managing food, getting in enough physical activity, and managing medications. This chapter also provides a series of practical tips to employ during the trip.

Selected Web Resources

➤ American Diabetes Association—"Living with Diabetes: When You Travel," http://www.diabetes.org/living-with-diabetes/treatment-and-care/medication/when-you-travel.html
This webpage addresses several areas on traveling with diabetes: the trip planning stage, packing, eating in the air, preparing for a medical emergency while away from home, storage of insulin, and crossing time zones. Advice for traveling abroad includes avoiding tap water overseas as it could lead to digestive problems or other illnesses, which could cause complications with diabetes. While most countries use the universal concentration of U-100 for insulin, travelers should confirm this information beforehand because, historically, concentrations in other countries were different, such as U-40 or U-80. If this is the case, it requires the patient to do a conversion of a U-100 dosage to reflect the different concentration of the U-40 or U-80 vial before drawing the appropriate amount of insulin to administer. The webpage also includes links to further information on traveling with diabetes supplies and avoiding dehydration.

➤ Defeat Diabetes Foundation—"Tips for Traveling with Diabetes," http://www.defeatdiabetes.org/about_diabetes/text.asp?id=Travel_Tips
This webpage offers tips for travel by road, air, and other modes of transportation. It includes additional information on traveling by plane, crossing time zones, visiting foreign countries, and dealing with discrimination. The section also advises the traveler to carry proper documentation or wear a medical alert bracelet, which designates a person as someone with diabetes. People should also carry current contact information for their primary care physician. The webpage recommends packing double what would normally be necessary in terms of medicine and supplies because travel delays frequently occur. It is also helpful to know the generic names of any drugs taken for diabetes and other any other conditions in case there is a need to refill a prescription. Another good idea is to travel with a companion who is aware of the person's diabetes and how to provide assistance.

➤ JDRF—"Planning a Trip," http://kids.jdrf.org/index.cfm?page_id=109788
This resource provides links to tips and checklists to ensure that children traveling with their families or on field trips are managing their diabetes properly. There

are lists of what to pack for a one-night sleepover, a camping trip that lasts a few days, or vacations of a week or more. Tips include the optimal way to pack insulin, such as cushioned between clothing, in an insulated container, in bags carried with the traveler and kept away from extreme heat or cold, and using two bags with the same medicine in case one is lost. Advice includes how to travel through airport security efficiently, as well as how to calibrate insulin dosages when crossing time zones. Two diabetes experts provide tips on how to hike and camp while managing juvenile diabetes.

➤ Joslin Diabetes Center—"Diabetes and Travel: 10 Tips for a Safe Trip," http://www .joslin.org/info/diabetes-and-travel-10-tips-for-a-safe-trip.html
This webpage offers a succinct summary of ten travel tips for the patient with diabetes or for someone who is traveling with a child or adult who has the condition. The tips include the following: (1) no matter the mode of travel, patients should always keep diabetes supplies close at hand and ensure they are safely packed so no breakage or other damage occurs due to jostling or extreme heat or cold; (2) as much as possible, patients should stick to a routine and try to eat meals at times they would eat if at home; (3) patients should keep documentation from health care providers about their condition and have it translated into the language of the country they are visiting; (4) patients should inform Transportation Security Agency officers of their condition before going through security lines; (5) they should be prepared at all times to treat low glucose with insulin, glucose tablets, or food; (6) they should research any types of food they will be eating with regard to carbohydrates, so insulin will be properly dosed; (7) patients should carry more diabetes supplies than needed in case travel delays occur; (8) they should consider time zone issues and work with their health care team to determine how to calibrate insulin properly; (9) they should test blood sugar often because inactivity or increased activity that is different from their normal routine can alter the amount of insulin needed; and (10) patients should make sure to inform fellow travelers that they have diabetes or wear a medical alert bracelet in case something happens and they are unable to communicate.

➤ National Diabetes Education Program—"Have Diabetes Will Travel," http://ndep .nih.gov/media/have_diabetes_will_travel_508.pdf
This links to a PDF of a succinct two-page information summary on tips while traveling, including planning ahead, packing properly, information about flying, and general tips about traveling on the road.

➤ Transportation Security Administration—"Passengers with Diabetes," http://www .tsa.gov/traveler-information/passengers-diabetes
This section of the TSA webpage for travelers with special needs provides tips for working with security officers when traveling by airline. The section addresses the kinds of medical supplies and equipment that a diabetic passenger might carry,

and it lists supplies that should be declared and separated from other belongings before screening begins:

- Liquids
- Gels
- Aerosols
- Medically necessary items in excess of 3.4 ounces
- Freezer packs
- Frozen gel packs

If the patient does not wish for his or her liquids, gels, or aerosols to be X-rayed or opened, he or she must inform the TSA officer, which may require a different type of property inspection and a pat-down. Unless the frozen gel packs or freezer packs are solid once they reach the screening area, they will be treated as liquids and subjected to the same scrutiny. The webpage advises patients using an insulin pump that they can be screened using imaging technology, so they do not need to disconnect from it. The patient needs to inform the TSA officer about the insulin pump before the screening process begins. A self-pat-down of the insulin pump may be performed by the patient, which is then followed by an explosive trace detection of his or her hands.

Selected Audiovisual Resources

➤ Diabetes1.org—"Tips for Managing Your Diabetes While Traveling," http://www.diabetes1.org/MultimediaLibrary/flvplayer.cfm/87
  This links to a short video that highlights how and what patients should pack when traveling by any mode of transportation; calibrating medication dosages depending upon time zone; contacting patients' medical insurance company before traveling to know what their options are should they become ill on the trip; and acclimating to new surroundings.

➤ 5minLife Videopedia—"How to Organize Your Diabetic Supplies When You Travel," http://www.5min.com/Video/How-to-Organize-Your-Diabetic-Supplies-When-You-Travel-482952905
  This five-minute video provides advice on traveling, including bringing duplicates or triplicates of medications; keeping all supplies with the patient and not in stored luggage; and bringing a travel letter from a health care provider detailing the medical supplies the patient is carrying.

➤ University of California Television—"Taking Control of Your Diabetes: Traveling with Diabetes," http://www.uctv.tv/search-details.aspx?showID=15232
  In this thirty-minute video, a person with type 1 diabetes, Adam Levbarg, shares his experiences traveling around the world while successfully managing his diabetes. He encourages those with diabetes to take proper precautions while traveling and not to avoid it out of concern for their health condition.

References

American Diabetes Association. 2012. "Living with Diabetes: When You Travel." American Diabetes Association. Accessed July 6. http://www.diabetes.org/living-with-diabetes/treatment-and-care/medication/when-you-travel.html.

Chait, J. 2009. "Taking Your Diabetes on a Cruise." Diabetes Self-Management. Updated March 4. http://www.diabetesselfmanagement.com/articles/general-diabetes-and-health-issues/taking_your_diabetes_on_a_cruise/all/.

Chandran, M., and S. V. Edelman. 2003. "Have Insulin, Will Fly: Diabetes Management During Air Travel and Time Zone Adjustment Strategies." *Clinical Diabetes* 21, no. 2: 82–85.

Joslin Diabetes Center. 2012. "Diabetes and Travel—10 Tips for a Safe Trip." Joslin Diabetes Center. Accessed July 6. http://www.joslin.org/info/diabetes-and-travel-10-tips-for-a-safe-trip.html.

Klobassa Davidson, N., and P. Moreland. 2011. "Traveling with Diabetes—Plan Ahead." Mayo Foundation for Medical Education and Research. June 24. http://www.mayoclinic.com/health/traveling-with-diabetes/MY01794.

Kruger, D. F. 2006. *The Diabetes Travel Guide*. 2nd ed. Alexandria, VA: American Diabetes Association.

Stahl, R. J. 2012. "Taking Care of Your Diabetes When You Are Away from Home." CVS Health Information Center. Accessed July 6. http://health.cvs.com/GetContent.aspx?token=f75979d3-9c7c-4b16-af56-3e122a3f19e3&chunkiid=462517.

Part IV

Related Health Complications and Care Resources

Chapter 17

Foot, Skin, and Gum Problems

Introduction

For people with types 1 and 2 diabetes, too much glucose in the blood over time can cause health complications. High blood glucose can cause nerve damage and poor blood flow. These two complications can then further cause foot, skin, and gum problems. Improper foot care can lead to infections and even gangrene, which may require amputation. Skin problems include fungal and bacterial infections as well as conditions that are more serious. Diabetes-related issues with the gums can cause disease, loss of teeth, and serious infections in the bone structure of the mouth. This chapter provides a basic overview of diabetes-caused foot, skin, and gum issues, the consequences of these conditions, and the care required to prevent problems.

Feet

Poor blood circulation and peripheral neuropathy caused by diabetes can lead to several types of conditions with the feet that should be addressed expediently, no matter how minor the issues initially appear, to prevent more severe complications from occurring later. Nerve damage caused by diabetes means that people are sometimes not even aware of problems with their feet, simply because they do not feel the same sensations as they did before the disease. Something as minor as a small cut, which may go undetected at the time it occurs, can ultimately lead to a serious infection because blood is not flowing fully to the lower extremities and feet to help the natural healing process (American Diabetes Association, 2012b). Left untreated, these infections can become so serious that amputation is necessary. Some of the more common foot conditions include calluses and corns, fungal infections, blisters, and ulcers.

Calluses and Corns

A callus on the foot is a hardened and thick area of the skin without distinct borders that can be located on any area of the foot, though usually on the sole or sides. Repetitive friction in a particular area of the foot forms the callus, which is generally caused by poor-fitting shoes, socks, or walking barefoot. Corns on the foot generally develop on a bony portion of the foot or in between the toes. Unlike calluses, corns have distinct borders, may be waxy in appearance, and be either soft or hard (Cleveland Clinic, 2010). Corns can also be painful, although that is not always evident to people with peripheral neuropathy, who usually do not feel much sensation in their feet. Calluses or corns left untreated or improperly treated, such as cutting or trimming them with a sharp instrument or using chemicals to peel away dead skin, can lead to an open ulcer on the foot (Hanson, 2011).

Fungal Infections

Conditions such as athlete's foot and fungus on the toenails can lead to complications that are more serious if not treated early. Wearing shoes offers the feet a wet and warm environment that promotes fungus growth. If there are cracks in the skin, it is possible for germs to cause fungal infections on the foot or toenails (Tan and Joseph, 2004). While over-the-counter medications can alleviate some of these issues, a physician should determine whether oral antibiotics are also needed.

Blisters and Ulcers

Blisters can occur on any area of the foot and are caused by ill-fitting shoes or socks. While not as serious as a corn, they can be very painful. Patients should not drain blisters manually because doing so can lead to further infection. An ulcer, which is more serious, is an actual opening or sore on the foot that can be caused by a minor cut or improper footwear (National Diabetes Education Program, 2012b). Because of poor circulation in the lower extremities, ulcers that would normally heal quickly can become serious if there is no medical intervention. A physician should examine any open wound on the foot and determine the best course of action to heal it.

Suggested Foot Care

If patients do not undertake basic foot care, there is a greater risk of minor issues quickly becoming more severe. One of the first steps to take proper care of the feet is to ensure appropriate blood glucose levels are maintained so there will be optimal circulation. Patients should inspect their feet daily for any changes or problems; however, if this is not possible due to mobility or eye problems, a family member or friend should do so (National Diabetes Education Program, 2011). Patients should avoid extremely hot water when bathing or placing heating pads on their feet because injury can occur if the sensation level is minimized by neuropathy.

Patients must also make sure to properly moisturize their feet because dry skin is a direct result of nerves not telegraphing to the feet that they need to sweat, and subsequent cracks can lead to germs entering the foot. Bathing or showering every day and keeping the feet clean are important, as is adding a thin coating of moisturizer to prevent dryness (de la Cruz, Valente, and Brosnan, 2007). Being conscientious about always wearing proper and well-fitting footwear, and never walking barefoot, can prevent calluses or corns from forming, as well as help avoid scrapes or cuts.

When spending time in a pool, it is recommended that patients wear swim shoes at all times.

Patients should have annual foot exams by a physician or podiatrist; more frequent visits may be necessary if additional complications exist, such as structural issues with the foot. A podiatrist can customize shoes with orthotic inserts to alleviate or prevent problems. Patients should take any problem with the feet seriously and seek medical advice and help.

Skin

Because of vascular and circulation issues, patients with diabetes are prone to various types of infections on the skin. Seeing a physician in the early stages can help either prevent infections initially or provide necessary treatment as soon as possible. Recognizing dermatological issues and seeking appropriate treatment early is imperative in preventing more complications that can be serious.

According to both the Cleveland Clinic (2010) and the American Diabetes Association (2012c), several of the more common skin conditions include fungal and bacterial infections as well as scleroderma diabeticorum, vitiligo, and diabetic dermopathy, necrobiosis lipoidica diabeticorum, eruptive xanthomatosis, digital sclerosis, disseminated granuloma annulare, and acanthosis nigricans.

Fungal and Bacterial Infections

Fungal infections can occur on the skin in areas that are prone to being moist and damp, such as under the breasts, in the groin area, on the genitals, or in between the toes. Bacterial infections can occur in the form of sties, boils, folliculitis, or carbuncles (Tan and Joseph, 2004). In addition, dry skin can occur anywhere on the body because of poor circulation. Patients should address dry skin early because cracks in the skin can allow germs to enter the body and cause an infection.

Scleroderma Diabeticorum

While type 2 diabetes patients are more prone to scleroderma diabeticorum, it occurs very rarely and usually in overweight people. It is a hardening of the skin on the upper back and the back of the neck. Topically, treatment includes application of ointments and lotions that soften the skin and make the area less prone to irritation. The optimal treatment, however, is to bring blood glucose levels under control, because uncontrolled glucose contributes to the condition (Polin, 2011).

Vitiligo

Type 1 patients are prone to vitiligo, a condition affecting the coloring of the skin. The cells that control pigment production suffer damage or are muted, the results of which are areas of skin that lose their natural color. The areas most prone to this condition include the face, chest, and abdomen. It can be treated topically with steroids (Cleveland Clinic, 2010).

Diabetic Dermopathy

Diabetic dermopathy affects the legs and is due to poor blood circulation to the lower extremities from damage to small blood cells caused by diabetes (American Diabetes Association, 2012c). Shiny patches or lesions will appear which are scaly in texture but which are generally not painful and will not cause itching. Patients who receive a diagnosis of diabetic dermopathy can take comfort in knowing this condition is considered harmless.

Necrobiosis Lipoidica Diabeticorum

Diabetes can cause the skin on the lower legs to become yellow with a waxy texture and a purple border due to damage to blood vessels, a condition known as necrobiosis lipoidica diabeticorum (Cleveland Clinic, 2010). This condition, which causes severe itching, is also painful. Patients should seek medical attention if the sore areas break open because further infection could occur if not treated.

Eruptive Xanthomatosis

Eruptive xanthomatosis is a condition known only to occur in patients with diabetes, as a result of poorly controlled glucose levels. Small-sized bumps occur on the skin, yellow in color, surrounded by red halos, and can cause itching (Cleveland Clinic, 2010). These small bumps can arise on the arms, hands, buttocks, and legs. Treatment consists of lowering blood glucose levels to normal and reducing cholesterol levels, because high triglycerides are a known contributor to this condition.

Digital Sclerosis

Due to poor circulation, a hardening of the skin surrounding the fingers and toes can occur, a condition called digital sclerosis. This hardening, in turn, causes stiffness and joint pain in the areas affected. Lotions and creams are a topical treatment for this condition, which will aid in softening the skin, but the optimal solution is to keep blood glucose levels under control (Cleveland Clinic, 2010).

Disseminated Granuloma Annulare

Disseminated granuloma annulare, a rashlike condition that is not harmful, often occurs on areas of the skin far from the trunk area of the body, such as the ears or fingers. The rash consists of arclike raised portions of the skin, which are red or brown in appearance. Prescription topical steroid drugs can help improve the condition, so patients should contact their health care provider if it causes discomfort (American Diabetes Association, 2012c).

Acanthosis Nigricans

Acanthosis nigricans is often a precursor to diabetes, so patients should take this condition seriously if they are currently diagnosed as prediabetic. The skin becomes darker and thicker in areas around the neck, groin, and armpits (Cleveland Clinic, 2010). There is no cure for the condition, but it generally improves with weight loss.

Suggested Skin Care

In addition to maintaining hygienic habits, such as bathing or showering daily, patients should remain vigilant when inspecting their body for any changes so that they can take immediate action before a new condition worsens. Because some conditions can lead to serious complications, patients with diabetes should check their skin daily for dryness, moisture, keratin between the toe webs, blisters, hemorrhages, erosions, and ulcers (Levin and Pfeifer, 2009). For any type of skin condition, no matter how minor it appears initially, patients should schedule a consult with a physician or diabetes nurse. Some conditions respond well to topical creams that contain antibiotics or steroids, and these may provide immediate relief.

Gums

Oral health and hygiene are imperative for patients because they are at a greater risk of experiencing minor to major complications with their teeth and gums due to circulation issues caused by the disease. Healing can take much longer when having routine procedures, such as after a teeth-cleaning appointment.

Periodontitis

Periodontitis, a major concern for people with diabetes, is an infection of both the gums and bone structure. Poor circulation causes the condition, a problem which can make the gums prone to infection from minor irritants or germs. Higher levels of glucose in a patient also cause increased bacteria to be present in the mouth, which can lead to infection. This, coupled with poor oral hygiene care, can lead to health problems (American Diabetes Association, 2012a).

Gingivitis

Gingivitis, a precursor to periodontitis, is an early phase of the disease, which causes puffiness around the gum area and frequent bleeding after tooth brushing or flossing. Early intervention can prevent the more serious periodontitis from occurring in patients with diabetes.

Suggested Gum Care

Patients who smoke should make their best effort to stop. Smoking increases the probability they will develop an oral infection, such as periodontitis, or other more serious conditions. Symptoms of gum disease, while not always painful, should be readily apparent upon visual inspection, such as swollen areas around the teeth, bleeding, bad breath, and teeth not fitting together as they did previously, whether natural teeth or dentures (American Diabetes Association, 2012a). Patients should regularly schedule visits to a dentist who is experienced with treating patients with diabetes. If patients notice any changes to the gum area between regularly scheduled appointments, they should make an additional appointment with their dentist to address these concerns immediately.

Summary

It is imperative that patients are vigilant in keeping their blood glucose stable because high levels can lead to unnecessary and burdensome health complications related to the feet, skin, and gums. Damage to the nerve endings in the feet due to diabetic neuropathy can lead to serious problems being masked because injuries, cuts, or scrapes may not be noticed. If untreated, serious infections can occur, which may lead to amputation. Fungal and bacterial infections can easily occur on sensitive areas of the skin if the patient fails to maintain good hygiene daily as well as normal glucose levels. Patients with diabetes are also prone to issues with their gums, which can lead to tooth loss or more serious infections in the mouth and jaw. Patients should make regular visits to their podiatrist, dermatologist, and dentist, who should be core members of the health care team.

Information Sources

Selected Print Resources

➤ Ahroni, Jessie, and Neil Scheffler. 2006. *101 Foot Care Tips for People with Diabetes.* Alexandria, VA: American Diabetes Association.
   This book addresses all areas of foot care concern for patients with diabetes with succinct and helpful suggestions for maintaining healthy feet.

➤ Beaser, Richard. 2005. *The Joslin Guide to Diabetes: A Program for Managing Your Treatment.* New York: Fireside.
   The *Joslin Guide* contains a chapter about foot care for the patient with diabetes. The chapter covers risk factors for developing foot problems, symptoms, and foot care guidelines.

➤ Hanson, Erik. 2011. *Diabetic Foot Care: A Guide for Patients and Healthcare Professionals.* Long Island City, NY: Hatherleigh.

Written for both health care providers and patients with diabetes, this comprehensive resource outlines all major components of foot care including prevention, treatment, maintenance, and locating physicians.

➤ Levin, Marvin E., and Michael A. Pfeifer. 2009. *The Uncomplicated Guide to Diabetes Complications*. 3rd ed. Alexandria, VA: American Diabetes Association. This title provides sections on skin complications and on oral and dental health. Each section describes complications that can occur with skin, feet, and gums and provides information on how to prevent the complications from occurring.

Selected Web Resources

➤ American Diabetes Association—"Living with Diabetes: Diabetes and Oral Health Problems," http://www.diabetes.org/living-with-diabetes/treatment-and-care/oral-health-and-hygiene/diabetes-and-oral.html
This webpage examines the aspects of how diabetes affects oral health and ways to prevent complications that are more serious. Gum disease, in particular, is something patients need to be cautious about because poorly controlled blood glucose can cause this condition, and having it, in turn, can produce higher glucose levels. It is very important for patients to notify dental care workers about their condition and their prescribed medications; the dental worker will also need to know whether blood glucose is at normal and stable levels before recommending any type of dental surgical procedures.

➤ American Diabetes Association—"Living with Diabetes: Foot Complications," http://www.diabetes.org/living-with-diabetes/complications/foot-complications/
This webpage provides a summary in easy-to-understand language on the major foot conditions for patients. These include neuropathy, which is caused by nerve damage so the feet cannot feel heat, cold, or injury; skin changes in the feet, such as increased dryness, peeling, or cracking; calluses, which occur more often in people with diabetes; foot ulcers, which may go unnoticed if there is neuropathy and can cause such severe infections that amputation is necessary; and poor circulation, which can be controlled by stopping smoking and keeping blood pressure and cholesterol low.

➤ American Diabetes Association—"Living with Diabetes: Skin Complications," http://www.diabetes.org/living-with-diabetes/complications/skin-complications.html
This webpage outlines and describes the major skin conditions that patients with diabetes are prone to experiencing. These general skin conditions include bacterial infections, such as sties, boils, folliculitis, carbuncles, and infections around the nails; fungal infections; and general or localized itching. The webpage also addresses specific diabetic-related skin conditions, including diabetic

dermopathy, necrobiosis lipoidica diabeticorum, blisters, eruptive xanthomatosis, digital sclerosis, disseminated granuloma annulare, and acanthosis nigricans.

➤ Cleveland Clinic—"Foot and Skin Related Complications of Diabetes," http://my.clevelandclinic.org/disorders/diabetes_mellitus/hic_foot_and_skin_related_complications_of_diabetes.aspx
This webpage outlines and describes conditions of both the feet and skin that occur as a result of having diabetes or prediabetes conditions. It provides detailed definitions of the most common foot and skin ailments as well as suggested treatment options. One section discusses how to avoid typical foot problems and when to contact a health provider for further assistance. This webpage addresses common skin conditions associated with diabetes in detail and includes a section on how some of these can be prevented or improved.

➤ National Diabetes Education Program—"Feet Can Last a Lifetime: A Health Care Provider's Guide to Preventing Diabetes Foot Problems," http://ndep.nih.gov/ media/feet_hcguide.pdf
While this resource is written for health care providers and their team, it does provide valuable information on the different types of foot ailments and what physicians are looking for during examinations. This fifty-page PDF also outlines the many ways patients can prevent foot problems from occurring and what to do should they experience these conditions.

➤ National Diabetes Education Program—"Take Care of Your Feet for a Lifetime," http://ndep.nih.gov/media/NDEP4_TextCareFeet-2c_508.pdf
This booklet provides systematic instructions on how patients should care for their feet and outlines the concerns patients with diabetes should address daily.

➤ National Diabetes Information Clearinghouse—"Prevent Diabetes Problems: Keep Your Feet and Skin Healthy," http://diabetes.niddk.nih.gov/dm/pubs/complications_feet/
Written in easy-to-read language, this webpage teaches patients about common skin and foot problems and how they can prevent problems from occurring. There are illustrations that provide further details on where to look on the foot for common ailments and multiple tips on how to be proactive in caring for the skin and feet.

Selected Audiovisual Resource

➤ National Library of Medicine—"Diabetes Foot Care," http://www.nlm.nih.gov/medlineplus/tutorials/diabetesfootcare/htm/index.htm
This interactive slideshow tutorial provides the basics on how to maintain healthy feet, including choosing appropriate footwear, preventing problems and injuries, caring for the feet, and promoting regular checkups with a physician.

References

American Diabetes Association. 2012a. "Living with Diabetes: Diabetes and Oral Health Problems." American Diabetes Association. Accessed July 12. http://www .diabetes.org/living-with-diabetes/treatment-and-care/oral-health-and-hygiene/ diabetes-and-oral.html.

———. 2012b. "Living with Diabetes: Foot Complications." American Diabetes Association. Accessed July 12. http://www.diabetes.org/living-with-diabetes/ complications/foot-complications/.

———. 2012c. "Living with Diabetes: Skin Complications." American Diabetes Association. Accessed July 12. http://www.diabetes.org/living-with-diabetes/ complications/skin-complications.html.

Cleveland Clinic. 2010. "Foot and Skin Related Complications of Diabetes." Cleveland Clinic. Last reviewed on March 15. http://my.clevelandclinic.org/disorders/ diabetes_mellitus/hic_foot_and_skin_related_complications_of_diabetes.aspx.

de la Cruz, G. J., S. Valente, and J. Brosnan. 2007. "How to Take Care of Your Feet When You Have Diabetes." *Nursing* 37: 14–15.

Hanson, E. 2011. *Diabetic Foot Care: A Guide for Patients and Healthcare Professionals*. Long Island City, NY: Hatherleigh Press.

Levin, M. E., and M. A. Pfeifer 2009. *The Uncomplicated Guide to Diabetes Complications*. 3rd ed. Alexandria, VA: American Diabetes Association.

National Diabetes Education Program. 2011. "Be Sweet to Your Feet if You Have Diabetes." National Institutes of Health, Centers for Disease Control and Prevention. Updated August. http://ndep.nih.gov/media/be_sweet_to_your_feet_ 508.pdf.

———. 2012. "Keeping Feet Healthy and Happy." National Institutes of Health, Centers for Disease Control and Prevention. Accessed November 28. http:// ndep.nih.gov/media/Keeping_ Feet_Healthy_Article.pdf.

Polin, B. S. 2011. "Diabetic Skin Conditions." Diabetic Lifestyle. Updated April 18. http://www.diabeticlifestyle.com/everyday-life/diabetic-skin-conditions.

Tan, J. S., and W. S. Joseph. 2004. "Common Fungal Infections of the Feet in Patients with Diabetes Mellitus." *Drugs and Aging* 21, no. 2: 101–112.

Chapter 18

Diabetic Retinopathy

Introduction

Eye diseases, such as cataracts, glaucoma, and diabetic retinopathy, can result from diabetic eye disease and cause vision loss or blindness, which are some of the more serious complications of diabetes. Cataracts, which develop at an earlier age in people with diabetes, cloud the eye's lens. Glaucoma causes an increase in fluid pressure inside the eye, resulting in optic nerve damage and consequently a loss of vision. Diabetic retinopathy, damage to the blood vessels in the retina, is the leading cause of new-onset blindness among adults in the United States.

Diabetes and Retinopathy

Diabetic retinopathy usually occurs in both eyes and results from changes and damage to the blood vessels located in the retina, a light-sensitive tissue located in the back of the eye. High levels of blood glucose cause damage to the small blood vessels in the retina by causing the lining of the blood vessels to thicken and develop leaks. Diabetes causes the blood vessels to become very weak, resulting in poor circulation in the vessels and in the growth of more abnormal vessels. It's important to learn about the types of diabetic retinopathy in addition to risk factors, symptoms, diagnosis, treatment, and prevention of this complication of diabetes.

Classification

There are four classifications of diabetic retinopathy. The disease progresses from a mild form called nonproliferative retinopathy to proliferative retinopathy, which is the most advanced stage of the disease (National Eye Institute, 2012).

- Mild nonproliferative retinopathy: High levels of blood glucose begin causing damage to the retinal blood vessels. Microaneurysms, which are balloon-like swellings in the retina that often leak fluid, begin occurring in the retina's tiny blood vessels.
- Moderate nonproliferative retinopathy: Some of the blood vessels nourishing the retina with blood become blocked.
- Severe nonproliferative retinopathy: As more blood vessels become blocked, the retina becomes deprived of its blood supply. New blood vessels begin growing.

- Proliferative retinopathy: The new blood vessels that form are abnormal and have fragile and thin walls, which can rupture easily. The blood from the ruptured vessels leaks into the vitreous humor causing blood to block the passage of light to the retina. Blood vessels also cause scar tissue, which begins to pull on the retina causing it to become detached. Proliferative retinopathy can result in severe vision loss and can lead to blindness.

In addition to blood leaking into the retina, resulting in vision loss, some people with diabetic retinopathy also experience macular edema. The macula is located in the center of the retina and contains blood vessels and nerve fibers. The macula is the area of the eye that is responsible for central vision. Macular edema results from fluid leaking into the macula center. The fluid in the macula results in swelling, thickening, and blurred vision, leading to vision loss (Joslin Diabetes Center, 2012). While macular edema usually occurs in the more advanced stages of the disease, it can occur at any phase of the disease.

Risk Factors

The prevalence of diabetic retinopathy is higher in patients with type 1 diabetes; however, anyone with diabetes is at risk for developing diabetic retinopathy. The longer the patient has had diabetes, the greater the risk of developing diabetic retinopathy, with those having diabetes for more than ten years at greatest risk. In addition to poor glucose control, having other associated medical conditions can also increase the risk of developing retinopathy. Those with high blood pressure, kidney disease, and high cholesterol are at greater risk. Pregnant women with either type 1 or type 2 diabetes are at increased risk and should receive regular screenings during the pregnancy for retinopathy. Anyone with diabetes should have a comprehensive dilated eye exam annually (Levin and Pfeifer, 2009).

Symptoms

It is important to know that patients may have perfect vision and no symptoms but still have retinopathy and be at risk for vision loss and blindness. As the disease progresses and swelling and loss of blood circulation to the macula occur, patients may experience varying degrees of blurred vision. Patients with proliferative retinopathy may experience floating lines or webs when blood vessels rupture. Large hemorrhages may result in vision reduced so greatly that patients can perceive only light or darkness. Patients with retinal damage may experience no symptoms at all or may experience blurred vision, fluctuating vision, floating webs, line distortion, or vision loss so severe that they have only light perception (Levin and Pfeifer, 2009).

Because there are usually no symptoms, and sometimes symptoms will disappear and then reoccur, having regular eye exams is very important. Left untreated, diabetic retinopathy can result in severe vision loss and in some cases blindness. Early treatment is the most effective method to delay the progression of the disease. Patients experiencing any eye symptoms or noticing any changes in their vision should schedule an eye exam immediately (Canadian Diabetes Association, 2012).

Diagnosis

Regular, comprehensive, dilated eye exams are essential for anyone with diabetes to help detect diabetic eye disease. Because there are usually no symptoms, an eye exam is necessary to uncover any problems. Also, early diagnosis is important because laser surgery can delay or halt the progression of the disease to prevent blindness; however, laser surgery cannot restore vision that has already been lost.

The comprehensive eye exam includes a visual acuity test, a dilated eye exam to examine the retina, and tonometry. The visual acuity test examines how well someone can see from certain distances. In the dilated eye exam, the ophthalmologist uses eyedrops to dilate the pupils and obtain a better view of the eye to examine it for disease. The ophthalmologist also examines the retina and optic nerve. A tonometer is an instrument used to measure pressure in the eye. These tests allow the ophthalmologist to check the retina for leaking blood vessels, macular edema, nerve tissue damage, and blood vessel changes.

If there are signs of macular edema, patients may have another test called a fluorescein angiogram. In this procedure, the patient receives an injection of dye into the arm and, as the dye flows through the retinal blood vessels, the test captures images of the dye. A fluorescein angiogram shows if there are any leaking blood vessels in the retina.

Treatment

There is no cure for diabetic retinopathy; however, laser treatment and vitrectomy, a surgical procedure requiring a tiny incision in the eye, can help reduce the loss of vision. If these treatments are performed early, they can greatly reduce the chances of blindness, but there is no treatment to restore vision that has already been lost to diabetic retinopathy.

Patients with nonproliferative retinopathy do not undergo any treatment unless macular edema develops. These patients should try to manage and control blood glucose levels, blood pressure, and blood cholesterol levels to delay or prevent the progression of the disease to proliferative retinopathy. If patients develop macular edema in the nonproliferative stages, then they may have treatment with a form of laser surgery called focal laser treatment. Focal laser treatment can improve lost vision in some cases, and the treatment also can reduce the risk of vision loss by 50 percent. The doctor will use the laser to burn areas where there is retinal leakage surrounding the macula; this procedure will slow fluid leakage, which would otherwise reduce the amount of retinal fluid (National Eye Institute, 2012).

When diabetic retinopathy advances to the proliferative retinopathy stage, patients undergo laser treatment to shrink abnormal blood vessels. Laser treatment destroys the damaged, closed capillaries of the retina that would promote the growth of the new, abnormal blood vessels and helps increase the amount of oxygen to the retina. Treatment should be performed before hemorrhaging occurs to prevent vision loss or blindness.

Patients who have a hemorrhage in the vitreous gel, which is the gel-like substance in the center of the eye that gives the eye its round shape, or who have a detached macula may need to undergo a vitrectomy for their sight to return. While the patient is under local or general anesthesia, the physician will start the vitrectomy with a small incision in the eye. The physician then uses an instrument to remove the blood-saturated vitreous gel and replaces that area with a salt solution (Levin and Pfeifer, 2009).

Prevention

While patients cannot prevent the occurrence of diabetic retinopathy, even with tightly controlled blood glucose levels, they can reduce their chances and delay onset by properly managing their blood glucose levels, blood pressure, and cholesterol levels. Laser surgery, if performed before vision loss, can also prevent the risk of blindness (National Eye Institute, 2012). To prevent blindness, it is essential for patients with either type 1 or type 2 diabetes to schedule an annual visit to an ophthalmologist who has diabetic retinopathy experience; if complications or changes in vision occur, more frequent visits may be necessary. The National Eye Institute recommends patients take their medications as prescribed; reach and maintain a healthy weight; engage in regular physical activity; control glycated hemoglobin (A1C), blood pressure, and cholesterol levels; stop smoking, and have a dilated eye exam annually to protect vision (National Eye Institute, 2012).

Summary

Glucose management is essential to prevent diabetic eye problems such as cataracts, glaucoma, retinopathy, and loss of vision and blindness. Diabetic retinopathy is the leading cause of new-onset blindness among adults in the United States. High blood glucose causes damage to the small vessels in the retina, which begin to thicken and leak. Over time, the affected blood vessels become very weak and circulation within them becomes poor. Diabetic retinopathy progresses from nonproliferative to an advanced stage called proliferative retinopathy. Because a patient may have no symptoms and still have retinopathy, any patient with diabetes should have a comprehensive eye exam annually to diagnose the condition early.

Information Sources

Selected Print Resources

➤ Collazo-Clavell, Maria. 2009. *Mayo Clinic The Essential Diabetes Book: How to Prevent, Control, and Live Well with Diabetes.* Rochester, MN: Mayo Clinic.
This title provides an explanation of how uncontrolled diabetes can lead to complications including retinopathy. The eye complications chapter includes information about the types of retinopathy, signs, symptoms, and treatment.

➤ Garnero, Theresa. 2008. *Your First Year with Diabetes: What to Do Month by Month.* Alexandria, VA: American Diabetes Association.
The resource is excellent for someone newly diagnosed with diabetes. The section on eye problems is succinct and provides new patients with an overview of diabetic eye problems and a checklist of methods to work effectively with diabetic retinopathy issues.

➤ Levin, Marvin E., and Michael A. Pfeifer. 2009. *The Uncomplicated Guide to Diabetes Complications.* 3rd ed. Alexandria, VA: American Diabetes Association.
This title provides readers with a detailed chapter on diabetic eye disease. The relevant chapter includes background information including how the eye works, effects of diabetes on the retina, macular edema, risk, prevention, control, symptoms, eye exams, and treatment. This resource also contains a chapter about the genetics of eye disease.

➤ Perrin, Rosemarie. 2007. *Living with Diabetes: Everything You Need to Know to Safeguard Your Health and Take Control of Your Life.* Toronto, Ontario, Canada: Sterling.
The resource includes information on controlling glucose to prevent complications. One section covers diabetic eye disease, including information on retinopathy, aggravating conditions, detection, treatment, glaucoma, and cataracts. The section also includes several helpful illustrations.

Selected Web Resources

➤ Canadian Diabetes Association—"Vision Health," http://www.diabetes.ca/diabetes-and-you/living/complications/vision-health/
This site provides an overview of the symptoms of retinopathy and information about prevention and screening, and contains a link to information for patients on keeping eyes healthy when they have diabetes.

➤ Diabetes UK—"Your Eyes and Diabetes," http://www.diabetes.org.uk/Guide-to-diabetes/Complications/Retinopathy/
The site explains what diabetic retinopathy is, including the different types of retinopathy; how it is treated; how to reduce risk; and detection.

➤ FamilyDoctor.org—"Diabetes: Eye Care," http://www.familydoctor.org/online/
famdocen/home/common/diabetes/living/047.printerview.html
FamilyDoctor.org includes information on diabetic eye disease, including diabetic
retinopathy. The webpage includes information on causes, prevention, and care
of diabetic eye disease.

➤ Joslin Diabetes Center—"Eyes and Vision," http://www.joslin.org/info/managing_
diabetes.html
Users of this webpage should scroll down to the "Eyes and Vision" section. In
this section they will find links to many aspects of eye health: information about
annual eye exams; why they should visit the eye doctor; diabetic retinopathy;
treatment; symptoms; diseases of the eye; and laser treatment of diabetic
retinopathy. The site provides patients with detailed information about diabetic
eye disease and retinopathy.

➤ MedlinePlus—"Diabetes: Eye Complications," http://www.nlm.nih.gov/medline
plus/tutorials/diabeteseyecomplications/htm/index.htm
Patients can view the interactive tutorial or read the text summary from this
webpage. Information includes how the eye works, diabetic retinopathy, treatment, and information about other diabetic eye problems.

➤ National Eye Institute—"Diabetic Eye Disease," http://www.nei.nih.gov/health/
diabetic/
This webpage contains links to a variety of helpful resources for the diabetic
patient. It includes links to information about diabetic retinopathy, diabetic eye
disease, news releases, videos, and illustrations. There is also a quiz patients
can take to assess their knowledge of diabetic eye disease, and the site includes
links to other helpful resources about diabetic retinopathy, cataracts, and
glaucoma.

➤ National Eye Institute—"Facts about Diabetic Retinopathy," http://www.nei.nih
.gov/health/diabetic/retinopathy.asp
Patients with diabetic retinopathy or those who wish to prevent the condition from
occurring will find this site beneficial. The site provides an overview of diabetic
retinopathy followed by information about the causes, risk factors, symptoms,
detection, treatment, and current research.

➤ National Eye Institute—"Information for Healthy Vision: Diabetic Eye Disease,"
http://www.nei.nih.gov/diabetes/
This National Eye Institute webpage provides patients with a succinct overview
of diabetic retinopathy. Patients can learn about diabetic retinopathy and its
causes, risk factors, symptoms, detection, and treatment. The site contains links
to information about the comprehensive dilated eye exam, information about
finding an eye care professional, and financial resources.

➤ Prevent Blindness America—"Diabetic Retinopathy," http://www.preventblindness
.org/diabetic-retinopathy
This site contains information about diabetic retinopathy. It explains risk factors,
stages of the condition, treatment, and financial assistance. It also contains a quiz
about diabetes and the eyes. Other sections of the site do not necessarily pertain to
diabetic eye disease but contain information that may be of interest to those wishing to learn how to protect their vision. There is a link to a glossary of eye terms.

➤ U.S. Department of Health and Human Services—"Diabetic Retinopathy: What
You Should Know," http://www.nei.nih.gov/health/diabetic/diabeticretino.pdf
This online booklet provides information for diabetic retinopathy patients. It
covers information about causes, symptoms, diagnosis, and treatment. The
booklet also contains tips on how patients can protect their vision and questions
to ask eye care professionals. The booklet also includes many helpful illustrations.

Selected Audiovisual Resources

➤ American Optometric Association—"Diabetic Retinopathy," http://www.aoa
.org/diabetic-retinopathy.xml
In addition to a written explanation of diabetic retinopathy, diagnosis, and treatment, this resource contains links to short videos about diabetic retinopathy.
There are videos about nonproliferative diabetic retinopathy, proliferative diabetic
retinopathy, and laser treatment. There is also a link to a Spanish version of the site.

➤ EyeSmart—"What Is Diabetic Retinopathy?," http://www.geteyesmart.org/
eyesmart/diseases/diabetic-retinopathy.cfm
This resource explains diabetic retinopathy, causes, symptoms, risk factors, diagnosis, and treatment. Patients can also view illustrations of the eye and several
short videos about diabetic eye problems.

➤ Healthy Roads Media—"Diabetic Eye Problems: An Introduction," http://www
.healthyroadsmedia.org/titles/EngIntroDiabeticEyeProbs/EngIntroDiabeticEye
Probs.htm
Healthy Roads Media provides several very short video clips of interest to patients
with diabetes. The video about diabetic retinopathy is just over a minute in length
and describes diabetic retinopathy and symptoms of the condition, and encourages
patients to obtain an annual eye exam.

➤ Insider Medicine—"If I Had Diabetes and Concerns Regarding My Eyes," http://
www.insidermedicine.com/archives/If_I_Had_Diabetes_and_Concerns_Regarding_
My_Eyes_Dr_Jeff_Gale_MD_Queens_University_4434.aspx
This takes the patient to a short video where Jeff Gale, Department of Ophthalmology, Queens University, describes what he would do to care for his eyes if he
had diabetes.

➤ MedlinePlus—"Diabetes: Eye Complications Tutorial," http://www.nlm.nih.gov/medlineplus/tutorials/diabeteseyecomplications/htm/index.htm
The site provides a self-paced audiovisual tutorial about diabetic eye complications. Users of the site can also print out a text summary of the tutorial.

➤ National Eye Institute—"Diabetic Eye Disease," http://www.nei.nih.gov/health/diabetic/
Patients can find a variety of educational materials linked from this site including a short video about diabetic eye disease. In the video, Rachel Bishop explains the importance of glucose control in the prevention of diabetic eye disease as well as the importance of annual eye exams. She also covers information about treatment of the condition.

➤ National Eye Institute—"Diabetic Eye Disease: A Self-Guided Module," http://www.nei.nih.gov/diabetes/flipchart/slide2_English.htm
This self-guided learning module provides slides and audio to explain information about eye care and prevent developing diabetic retinopathy. The module explains how diabetes damages the eyes and the importance of an annual eye exam, and provides tips on protecting vision.

➤ NIHSeniorHealth.gov—"Diabetic Retinopathy," http://nihseniorhealth.gov/videolist.html#diabetes
This webpage contains several videos for people with diabetes. There are three short videos about diabetic retinopathy under the same heading on this page.

References

Canadian Diabetes Association. 2012. "Vision Health." Canadian Diabetes Association. Accessed July 6. http://www.diabetes.ca/diabetes-and-you/living/complications/vision-health/.

Joslin Diabetes Center. 2012. "Diabetic Retinopathy." Joslin Diabetes Center. Accessed July 9. http://www.joslin.org/info/diabetic_retinopathy.html.

Levin, M. E., and M. A. Pfeifer 2009. *The Uncomplicated Guide to Diabetes Complications.* 3rd ed. Alexandria, VA: American Diabetes Association.

National Eye Institute. 2012. "Facts about Diabetic Retinopathy." National Eye Institute, National Institutes of Health. Accessed July 6. http://www.nei.nih.gov/health/diabetic/retinopathy.asp.

Chapter 19

Cardiovascular Complications

Introduction

Uncontrolled glucose can damage organs and affect the heart and blood vessels leading to serious cardiovascular complications. Patients with diabetes are two to four times more likely to develop cardiovascular disease than those without diabetes (HeartHub, 2012). Cardiovascular disease accounts for 65 percent of all deaths in patients with diabetes and is the leading cause of diabetes-related deaths (Levin and Pfeifer, 2009). Cardiovascular disease is a broad term that refers to a variety of diseases affecting the heart, including diseases of the heart muscle, the coronary arteries that carry oxygen to the heart, the heart valves, the heart's electrical system, and the arteries, veins, and capillaries.

Patients with diabetes may develop cardiovascular disease and complications such as coronary artery disease, heart attack, congestive heart failure, stroke, high blood pressure, or peripheral artery disease. Having prediabetes also places patients at an increased risk for developing cardiovascular disease. This chapter explains the risk factors for cardiovascular complications, describes some of the common cardiac conditions associated with diabetes, and explains methods patients with diabetes can employ to prevent or delay these complications.

Coronary Artery Disease

When a narrowing or blockage of the coronary arteries occurs and causes a reduction or complete blockage of blood flow to the heart, the result is called coronary artery disease. The blockages can result in a heart attack or damage to the heart muscle, severely restricting the ability of the heart to pump. The narrowing of the vessels is usually caused by atherosclerosis, known as a hardening or clogging of the arteries. Atherosclerosis is a buildup of cholesterol and fatty deposits that accumulates in the arteries over many years (Levin and Pfeifer, 2009).

Symptoms

Angina, also known as chest pain or chest pressure, is the most common symptom of coronary artery disease. Patients may feel pain or pressure under the breastbone or in the shoulder, arm, or jaw. The pain is usually worse upon exertion and may ease when resting. Emotional distress may also cause chest pain to occur. Anyone experiencing angina should immediately seek emergency medical treatment. Other symptoms of coronary artery disease include difficulty breathing or shortness of breath, nausea and vomiting, sweating, dizziness, fainting, and rapid or irregular heart rhythm (Levin and Pfeifer, 2009; Cleveland Clinic, 2012).

Treatment

Treatment for coronary artery disease includes medications, catheterization, or surgery. Oral medications include aspirin, nitroglycerin, beta blockers, angiotensin-converting enzyme (ACE) inhibitors, and angiotensin-receptor blockers. Those with blockages may undergo cardiac catheterization to allow the surgeon to perform a balloon angioplasty or to insert stents. Patients with extensive blockages may require open-heart surgery during which the surgeon would perform a coronary artery bypass graft (CABG) (Mayo Clinic, 2010).

Risk Factors

There are many nonmodifiable risk factors, including age, gender, menopause, family history, and race. Modifiable risk factors include blood glucose, high cholesterol level, high blood pressure, and smoking. People with diabetes should control cholesterol and blood pressure levels and quit smoking or avoid starting smoking. People who have had diabetes for more than twenty years are also more likely to develop heart disease than those without diabetes (Mayo Clinic, 2010).

Prevention

Nonmodifiable risk factors cannot be changed; however, people with diabetes can lower their risk of developing coronary artery disease by working closely with their health care team to manage their glucose levels, blood pressure, and LDL cholesterol within appropriate ranges. Those who smoke should quit smoking. Patients should aim for these target ranges:

- Blood glucose: A1C 7.0 percent or below
- Blood pressure: 130/80 mm Hg or below
- LDL cholesterol: 100 mg/dL or below

Heart Attack

A myocardial infarction, also called heart attack, occurs when the flow of oxygen and nutrient-rich blood to the heart suddenly becomes blocked. If blood flow does not resume quickly, the affected area of heart muscle tissue begins to die. Most often, heart attacks occur as a result of coronary artery disease. Plaque builds up in the coronary arteries over many years causing atherosclerosis, which can rupture and bleed, causing a blood clot to form. If large enough, the clot can block the blood flow through the coronary artery, resulting in a blockage. If the blockage is not treated quickly, the heart muscle being fed by that artery begins to die (National Heart Lung and Blood Institute, 2011).

Risk Factors

Risk factors for heart attack include age of over forty-five for men and fifty-five for women, family history of heart disease, high blood pressure, abnormal cholesterol levels, lack of physical activity, being overweight or obese, smoking, and being insulin resistant or having diabetes (National Heart Lung and Blood Institute, 2011).

Symptoms

The symptoms of a heart attack include (Levin and Pfeifer, 2009) the following:

- Chest pain or discomfort that does not go away after resting
- Pain or discomfort in the arms, back, jaw, neck, or stomach
- Shortness of breath
- Profuse sweating
- Indigestion, nausea, and vomiting
- Light-headedness, fainting, or near fainting
- Palpitations
- Fatigue

Diabetes can cause such significant nerve damage that sometimes patients will not feel the chest pain or discomfort associated with a heart attack (American Diabetes Association, 2012). Also, women sometimes do not experience chest pain and instead may feel back or neck pain, indigestion, heartburn, nausea, vomiting, extreme fatigue, or shortness of breath. Symptoms of light-headedness and fainting occur more often in women than they do in men.

Treatment

Immediate emergency treatment is essential to resume the flow of blood through the coronary artery and prevent or limit damage to the heart muscle tissue. If medical personnel suspect a heart attack, they will initiate treatment immediately, including oxygen therapy, aspirin, and nitroglycerin. After confirmation of the diagnosis, the patient will receive thrombolytic medication, which is used to dissolve clots (also known as a clot buster). Other procedures to treat a heart attack include angioplasty and CABG (National Heart Lung and Blood Institute, 2011).

Congestive Heart Failure

Congestive heart failure occurs when the heart muscle has progressively become weaker so that it is unable to pump enough blood to the body's organs. Heart failure can affect the right side of the heart, the left side of the heart, or most often both sides of the heart. Congestive heart failure results from heart muscle dying due to lack of blood flow from a blockage, heart muscle damage from heart attacks, leaky or narrow heart valves, or heart muscle problems (National Heart Lung and Blood Institute, 2012).

Risk Factors

Risk factors for congestive heart failure include the following:

- Age: sixty-five years or older
- Gender: men subject to higher risk than women
- Ethnicity: African Americans subject to increased risk
- Weight: being overweight or obese increases risk
- Having high blood pressure
- Having coronary artery disease
- Damage to the heart muscle from a previous heart attack
- Having diabetes
- Alcoholism, especially in women

Patients with diabetes are at increased risk of developing congestive heart failure because high blood pressure, coronary artery disease, and other heart problems are also associated with diabetes. Patients with diabetes are four to five times more likely to develop congestive heart failure than those who do not have diabetes (Levin and Pfeifer, 2009).

Symptoms

The signs and symptoms of congestive heart failure include (National Heart Lung and Blood Institute, 2012):

- Fatigue and weakness
- Shortness of breath
- Fluid retention
- Swelling of the ankles, feet, legs, abdomen, and neck veins
- Palpitations
- Coughing
- Nausea

Treatment

Treatment of congestive heart failure usually includes medications. Those with the condition may be prescribed one or more of the following medications:

- ACE inhibitors
- Angiotensin II receptor blockers (ARBs)
- Digoxin

- Beta blockers
- Diuretics
- Aldosterone antagonists

Lifestyle changes can also help control the symptoms of congestive heart failure. Patients with the condition should eat a heart-healthy diet. Because patients with congestive heart failure experience edema, they should significantly reduce salt intake as it also causes fluid buildup. People with heart failure should also monitor their fluid intake. The National Heart Lung and Blood Institute recommends that patients with congestive heart failure should lose weight, if needed, and maintain a healthy weight, engage in physical activity as directed by a doctor, stop smoking, and get plenty of rest (National Heart Lung and Blood Institute, 2012).

Prevention

To prevent congestive heart failure, those with the condition should endeavor to lower glucose levels and control any of the modifiable risk factors. Patients should eat a healthy diet and engage in regular physical activity. Also, patients should work with their health care provider and take their prescribed medications as directed. Those who smoke should stop.

Stroke

People with diabetes are two to four times more likely to have a stroke than those who do not have diabetes. A stroke occurs when the blood supply to the brain suddenly becomes blocked, usually due to a blood clot. A stroke causes damage to brain tissue, which can cause complications such as movement problems, pain, numbness, cognitive problems, and difficulty speaking (Levin and Pfeifer, 2009). People with diabetes are more likely to have severe complications or die from stroke than those who do not have diabetes; diabetics are also at greater risk of having additional strokes.

Risk Factors

In addition to having diabetes, risk factors for stroke include (Levin and Pfeifer, 2009):

- Age: being over age fifty-five
- Ethnicity: African Americans subject to increased risk
- Gender: men subject to increased risk
- Having had a previous stroke or a transient ischemic attack
- Family history of stroke
- Having heart disease
- Having high blood pressure
- Being overweight or obese

- Having abnormal cholesterol levels
- Tobacco, alcohol, or drug use

Symptoms

Warning signs and symptoms of stroke develop quickly. When blood supply to an area of the brain develops a blockage, the patient will have symptoms relating to the function of that particular brain area. Some signs and symptoms of a stroke include (Levin and Pfeifer, 2009) the following:

- Weakness or numbness on one side of the body or face
- Confusion or difficulty understanding
- Dizziness or loss of balance
- Loss of vision or double vision
- Sudden, severe headache
- Difficulty talking

Those with diabetes should know the warning signs and symptoms of stroke and call for emergency help immediately if experiencing any of the symptoms. Immediate treatment can reduce the length of time that blood flow is blocked, helping prevent permanent damage from occurring in the brain.

Treatment

Clot-busting drugs given immediately help minimize damage to brain tissue, thus reducing the risk of permanent complications. Surgical treatment of the blocked vessels includes carotid artery surgery or carotid stenting. Depending on the type of complications resulting from the stroke, patients may also see other health care providers for additional treatment including physical, occupational, or speech therapy.

Prevention

To prevent stroke, patients should endeavor to maintain glucose levels in the target range and control any of the modifiable risk factors associated with stroke. Also, patients should work with their health care provider and take their prescribed medications as directed.

High Blood Pressure

High blood pressure, also known as hypertension, is a complication that occurs frequently in people with diabetes, with two out of three patients diagnosed with the condition. Uncontrolled high blood pressure can lead to additional complications such as heart attack, stroke, eye problems, and kidney damage. The recommended target blood pressure for someone with diabetes is less than 130/80 mm Hg (American Diabetes Association, 2012).

Risk Factors

In addition to having diabetes, risk factors include the following:

- Age: the older, the greater the risk
- Ethnicity: African Americans and Native Americans subject to increased risk
- Gender: men subject to increased risk
- Family history
- Being overweight or obese
- An unhealthy diet
- High stress level

Symptoms

There are no symptoms of high blood pressure, so people with diabetes should get regular checks of their blood pressure. The American Diabetes Association (2012) recommends patients with diabetes should check their blood pressure two to four times a year.

Treatment

The recommended treatment for high blood pressure is engaging in a healthy lifestyle and medication, if lifestyle changes do not bring blood pressure within the recommended range. Lifestyle changes include modifying risk factors that are controllable through eating a healthy diet and regular exercise (American Diabetes Association, 2012). Patients with high blood pressure should also quit smoking; they should also drink alcohol only in moderation by limiting to consuming no more than one serving for women or two servings for men per day.

Peripheral Artery Disease

Peripheral artery disease (PAD) develops when blood vessels in the legs become narrowed or completely blocked by plaque buildup, which causes blood flow to the legs and feet to diminish (Levin and Pfeifer, 2009). Many people are not aware they have PAD, which is very dangerous because the condition can lead to stroke, heart attack, or ulcerations that if infected can result in amputation of the affected limb.

Risk Factors

People with diabetes are twenty times more likely to develop PAD than those without diabetes (Levin and Pfeifer, 2009). In addition to having diabetes, other risk factors for PAD include the following (American Diabetes Association, 2012):

- Age: being over age fifty
- Family history of heart disease or stroke
- Having heart disease or high blood pressure

- Being overweight or obese
- Having abnormal cholesterol levels
- Tobacco use

Symptoms

Often, patients with PAD do not experience symptoms. If they do have them, the symptoms may be mild. The symptoms may vary in each person but often include the following:

- Leg pain (often referred to as claudication) that is often worse when walking
- Foot pain that develops while lying down
- Numbness, tingling, or coolness in the legs or feet
- Sores that are slow to heal
- Hair loss on the leg or toes

Treatment

Patients with PAD should try to control their glucose levels, manage their blood pressure, and monitor their cholesterol. Some doctors may prescribe aspirin to patients with PAD to reduce the risk of heart attack and stroke. A doctor will assess the situation and recommend if a procedure is necessary. Surgical procedures such as angioplasty and artery bypass graft can help in the treatment of PAD. During an angioplasty a surgeon will insert a small tube attached to a balloon into an artery. The surgeon inflates the balloon, which opens the artery, and a stent holds the artery open. During an artery bypass graft a surgeon removes a blood vessel from one part of the body and attaches it to another artery to bypass the blocked artery (American Diabetes Association, 2012).

Prevention

To prevent PAD, patients should work toward keeping glucose levels within the target range and controlling any of the modifiable risk factors associated with the condition. Patients should also recognize the symptoms of PAD and visit their health care provider regularly to prevent complications.

Summary

It is important for patients to manage their blood glucose levels to prevent damage to the heart and blood vessels. The damage can lead to serious cardiovascular complications in patients with diabetes. Patients with diabetes are at a greater risk of developing coronary artery disease, heart attack, congestive heart failure, stroke, high blood pressure, or peripheral artery disease. Patients should focus on modifiable risk factors to reduce their chances of developing diabetes-related cardiovascular disease.

Information Sources

Selected Print Resources

➤ American Diabetes Association. 2004. *A Field Guide to Type 2 Diabetes: The Essential Resource from the Diabetes Experts.* Alexandria, VA: American Diabetes Association.
  The guide provides an overview of high blood pressure and cholesterol and contains useful guides for lowering blood pressure and keeping cholesterol within appropriate ranges.

➤ Collazo-Clavell, Maria. 2009. *Mayo Clinic The Essential Diabetes Book: How to Prevent, Control, and Live Well with Diabetes.* Rochester, MN: Mayo Clinic.
  The author provides an overview of long-term diabetes complications, including information on heart and blood vessel disease. There is information about coronary artery disease, heart attack, stroke, peripheral artery disease, and prevention of these diseases.

➤ Hieronymus, Laura, and Christine Tobin. 2008. *8 Weeks to Maximizing Diabetes Control: How to Improve Your Blood Glucose and Stay Healthy with Type 2 Diabetes.* Alexandria, VA: American Diabetes Association.
  This resource contains a short overview chapter of diabetes-related cardiovascular disease. Most important to diabetes patients in this resource are chapters that discuss reducing risk of developing cardiovascular disease and other complications.

➤ Levin, Marvin E., and Michael A. Pfeifer. 2009. *The Uncomplicated Guide to Diabetes Complications.* 3rd ed. Alexandria, VA: American Diabetes Association.
  This resource provides an excellent overview of cardiovascular complications in patients with diabetes. Furthermore, patients can learn how they can prevent these often life-threatening complications from occurring.

➤ Mertig, Rita Girouard. 2011. *What Nurses Know... Diabetes.* New York: Demos Health.
  Mertig provides an overview of diabetes-related complications including information about heart and blood vessel disease. She provides many useful tips on how to prevent complications by actively changing modifiable risk factors through a healthy lifestyle.

➤ Metzger, Boyd E. 2006. *American Medical Association Guide to Living with Diabetes: Preventing and Treating Type 2 Diabetes: Essential Information You and Your Family Need to Know.* Hoboken, NJ: Wiley.
  Metzger's book provides a comprehensive overview of diabetes-related heart conditions. Patients will find the explanation of the various diagnostic tests and procedures of value.

➤ Perrin, Rosemarie, and Seth Braunstein. 2007. *Living with Diabetes: Everything You Need to Know to Safeguard Your Health and Take Control of Your Life.* New York: Sterling.
This book contains information about diabetes-related cardiovascular disease, risk factors for developing heart complications, and information about preventing heart disease, stroke, and peripheral artery disease. The resource also contains some helpful illustrations of the heart and arteries.

Selected Web Resources

➤ American Diabetes Association—"Living with Diabetes: Heart Disease," http:// www.diabetes.org/living-with-diabetes/complications/heart-disease/
The webpage contains links to information about diabetes and cardiovascular disease and how people with diabetes can lower their chances of developing cardiovascular complications. It provides information about controlling glycated hemoglobin (A1C), blood pressure, and cholesterol levels to be heart healthy. The site also links to additional information about coronary artery disease, heart failure, stroke, and peripheral artery disease and how these conditions are diagnosed and treated.

➤ Canadian Diabetes Association—"Heart Disease and Stroke," http://www.diabetes .ca/diabetes-and-you/living/complications/heart-disease-stroke/
This webpage contains an overview of diabetes-related heart disease and stroke. The page lists target levels of blood glucose, blood pressure, and cholesterol, followed by information on controlling each of them. Patients can learn how to reduce risk by employing the helpful tips. The page also provides a link to a cardiovascular risk self-assessment tool.

➤ FamilyDoctor.org—"Diabetes and Heart Disease," http://familydoctor.org/ online/famdocen/home/common/diabetes/complications/647.html
This webpage contains an overview of diabetes and heart disease followed by a list of healthy lifestyle tips to prevent diabetes-related cardiac complications. It covers information about blood glucose control, healthy weight, cholesterol levels, physical activity, blood pressure control, and smoking cessation. There is also an audio version of the site included and links for finding additional information.

➤ HeartHub for Patients—"Diabetes," http://www.hearthub.org/hc-diabetes.htm
This webpage contains interactive modules for patients with diabetes to learn more about heart health. It presents information about the types of diabetes and cardiovascular risk factors. The media library holds a variety of illustrations pertaining to diabetes and cardiovascular complications.

➤ The Hormone Health Network—"Diabetes, Dyslipidemia, and Heart Protection," http://www.hormone.org/Resources/Patient_Guides/upload/FS_DIA_Diabetes_ Dyslipidemia_EN-web.pdf

This downloadable fact sheet provides an overview of dyslipidemia and the reasons why it should concern people with diabetes. It also presents information on why it is important to control lipid levels and includes tips on how patients can improve lipid levels to keep their heart healthy. The sheet includes a list of resources for locating additional information.

➤ Joslin Diabetes Center—"Heart and Cardiovascular Health," http://www.joslin .org/info/managing_diabetes.html
On this webpage, patients should scroll down to the "Heart and Cardiovascular Health" section. The page provides links to a range of information on diabetes, cardiovascular health, and tips for preventing complications. There are also links to information about cardiovascular disease in diabetes, prevention of the condition, and controlling cholesterol.

➤ National Diabetes Information Clearinghouse—"Diabetes, Heart Disease, and Stroke," http://diabetes.niddk.nih.gov/dm/pubs/stroke/index.aspx
The site provides patients with an easy-to-read overview of the connection between diabetes and cardiovascular disease, associated risk factors, prevention, and treatment information. It covers information about diabetes, prediabetes, metabolic syndrome, stroke, heart, and blood vessel disease, as well as prevention tips and treatment information for each.

➤ National Diabetes Information Clearinghouse—"Prevent Diabetes Problems: Keep Your Heart and Blood Vessels Healthy," http://diabetes.niddk.nih.gov/dm/ pubs/complications_heart/index.htm
This webpage contains an easy-to-read overview about diabetic cardiac issues and what patients can do to prevent complications. It explains diabetes-related cardiovascular complications as well as provides information about the heart and blood vessels. There is also information about warning signs of problems and what patients can do to prevent problems from developing. There is a guide to the pronunciation of terms as well as links for finding additional information.

Selected Audiovisual Resources

➤ American Diabetes Association—"Living with Diabetes: Heart Disease," http:// www.diabetes.org/living-with-diabetes/complications/heart-disease/
The webpage provides an audio file of the text on the page, so patients can click on a topic and listen to information about cardiovascular disease. See the description in the Selected Web Resources regarding the information included in this site.

➤ American Heart Association—"Diabetes Media Library," http://www.medmovie .com/mmdatabase/MediaPlayer.aspx?ClientID=89
This webpage contains a variety of illustrations and animations relevant to patients with diabetes. The focus of the information is on avoiding cardiovascular

complications associated with diabetes and includes topics such as high cholesterol, high blood pressure, smoking cessation, healthy eating, and physical activity.

➤ Canadian Diabetes Association—"Protect Your Heart with Our Cardiovascular Risk Self-Assessment Tool," http://www.diabetes.ca/diabetes-and-you/healthy-guidelines/cardio/
This webpage contains a short video explaining the assessment tool's questions, with a link to them, and provides tips on how to reduce risk.

➤ MedlinePlus—"Interactive Health Tutorials," http://www.nlm.nih.gov/medline plus/tutorial.html
Patients with diabetes can click on the links for individual topics to access these interactive tutorials and learn more about some of the cardiovascular conditions associated with diabetes, including congestive heart failure, heart attack, and high blood pressure. The webpage lists tutorials on heart failure, heart attack, and high blood pressure alphabetically under "Diseases and Conditions."

References

American Diabetes Association. 2012. "Living with Diabetes: Types of Heart Disease." American Diabetes Association. Accessed July 6. http://www.diabetes.org/living-with-diabetes/complications/heart-disease/types-of-heart-disease .html.

Cleveland Clinic. 2012. "Diseases and Conditions." Cleveland Clinic. Accessed July 6. http://my.clevelandclinic.org/heart/disorders/cad/cadsymptoms.aspx.

HeartHub. 2012. "Diabetes." American Heart Association. Accessed July 6. http://www.hearthub.org/hc-diabetes.htm.

Levin, M. E., and M. A. Pfeifer. 2009. *The Uncomplicated Guide to Diabetes Complications*. 3rd ed. Alexandria, VA: American Diabetes Association.

Mayo Clinic. 2010. "Coronary Artery Disease." Mayo Foundation for Medical Education and Research. June 29. http://www.mayoclinic.com/health/coronary-artery-disease/DS00064.

National Heart Lung and Blood Institute. 2011. "What Is a Heart Attack?" National Institutes of Health, U.S. Department of Health and Human Services. Last updated March 1. http://www.nhlbi.nih.gov/health/health-topics/topics/heart attack/.

———. 2012. "What Is Heart Failure?" National Institutes of Health, U.S. Department of Health and Human Services. Last updated January 9. http://www.nhlbi.nih .gov/health/health-topics/topics/hf/.

Chapter 20

Mental Health Issues

Introduction

Patients may experience various emotions, from denial to frustration, anger, sadness, anxiety, or fear, when they first receive a diagnosis of diabetes. People with diabetes have a higher rate of clinical depression compared to people who do not have the condition. Depression can interfere with how patients manage their diabetes. This chapter provides a brief background about diabetes and mental health and includes strategies for patients to help them cope with the disease.

Stress and Anger

For those newly diagnosed with diabetes, whether children or adults, there are various stages they may go through when grappling with life-changing information regarding their health. Initial reactions might include stress and anger. Knowing that diabetes is a chronic condition, and not something that can be cured, can add to a person's stress level, which in turn can have negative physiological effects on the body. For instance, when a person is under stress for whatever reason, not just being diabetic, the body releases hormones into the bloodstream that can lead to hyperglycemia (Mayo Clinic, 2012). Likewise, feelings of anger and helplessness can also affect a person physiologically, putting stress on all organs of the body (Napora, 2012).

According to Napora (2012), some of the symptoms of stress and anger to watch for in a person with diabetes include the following:

- Change in sleeping habits—too little or too much
- Change in eating habits—too little or too much
- Weight change
- Frequent crying
- Memory and concentration problems
- Anxious thoughts
- Irritability
- Physiological problems, such as heart palpitations, upset stomach, diarrhea, constipation, sweating, feeling faint, trembling, and teeth grinding
- Sexual dysfunction
- Avoiding work or relationships

Sometimes the cause of diabetes-specific stress and anger is the daily work it takes to cope with the disease as effectively as possible while still living a normal life with family and friends. Coping skills that help with both stress and anger management for patients begin with determining their personality type, such as type A or type B, to use as a baseline for how they handle emotions, positive or negative. One effective stress management technique is meditation for only ten to thirty minutes a day. Muscle relaxation techniques coupled with visualization and guided imagery to envision in detail an optimal outcome for a stressful situation is helpful. Joining an exercise group or a yoga class, after obtaining medical clearance to do so, can also be useful techniques to channel stress and anger in a positive direction.

Managing stress and anger is just as important as managing blood glucose levels and administering medications on a regular basis. Stress, frustration, and anger can occur at home or at work, where cultural expectations demand that people put in long hours and take few vacation days, both of which can have long-term negative effects upon patients with a chronic condition such as diabetes. It is important to recognize that part of a person's daily regimen should include incorporating both healthy physical and psychological coping habits when dealing with stress and anger, because it will ultimately improve overall health.

Denial and Depression

It can be very dangerous for patients to deny anything is wrong with their health because such denial may mean the patients are neglecting to monitor blood glucose levels, take medications, and make appropriate lifestyle changes that could ameliorate symptoms. Patients might want to overeat or make poor health decisions. While this is a natural initial reaction when hearing negative news, patients with diabetes must take charge of their health and modify their lifestyle as expediently as possible.

For some patients, their symptoms of stress, frustration, anger, and denial can evolve into more serious mental health problems, such as depression. It is possible that diabetes itself will cause depression because of the physiological changes it causes throughout the body. Studies are currently investigating the link between diabetes and depression.

While depression and stress symptoms are very similar, the depressive symptoms are generally more severe and last longer. Thoughts of suicide, loss of happiness in doing activities which once brought pleasure, and overwhelming guilt are all serious signs of depression. At this stage, if it seems likely that the patient is experiencing depression, it is important to seek medical intervention for him or her. A health care professional, such as a psychiatrist, psychologist, social worker, counselor, or psychiatric nurse, should make the diagnosis of depression. In some cases, the health care profession may recommend psychological and counseling therapy. In addition, a medical doctor may deem prescription antidepressant medications necessary for a short or long-term interval to ameliorate depressive symptoms.

Anxiety

Related to depression, anxiety is a feeling of worry that is out of proportion to the situation. While it is advantageous for patients with diabetes to be vigilant and concerned about their health because it prompts them to take appropriate action in support of their well-being, there are times when this worry becomes so large that it affects a person's mental health. Studies indicate that those with diabetes are more prone to anxiety, which may be a result of the physiology of the disease combined with genuine concern and worry about the condition (Canadian Diabetes Association, 2012). Some of the telltale signs and symptoms of excessive anxiety include the following (Canadian Diabetes Association, 2012):

- Restlessness
- Feeling of being keyed up or on edge
- Feeling a lump in your throat
- Difficulty concentrating
- Fatigue
- Irritability
- Impatience
- Being easily distracted

- Muscle tension
- Trouble falling or staying asleep (insomnia)
- Excessive sweating
- Shortness of breath
- Stomachache
- Diarrhea
- Headache

If left untreated, anxiety can become depression. It is recommended that patients with these symptoms contact a mental health professional for further investigation and diagnosis. To combat anxiety, psychiatrists, psychologists, or counselors can enlist talk therapy or prescribe antianxiety medication to ameliorate the symptoms.

Eating Disorders

Young adults with type 1 diabetes, especially women, are prone to developing a specific eating disorder that is sometimes referred to as diabulimia (JDRF, 2007). By skipping or changing the dosage of their insulin, these patients lose weight. According to the Canadian Diabetes Association (2012), research studies indicate that 10 to 20 percent of girls in their midteens and 30 to 40 percent of older teen girls with diabetes restrict or skip entirely insulin dosages so they can control their weight. Other types of eating disorders may also coexist with diabetes, such as anorexia or compulsive overeating.

Management of type 1 diabetes is already a challenge for young adults; however, by altering insulin intake, the chances of experiencing a major health crisis, such as permanent kidney or nerve damage, increases dramatically. It is important for adults to be cognizant of this eating disorder and be vigilant for the following signs and symptoms, which could indicate a teenager or young adult is changing prescribed dosages of insulin (Wheeler, 2012):

- Extremely high glycated hemoglobin (A1C) test results
- Frequent episodes of diabetic ketoacidosis
- Frequent hospital or emergency room visits
- Change in eating habits
- Concerns about weight and body shape
- Frequent urination
- Low energy levels
- Irregular or no menses
- Establishing a pattern of extreme exercise coupled with frequent hypoglycemia

If caregivers observe any of these symptoms, they should seek the help of a health care professional or counselor who specializes in eating disorders and request an evaluation of the child or teenager to determine if further treatment is necessary.

Summary

Understanding the relationships between stress, anger, frustration, denial, depression, and anxiety with physical well-being is an important component in the overall management of diabetes. Sustaining a healthy and positive outlook while simultaneously managing diabetes is a challenge, and seeking outside help in the form of support groups, one-on-one counseling, pastoral care, or medication is nothing to be ashamed of but rather is a sign of strength by taking control of individual health in a proactive and effective manner.

Information Sources

Selected Print Resources

➤ Goldberg, Linn, and Diane L. Elliot. 2002. *The Healing Power of Exercise: Your Guide to Preventing and Treating Diabetes, Depression, Heart Disease, High Blood Pressure, Arthritis, and More.* New York: Wiley.
  This book outlines the benefits of various types of exercise and how regular physical activity can have a positive effect on diabetes and depression. There are suggestions on how to customize exercise plans that work for different types of conditions.

➤ Gregg, Jennifer A., Glenn M. Callaghan, and Steven C. Hayes. 2007. *The Diabetes Lifestyle Book: Facing Your Fears and Making Changes for a Long and Healthy Life.* Oakland, CA: New Harbinger.

This resource addresses the daily management of the medical concerns of diabetes and the attendant psychological effects. To aid the patient in making positive life changes and coping with diabetes in a healthy way, the book suggests a psychological regimen called acceptance and commitment therapy.

➤ Napora, Joseph P. 2010. *Stress-Free Diabetes: Your Guide to Health and Happiness.* Alexandria, VA: American Diabetes Association.
Author Napora provides practical tips and strategies for dealing effectively with stress to aid in managing diabetes. The four major goals of the book are to help patients with diabetes prioritize stress reduction as part of their overall disease management; to illustrate what the symptoms of stress are and how it affects overall health; to demonstrate how a more mindful approach to managing diabetes helps to reduce stress; and to provide both a structure and the tools necessary for preventing or treating the stress associated with both diabetes and life.

➤ Polansky, William H. 1999. *Diabetes Burnout: What to Do When You Can't Take It Anymore.* Alexandria, VA: American Diabetes Association. `
A humorous take on a serious subject, this resource provides various tips and mechanisms for the person with diabetes to deal with the daily regimen of managing the disease and the related stresses that naturally occur, both for individual patients and with regard to their relationship with family and friends.

➤ Roszler, Janis. 2006. *Diabetes on Your Own Terms.* New York: Da Capo.
Individuals who feel that they have no control over their disease can experience stress, frustration, denial, anger, and depression. This book outlines strategies and techniques for wresting the control away from the disease and living a much more positive and fruitful life. A chapter addressing stress demonstrates how it adversely affects health and provides suggestions for reducing it, such as getting enough sleep each night, participating in physical activities during the day, engaging in water therapy or aromatherapy, learning how to meditate, and maintaining healthy relationships with partners and friends. If patients suspect they may be suffering from something more serious than stress, such as depression, it is advised they seek professional help.

➤ Rubin, Richard, Gary M. Arsham, Catherine Feste, David G. Marrero, and Stefan H. Rubin. 2003. *101 Tips for Coping with Diabetes.* Alexandria, VA: American Diabetes Association.
This book, written in a simple question-and-answer format, provides helpful advice on how to most effectively handle some of the various psychological aspects of diabetes, including stress management, depression, and anger.

➤ Rubin, Richard R., June Biermann, and Barbara Toohey. 1999. *Psyching Out Diabetes: A Positive Approach to Your Negative Emotions.* 3rd ed. New York: McGraw-Hill.

This book examines the psychological phases that can occur after receiving a diagnosis of diabetes, such as fear, guilt, anger, and depression, and outlines coping skills to overcome these emotions so the patient can better manage the disease.

➤ Warshaw, Hope. 2009. *Real-Life Guide to Diabetes: Practical Answers to Your Diabetes Problems*. Alexandria, VA: American Diabetes Association.
A chapter of this book contains information about stress and depression associated with diabetes and how to deal with diabetes management burnout.

Selected Web Resources

➤ American Diabetes Association—"Living with Diabetes: Mental Health," http://www.diabetes.org/living-with-diabetes/complications/mental-health/
Because diabetes requires people to be extra vigilant about their physical health, they often take for granted or neglect the importance of maintaining their mental health. Having a chronic condition can make people so hyperfocused on their bodies and its functionality that they do not see there can also be a positive connection between a healthy mental state and a healthy body. This webpage addresses three main areas of concern: anger, denial, and depression. Each main issue has a link that leads to an examination of the subject in greater detail, including real-life examples and helpful suggestions on how to address these common reactions to having diabetes.

➤ American Diabetes Association—"Living with Diabetes: Mental Health: Depression," http://www.diabetes.org/living-with-diabetes/complications/mental-health/depression.html
According to the American Diabetes Association, studies indicate those people with diabetes are more prone to depression than those without the condition. Having to address the physical concerns of diabetes on a daily basis can take its toll on any person. This webpage examines the causative effects of diabetes and depression and how, conversely, depression can cause ill effects for people with diabetes because the depression makes patients less motivated to take care of the disease properly. It outlines areas of serious concern and recommends when and how to take action.

➤ Canadian Diabetes Association—"Diabetes and Depression," http://www.diabetes.ca/diabetes-and-you/living/complications/depression/
Depression with diabetes may be a result of the rigors of dealing with the disease, the metabolic effects of the disease on the brain, or a combination of the two. The webpage discusses in detail the early warning signs and symptoms of depression in patients, as well as possible treatments, which include both talk therapy and medications. The page also presents a general discussion on anxiety and eating disorders.

➤ Clinical Center, National Institutes of Health—"Coping with Chronic Illness," http://www.vaprojectaccess.org/file.php/1/NIH_Coping_with_Chronic_Illness_ 1_.pdf

This informational booklet is useful for helping both patients and their family members cope with a chronic illness. It addresses reactions to illness, which include experiencing conflicting emotions, such as anger, denial, confusion, fear, grief, and guilt. This downloadable resource gives practical advice on how to cope with chronic illness, such as acceptance; taking control through knowledge, planning, and problem solving; and joining support networks.

➤ Joslin Diabetes Center—"Eating Disorders/'Diabulimia' in Type 1 Diabetes," http:// www.joslin.org/info/Eating_Disorders_Diabulimia_in_Type_1_Diabetes.html

This webpage provides a succinct summary of the origin and manifestation of eating disorders in children and teenagers, most of whom are female. Young women with type 1 diabetes are twice as likely to develop an eating disorder as their counterparts without the disease, so adults should be vigilant if they see any telltale signs. Compounding the seriousness of handling diabetes, any alteration to prescribed insulin levels can have devastating health results, including diabetic ketoacidosis (DKA), which can sometimes be fatal.

➤ Joslin Diabetes Center—"Mental Health and Counseling Services," http://www .joslin.org/care/mental_health_and_counseling_services.html

This webpage includes a succinct synopsis of the various emotional issues related to having diabetes and a link to helpful discussion boards where people can reach out to other patients for advice. The Joslin Diabetes Center focuses on the following mental health areas for support:

- Adjustment to the diagnosis
- Concerns about not being able to maintain the diabetes care plan
- Eating problems or disorders
- Burnout from dealing with the disease
- Depression
- Anxiety

- Life transitions
- Work and family stress
- Marital issues
- Family adjustment
- A child's school difficulties or behavior problems
- Parenting issues

References

Canadian Diabetes Association. 2012. "Diabetes and Depression." Canadian Diabetes Association. Accessed July 13. http://www.diabetes.ca/diabetes-and-you/living/complications/depression/.

JDRF. 2007. "Diabulimia." JDRF. July 26. http://www.jdrf.org/index.cfm?page_id=107141.

Mayo Clinic. 2012. "Hyperglycemia in Diabetes." Mayo Foundation for Medical Education and Research. June 14. http://www.mayoclinic.com/health/hyperglycemia/DS01168/DSECTION=causes.

Napora, J. 2012. "Living with Diabetes: Managing Stress and Diabetes." American Diabetes Association. Accessed July 13. http://www.diabetes.org/living-with-diabetes/parents-and-kids/everyday-life/managing-stress-and-diabetes.html.

Wheeler, R. B. 2012. "Diabulimia: Skipping Insulin to Lose Weight." Everydayhealth. Last updated February 13. http://www.everydayhealth.com/type-1-diabetes/diabulimia.aspx.

Chapter 21

Diabetic Neuropathy

Introduction

Another complication of prolonged uncontrolled high glucose levels is diabetic neuropathy. Diabetic neuropathy is damage to the nerves resulting from excess glucose injuring the walls of blood vessels that supply the nerves and the nerve fibers in the body. Neuropathy is a nerve disorder that may be extremely debilitating and produces a variety of symptoms, the most common being pain, tingling, or numbness in the extremities. Symptoms of diabetic neuropathy vary depending on the location of the neuropathy. Nerve problems can even occur in the organs, causing problems with the digestive system, urinary tract, heart, sex organs, and in the blood vessels, causing mild or even fatal complications. This chapter provides an overview of the types, causes, symptoms, treatment, care, and prevention of diabetic neuropathy.

Neuropathy is a broad term that includes many different nerve conditions including peripheral neuropathy, autonomic neuropathy, and motor neuropathy. Diabetic neuropathy is one of the most common long-term complications of diabetes, afflicting 60 to 70 percent of people with diabetes (Mertig, 2011). Proper glucose management can reduce the risk of developing diabetic neuropathy. It is important to note, however, that neuropathy can have causes other than diabetes, and symptoms that seem like they may be diabetes related may actually be caused by other medical problems (American Diabetes Association, 2005).

Peripheral Neuropathy

Peripheral neuropathy, also known as sensory neuropathy or distal symmetric neuropathy, is the most common type of diabetic neuropathy. Peripheral neuropathy is a general term for damage to nerves that are in the peripheral nervous system, which includes toes, feet, legs, hands, and arms. Neuropathy tends to affect the feet before other areas.

Peripheral neuropathy can lead to significant complications. Change in gait, which is the way a person walks, results from muscle weakness and loss in reflexes from peripheral neuropathy. Changes in gait may then cause foot conditions such as hammertoes, midfoot collapse, blisters, or sores. Those with neuropathy may not feel foot injuries and such conditions may go untreated resulting in the spread of infection to the bone. If this advanced state of infection occurs, an amputation of the foot may be necessary to stop the spread of infection (National Diabetes Information Clearinghouse, 2012).

Symptoms

Symptoms of peripheral neuropathy generally are worse at night and range from mild to severe. Symptoms of the condition often include the following:

- Numbness
- Insensitivity to pain or temperature
- Tingling, burning, or prickling sensation
- Sharp pains or cramps
- Sensitivity to touch
- Loss of balance and coordination

Autonomic Neuropathy

Another type of neuropathy, called autonomic neuropathy, affects the autonomic nerve areas of the body that control the heart, blood pressure, perspiration, glucose levels, and certain internal organs. Because autonomic neuropathy can affect these organs, a variety of different problems may result, including but not limited to gastrointestinal problems, respiratory difficulty, urinary and sexual problems, and vision impairment (Mertig, 2011).

Symptoms

Symptoms depend on where the nerve damage is located and what parts of the body those nerves control.

Digestive system:

- Indigestion
- Heartburn
- Vomiting
- Bloating
- Diarrhea
- Constipation
- Feeling that food sits in the stomach too long

Urinary tract:

- Frequent urination
- Infrequent urination
- Loss of bladder control or leaking urine
- Frequent bladder infections

Sexual organs, in men:

- Decrease in sexual response
- Difficulty achieving or maintaining an erection

Sexual organs, in women:

- Difficulty feeling aroused
- Vaginal dryness
- Difficulty having an orgasm

Cardiovascular system:

- Feeling dizzy
- Fainting
- Rapid heartbeat

Sweat glands:

- Profuse sweating, particularly at night or while eating
- No longer sweating even when very hot

Eyes:

- Trouble driving at night
- Decreased pupil size

Hypoglycemia Unawareness

People with diabetes usually experience noticeable symptoms when their blood glucose levels drop below 70 mg/dL. These symptoms may not occur in people with autonomic neuropathy who have a condition called hypoglycemia unawareness. This condition results in hypoglycemia being difficult to recognize, often delaying treatment of the low blood glucose level (National Diabetes Information Clearinghouse, 2012).

Motor Neuropathy

Motor neuropathy is a very rare form of diabetic neuropathy affecting the nerves that carry signals to the muscles that cause motion. This type can affect walking and moving the fingers and hands (Joslin Diabetes Center, 2012).

Proximal Neuropathy

Proximal neuropathy is more common in older patients and in those who have type 2 diabetes. This type of neuropathy is also known as lumbosacral plexus neuropathy, femoral neuropathy, or diabetic amyotrophy. Proximal neuropathy typically affects one side of the body and manifests as pain in the thighs, hips, buttocks, or legs. This type of neuropathy causes weakness in the areas affected, resulting in the person having difficulty going from a sitting position to standing; the person will often need help to stand (National Diabetes Information Clearinghouse, 2012).

Focal Neuropathy

Focal neuropathy is a very painful form of neuropathy that usually affects older patients with diabetes. This type of neuropathy develops suddenly and affects a specific nerve or nerve group found in the head, eyes, face, pelvis, back, abdomen, torso, or leg. Fortunately, focal neuropathy usually improves gradually over time (Levin and Pfeifer, 2009).

Symptoms

The symptoms of focal neuropathy include the following (National Diabetes Information Clearinghouse, 2012):

- Difficulty focusing the eye
- Double vision
- Aching behind the eye
- Bell's palsy (facial paralysis on one side)
- Pain, often in the lower back, pelvis, front of the thigh, chest, stomach, side, shin, foot, or abdomen

Risk Factors

In addition to uncontrolled high levels of glucose, risk factors for developing diabetic neuropathy include the following:

- Age: the older the person, the greater the chance of developing diabetic neuropathy
- Duration: the longer the person has had diabetes, the greater the chance of developing neuropathy (The greatest risk is among people who have had diabetes for twenty-five years or longer, but neuropathy can begin anytime.)
- Having high cholesterol
- Having high blood pressure
- Being overweight or obese

Diagnosis

Doctors diagnose neuropathy based on symptoms, physical exam, and diagnostic test results. During a physical exam the doctor tests blood pressure, heart rate, muscle strength, reflexes, and reaction to position changes, vibration, and touch. There are a variety of tests a doctor may order to confirm the presence of diabetic neuropathy in patients who have signs of the condition (Joslin Diabetes Center, 2012):

- Electromyography: This test measures the response of muscles to electrical impulses.
- Nerve conduction studies: These tests study the flow of electrical current through the nerves.
- Heart rate variability check: This test shows how the heart responds to changes in blood pressure, posture, and deep breathing.
- Ultrasound: This test uses sound waves to produce images of the organs being studied.

The patient should remember to request an annual foot exam as well to look for signs of peripheral neuropathy. The foot exam should include a comprehensive evaluation of the skin, circulation, and sensation in the feet. In such a sensation test, the doctor uses a nylon monofilament attached to a handle to touch the foot. This test determines whether the patient can sense the pressure of the touch. Those who cannot feel pressure may have lost sensation and may be at risk for developing foot sores that may not heal. The doctor will also test reflexes and vibration perception (National Diabetes Information Clearinghouse, 2012).

Treatment

Diabetic neuropathy has no cure. The most effective ways to control the condition are through managing blood glucose levels and healthy lifestyle changes, which include the following:

- Eating a healthy, well-balanced diet
- Engaging in regular physical activity and exercise as prescribed by a health care provider
- Losing weight or maintaining a healthy weight
- Lowering and controlling blood pressure
- Quitting smoking
- Avoiding or limiting alcohol to no more than two servings per day for men and no more than one serving per day for women.
- Protecting the feet by abiding by the rules in the list that follows:
- Washing feet daily with lukewarm water and mild soap
- Keeping feet and between the toes dry and using medicated powder
- Applying cream or lanolin lotion to the feet and heels daily
- Performing daily checks to look for redness and swelling of the feet
- Performing proper toenail clipping by cutting toenails straight across
- Protecting feet by not going barefoot
- Protecting feet from excessive heat or cold (*see also* CHAPTER 17, FOOT, SKIN, AND GUM PROBLEMS)

There are medications and treatments available to ameliorate the pain, discomfort, and other symptoms associated with diabetic neuropathy. Some physicians recommend taking acetaminophen, aspirin, or ibuprofen throughout the day, before pain becomes severe. Once the pain becomes severe, it may be more difficult to achieve pain relief. Other medications include duloxetine and pregabalin, which treat the pain associated with neuropathy. Antiepileptic medications and antidepressants interrupt pain transmission, but antidepressants may take several weeks before the patient feels the effect (Levin and Pfeifer, 2009). Additional treatments include lidocaine patches and oral mexiletine, transcutaneous nerve stimulation, and biofeedback. Transcutaneous electrical nerve stimulation (TENS) is a safe and painless delivery of electrical impulses along nerve pathways that prevents pain signals from reaching the brain. Biofeedback is a special type of therapy that uses a machine to teach a person how to control his or her response to pain.

Summary

Excess glucose injures the nerves and blood vessels in the body, which can result in diabetic neuropathy. Diabetic neuropathy can be extremely painful and debilitating. Symptoms of the condition vary and include pain, tingling, and numbness. The condition can even occur in organs causing complications with the digestive system, urinary tract, heart, sex organs, and blood vessels. People with diabetes can prevent or delay the development of neuropathy by managing blood glucose levels and keeping them within normal range.

Information Sources

Selected Print Resources

➤ American Diabetes Association. 2010. *Diabetes A to Z: What You Need to Know about Diabetes—Simply Put*. Alexandria, VA: American Diabetes Association.
This resource contains a short yet succinct section about diabetic nerve damage. The resource uses illustrations and clear explanations to teach patients about the different types of nerves. There is a section explaining distal symmetric polyneuropathy and its symptoms followed by an overview of autonomic neuropathy and its associated symptoms. The book includes several tips for patients on how they can prevent or limit nerve damage.

➤ Beaser, Richard. 2005. *The Joslin Guide to Diabetes: A Program for Managing Your Treatment*. New York: Fireside.
The book contains a section discussing the long-term complications of diabetes and includes a small section about neuropathy. It includes an overview of neuropathy followed by information about sensory neuropathy and autonomic neuropathy. Patients can also read about treatments for the condition and learn self-care techniques.

➤ Colvin, Rod, and James Lane. 2011. *The Type 2 Diabetes Handbook: Six Rules for Staying Healthy with Type 2 Diabetes*. Omaha, NE: Addicus.
This resource provides a section on diabetes-related complications and how patients can avoid developing them. This book includes information about nerve damage, peripheral neuropathy, proximal neuropathy, autonomic neuropathy, and focal neuropathy. There is a diagram of the body that outlines the different types and the nerves and areas affected.

➤ Cushing, Mims, and Norman Latov. 2009. *You Can Cope with Peripheral Neuropathy: 365 Tips for Living a Full Life*. New York: Demos Medical.
While the book is aimed at anyone with peripheral neuropathy, not just those with diabetes, patients will find this resource useful for dealing with the condition. The book focuses on providing tips to sufferers of neuropathy on how to manage

their condition and perform daily activities. Tips include how to care for hands and feet, exercising, living easily, maintaining wellness, hobbies, and travel.

➤ Latov, Norman. 2007. *Peripheral Neuropathy: When the Numbness, Weakness, and Pain Won't Stop.* New York: Demos Medical.
This book contains general information about neuropathy aimed at anyone suffering from the condition regardless of the cause. There is a small section on diabetic neuropathy, one of many causes of neuropathy. This resource is useful because it is a more in-depth resource about peripheral neuropathy and explains the function and organization of the peripheral nerves. Also useful for those suffering from the condition are sections on the management of neuropathy and patient stories. The resource concludes with a useful list of additional resources for patients with neuropathy.

➤ Levin, Marvin E., and Michael A. Pfeifer. 2009. *The Uncomplicated Guide to Diabetes Complications.* 3rd ed. Alexandria, VA: American Diabetes Association.
This resource provides an excellent overview of nerve complications in patients with diabetes. The book contains several chapters overviewing diabetes-related neuropathy in patients. One section contains in-depth information about peripheral neuropathy, its symptoms, diagnosis, treatment, and self-care. There is also a section detailing symptoms of diabetic autonomic neuropathy and its symptoms and treatment. Of particular use is a table outlining self-care activities for people who have neuropathy. The table provides tips for managing bladder and sexual dysfunction, gastroparesis, intestinal problems, cardiovascular dysfunction, impaired hypoglycemia regulation, impaired sweating, and impaired pupils.

➤ Mertig, Rita Girouard. 2011. *What Nurses Know...Diabetes.* New York: Demos Health.
Mertig's book contains an excellent overview of the long-term complications of diabetes and includes a succinct overview of diabetic neuropathy. The book begins with an overview of what neuropathy is, followed by information on peripheral neuropathy, Charcot's joint, and autonomic neuropathy. The section on autonomic neuropathy contains information on gastroparesis, neurogenic bladder, hypoglycemia unawareness, sudomotor neuropathy, postural hypertension, and sexual dysfunction related to neuropathy.

Selected Web Resources

➤ American Academy of Neurology Foundation—"Diabetic Nerve Pain: A Guide for Patients and Families," http://patients.aan.com/globals/axon/assets/8384.pdf
This is a link to a downloadable booklet for diabetic neuropathy patients and their family members. This resource explains what diabetic nerve pain is along with treatment, care, and alternative and complementary approaches to pain

relief. It also stresses the importance of exercise and taking care of the feet. The booklet includes information on finding support and contains links to additional resources.

➤ American Diabetes Association—"Living with Diabetes: Neuropathy (Nerve Damage)," http://www.diabetes.org/living-with-diabetes/complications/neuropathy/
This webpage contains links to information about peripheral, autonomic, and other types of neuropathy. It also contains information about steps patients can take to prevent or delay nerve damage. The page also provides a link to an audio version of the text.

➤ Centers for Disease Control and Prevention—"Take Charge of Your Diabetes: Nerve Damage," http://www.cdc.gov/diabetes/pubs/tcyd/nerve.htm
This short and easy-to-read informational webpage explains the signs of diabetic nerve damage and how to protect nerves from damage. The site contains a list of tips for avoiding diabetic nerve damage.

➤ Diabetes UK—"Nerves (Neuropathy)," http://www.diabetes.org.uk/Guide-to-diabetes/Complications/Nerves_Neuropathy/
The webpage explains neuropathy and its effects on the skin, muscles, stomach, intestines, bladder, blood vessels, and sweat glands. It also includes sections on different types of neuropathy: sensory, autonomic, motor, and gastroparesis. The page also presents several tips on avoiding complications.

➤ FamilyDoctor.org—"Diabetic Neuropathy," http://familydoctor.org/online/famdocen/home/common/diabetes/complications/050.html
This webpage includes a description of diabetic neuropathy, prevention techniques, treatment information, and foot care information.

➤ Joslin Diabetes Center—"Diabetic Neuropathy: What You Need to Know," http://www.joslin.org/info/diabetic_neuropathy_what_you_need_to_know.html
This Joslin Diabetes Center webpage provides information about the causes and symptoms of neuropathy and treatment options for patients who develop diabetic neuropathy.

➤ Mayo Clinic—"Diabetic Neuropathy," http://www.mayoclinic.com/health/diabetic-neuropathy/DS01045
This webpage provides links to an in-depth discussion on diabetic neuropathy. Patients can learn about symptoms, causes, risk factors, complications, tests, treatments, and prevention of diabetic neuropathy. In addition, this page includes links to information about alternative medicine, coping, and support.

➤ MedlinePlus—"Diabetic Nerve Problems," http://www.nlm.nih.gov/medlineplus/diabeticnerveproblems.html
This webpage contains links to various websites that have information on diabetic neuropathy. Because there are many complications resulting from neuropathy,

depending on where the nerve damage is located, users can find information about various types of diabetes-related nerve complications and conditions.

➤ National Diabetes Information Clearinghouse—"Diabetic Neuropathies: The Nerve Damage of Diabetes," http://diabetes.niddk.nih.gov/dm/pubs/neuropathies/index.htm
This easy-to-read informational webpage contains information about symptoms, types, diagnosis, treatment, and prevention of diabetic neuropathy.

➤ National Diabetes Information Clearinghouse—"Prevent Diabetes Problems: Keep Your Nervous System Healthy," http://diabetes.niddk.nih.gov/dm/pubs/complications_nerves/index.htm
This webpage, which is easy to read, explains diabetes complications and how patients can prevent nerve damage.

Selected Audiovisual Resources

➤ American Academy of Neurology—"Patient Education Videos: Diabetic Nerve Pain," http://patients.aan.com/go/videos
This webpage links to a video version of the booklet *Diabetic Nerve Pain: A Guide for Patients and Families*. The video explains what diabetic nerve pain is along with treatment, care, and alternative and complementary approaches to pain relief. It explains the goals of treatment along with the importance of exercise and information about foot care.

➤ MedlinePlus—"Diabetes Foot Care," http://www.nlm.nih.gov/medlineplus/tutorials/diabetesfootcare/htm/index.htm
This online tutorial provides patients with information on how diabetes can affect the feet and includes information about diabetic neuropathy. The video explains the harmful consequences of diabetic neuropathy to the feet and how management of the condition is crucial to avoid infections that can lead to gangrene, which would result in amputation. The section on foot management and care is especially beneficial.

References

American Diabetes Association. 2005. *American Diabetes Association Complete Guide to Diabetes*. Alexandria, VA: American Diabetes Association.

Joslin Diabetes Center. 2012. "Diabetic Neuropathy (Nerve Damage)—An Update." Joslin Diabetes Center. Accessed July 6. http://www.joslin.org/info/diabetic_neuorpathy_nerve_damage_an_update.html.

Levin, M. E., and M. A. Pfeifer. 2009. *The Uncomplicated Guide to Diabetes Complications*. 3rd ed. Alexandria, VA: American Diabetes Association.

Mertig, R. G. 2011. *What Nurses Know… Diabetes*. New York: Demos Health.

National Diabetes Information Clearinghouse. 2012. "Diabetic Neuropathies: The Nerve Damage of Diabetes." National Institute of Diabetes and Digestive and Kidney Diseases, National Institutes of Health. Last updated June 25. http://diabetes.niddk.nih.gov/dm/pubs/neuropathies/.

Chapter 22

Diabetic Nephropathy

Introduction

Diabetic nephropathy, also known as diabetic kidney disease or diabetic renal disease, is the leading cause of kidney failure and is a leading cause of morbidity and mortality for patients with diabetes. Nephropathy is more common in patients with type 1 diabetes; however, many patients with type 2 diabetes also develop the condition within ten years of being diagnosed with diabetes (Melmed, 2011). High blood glucose along with high blood pressure typically seen in diabetes patients causes damage to the glomeruli, the small filters in the kidneys. Protein begins to leak out in the urine and wastes, and fluid accumulates in the blood. This chapter provides an overview of diabetic nephropathy, including causes, risk factors, signs and symptoms, prevention, management, and treatments, followed by an annotated list of authoritative print, audiovisual, and web resources for additional information.

Kidneys

The kidneys are two bean-shaped organs, each the size of a fist, located near the middle of the back, one on each side of the spine. Each kidney contains approximately one million nephrons, each consisting of a small filtering unit containing a microscopic cluster of blood vessels called a glomerulus and a tubule that collects fluid. The glomeruli filter the blood, allowing excess water and waste to pass into the tubule and become urine, which will eventually drain from the kidneys through the ureters into the bladder (National Kidney and Urologic Diseases Information Clearinghouse, 2010).

In addition to the kidneys' major function of removing waste products and excess fluid, the kidneys also regulate the body's salt, potassium, and acid content. The kidneys produce hormones necessary for the functioning of organs and the body; for example, the kidneys produce erythropoietin, a hormone necessary for the stimulation of red blood cell production. They also produce hormones that regulate blood pressure and control the metabolism of calcium (National Kidney Foundation, 2012a).

Diabetes and Kidney Disease

Diabetes can cause kidney disease; however, other disorders can also be a cause of this type of disease. Some other causes of kidney disease include tumors, kidney disorders, infectious disease, and drug injury. So if a patient has signs of kidney disease, it is important for the health care provider to investigate whether the cause is from diabetes or another condition. When diabetes is the cause of kidney disease, it is called diabetic nephropathy. In diabetic nephropathy, excess glucose from uncontrolled diabetes causes damage to the small blood vessels in the body, damaging the blood vessels located in the kidneys. The damage to the blood vessels causes the kidneys to not filter blood properly.

In addition to blood vessel damage due to diabetes, diabetes can injure the nerves in the body and the urinary tract. Patients with diabetic nerve damage may not feel their bladder is full. The pressure from the full bladder can then damage the kidneys. Also, if urine remains in the bladder, a urinary tract infection may occur. The bladder infection can spread to the kidneys causing further damage (National Kidney Foundation, 2007a).

When there is damage to the kidneys from diabetes, over time, a protein in the blood called albumin will leak out into the urine in very small amounts. This condition is known as microalbuminuria. As the condition progresses, larger amounts of the protein albumin leak out, known as macroalbuminuria. At the macroalbuminuria stage, the kidneys' ability to filter the blood properly fails, which can cause the patient's blood pressure to rise. Recognizing microalbuminuria early is important so patients can begin to manage the disease and delay or halt its progression to macroalbuminuria and kidney failure.

Nephrotic Syndrome

Nephrotic syndrome, which is not a disease but a group of related signs and symptoms, can also occur in patients with diabetes. Nephrotic syndrome occurs when the glomeruli experience damage and begin leaking protein into the urine. A patient with nephrotic syndrome may have high levels of albumin in the urine but low levels of albumin in the blood. This deficiency in blood protein results in a fluid dysregulation in the body (National Kidney and Urologic Diseases Information Clearinghouse, 2012b). Also, the patient often will have high cholesterol and experience edema from fluid dysregulation, especially around the eyes, feet, and hands. If the underlying cause of nephrotic syndrome is not or cannot be treated, the patient may develop chronic kidney disease and, as it progresses, the kidneys may fail, resulting in the need for either dialysis or a kidney transplant (National Kidney and Urologic Diseases Information Clearinghouse, 2012a).

Risk Factors

There are a variety of risk factors associated with developing diabetes-related kidney disease. In addition to having type 1 or type 2 diabetes, risk factors for developing kidney disease include the following:

- Uncontrolled, high glucose levels
- Obesity
- High blood pressure
- High cholesterol (contributes to the progression of the disease)
- Older age (sixty-five and older)
- Family history of kidney disease
- Smoking (Patients should not begin smoking and those who do smoke should stop immediately.)
- Ethnicity (African Americans, Native Americans, Hispanic Americans, Asians, and Pacific Islanders)

Symptoms

Generally patients will not have any signs or symptoms of kidney disease until they have lost 70 to 90 percent of their kidney function, so in the early stages most patients do not experience any signs or symptoms. When kidney function falls below 25 percent, uremia develops as excess nitrogen compounds accumulate in the blood and tissues. The excess accumulation of the compounds results in a buildup of fluid, known as edema. The fluid overload then causes the patient to have high blood pressure (Levin and Pfeifer, 2009).

Diagnosis

Early diagnosis is essential so that the patient can begin to receive the treatments that will delay the development of diabetic kidney disease. The earliest sign of diabetic kidney disease is an increase in the amount of microalbumin in the urine, called albuminuria. Urinalysis screenings can measure microalbuminuria; these screenings test a patient's urine to detect substances that are indicative of kidney disease (National Kidney and Urologic Diseases Information Clearinghouse, 2010). There are three types of urinalysis screening:

Signs and Symptoms of Kidney Disease

Early signs and symptoms include the following:

- Excretion of albumin in the urine
- Weight gain
- Ankle swelling
- Increased nocturnal urination
- High blood pressure
- Enlarged kidneys

According to Levin and Pfeifer (2009), late signs and symptoms of kidney disease are as follows:

- Blood urea nitrogen (BUN) levels increase
- Creatinine levels increase in the blood
- Nausea, vomiting, and loss of appetite
- Weakness
- Increased fatigue
- Itching
- Muscle cramps
- Anemia
- Decreased need for insulin

1. Twenty-four-hour urine collection: Twenty-four-hour urine collection is a home-based test. On the first day, patients urinate in the toilet when they first wake up in the morning. For the next twenty-four hours, when patients urinate they must collect the urine in a container, including the first urine on day two. The patients keep the urine refrigerated throughout the collection period. Upon completion, they return the urine-filled container to their health care facility.

2. Timed urine collection: Similar to a twenty-four-hour urine collection, in this test the patient collects a urine sample for a specific time period. Shorter time-period collections may occur in a health care facility; longer collections may take place at home.

3. Spot collection: This screening often takes place in a medical office setting in the early morning and measures the albumin-to-creatinine ratio in the urine.

Because factors such as exercise, infection, fever, congestive heart failure, hyperglycemia, hypertension, pyuria (pus in the urine), and hematuria (blood in the urine) influence the amount of albumin in the urine, the American Diabetes Association (2005) recommends there be two out of three abnormal albumin tests in a six-month period before considering the diagnosis of diabetic kidney disease.

- BUN: The blood urea nitrogen test is a simple blood test that measures the amount of urea nitrogen in the blood. Urea nitrogen is a waste product when protein breaks down. Higher than normal levels may indicate kidney problems.
- Creatinine: Either a blood test or a urine test can measure creatinine. Creatinine is a waste product of creatine, which is a part of muscle. Higher than normal levels may indicate kidney problems.
- Electrolytes: An electrolyte test is another blood test, this time looking for problems with the body's fluid and electrolyte balance.
- Glomerular filtration rate (GFR) of the kidneys: The GFR test measures how well the kidneys filter creatinine, a waste product. The GFR is a measure of overall kidney health and involves using a formula that takes into consideration the creatinine level along with patient age, race, and sex. Patients should have a GFR test annually.
- Glycosylated hemoglobin (HbA1C): The HbA1C blood test checks for blood sugar control over the past three months.
- Kidney ultrasound: The kidney ultrasound is a test that uses high-frequency sound waves to produce a picture of the kidneys. This test can rule out non-diabetic causes of kidney disease.
- Kidney biopsy: The kidney biopsy is a diagnostic test that involves collecting a small piece of kidney tissue and examining it through a microscope. The biopsy evaluates the extent of kidney disease but usually takes place only if there is doubt about the diagnosis.

Kidney Disease Stages

Chronic kidney disease has five stages, each of which is based on degree of kidney damage and the GFR. A doctor will determine the patient's kidney disease stage and base treatment on the stage of kidney disease. The goal of treatment is to slow the progression of the disease to the next stage. Stages 1 and 2 are early stages of kidney disease, and stage 5 is classified as kidney failure. The following list shows diagnosis progression (Levin and Pfeifer, 2009):

- Microalbuminuria: There are small amounts of albumin in the urine.
- Chronic kidney disease, stage 1: Protein is present in the urine, GFR is normal or slightly increased. Some damage to the kidney has occurred.
- Chronic kidney disease, stage 2: There is a mild decrease in GFR and damage to the kidneys.
- Chronic kidney disease, stage 3: There is a moderate decrease in GFR.
- Chronic kidney disease, stage 4: There is a severe reduction in GFR, and the patient should start to prepare for either dialysis or transplantation eventually.
- Chronic kidney disease, stage 5: This stage is kidney failure. The kidneys are not working well enough to maintain health, so the patients needs dialysis or a transplant.

Anemia

As mentioned, in addition to removing waste products and excess fluid, the kidneys also produce hormones. In particular, they produce a hormone called erythropoietin (EPO). EPO is responsible for signaling the bone marrow to make more red blood cells. When the kidneys have damage, they make less EPO; with less EPO, the bone marrow will make fewer red blood cells. The production of fewer red blood cells results in a condition known as anemia. Red blood cells are the cells that carry oxygen throughout all parts of the body. As anemia develops, the body gets less oxygen and the person with anemia experiences increased fatigue, loss of energy, shortness of breath, pale skin, headaches, trouble concentrating, and often feels cold (Kidney School, 2012).

In addition, anemia begins to develop in the early stages of kidney disease, before the kidneys actually fail. Even when the kidneys are still working at 45 percent, they produce less EPO, resulting in anemia. As the kidney disease progresses, anemia worsens. Most people who develop kidney failure develop anemia as well (Kidney School, 2012).

Before 1989, people with kidney disease and anemia would require multiple blood transfusions to treat anemia. Now, synthetic erythropoiesis-stimulating agents (ESAs) are available. These drugs act to stimulate the bone marrow to produce red blood cells, resulting in reduced fatigue, increased appetite, and improved energy levels in patients (Kidney School, 2012).

Treatments

The goal of initial treatment is to delay the progression of kidney disease to the next stage and ultimately delay kidney failure. For diabetic patients, the first goal of treatment is to prevent or slow damage to the kidneys by keeping glucose under control (National Kidney Foundation, 2007a). The American Diabetes Association recommends maintaining an A1C level of below 7 to prevent or delay the progression of kidney disease (Levin and Pfeifer, 2009). The lower the A1C, the lower the risk of development or progression of the disease.

Because high blood pressure increases the chance of progression of kidney disease, control of blood pressure is also important. Patients with diabetic kidney disease should aim for a target blood pressure of lower than 130/80 mm Hg (American Diabetes Association, 2011). In addition, patients with protein or albumin in their urine should be treated with an angiotensin-converting enzyme (ACE) inhibitor or an angiotensin receptor blocker (ARB), which controls blood pressure (Levin and Pfeifer, 2009). Because some research shows that ACE inhibitors and ARBs can protect kidney function, some health care providers will prescribe them even if the patient has normal blood pressure (National Kidney Foundation, 2007a).

In addition to controlling blood glucose and blood pressure, people with kidney disease should eat a healthy diet low in protein because research studies demonstrate this can delay the progression of kidney damage. Patients should also eat a diet low in salt, low in unsaturated fat, and low in cholesterol to manage their blood pressure and cholesterol (Levin and Pfeifer, 2009).

Kidney Failure

Once kidney disease progresses to kidney failure, also known as stage 5, or end stage, the kidneys no longer work well enough to sustain life. For patients who progress to end-stage kidney disease, three therapeutic options are available: hemodialysis, peritoneal dialysis, or kidney transplantation. The health care provider takes into consideration multiple factors to determine which treatment option best meets the need of the patient (National Kidney Foundation, 2007a).

Dialysis

End-stage kidney disease patients have two options for dialysis treatment: hemodialysis and peritoneal dialysis. Dialysis is used to remove waste, salt, and excess water; maintain a normal balance of chemicals in the blood; and maintain a normal blood pressure (National Kidney Foundation, 2012a). It is important for patients to realize that dialysis must take place for the rest of their life or until they undergo a kidney transplant. Dialysis does not cure kidney disease; rather, it performs many of the functions of the kidneys.

Hemodialysis

Hemodialysis performs some of the functions of the kidneys by using a machine to remove waste and extra fluids from the body. The dialysis machine uses a special filter known as a dialyzer, or artificial kidney.

Before dialysis can begin, access to the blood vessels is made during a minor surgical procedure. The patient's blood flows out into the hemodialysis machine, is filtered by the dialyzer, and then returns to the patient via a venous line (National Kidney Foundation, 2007b). The length of hemodialysis treatments often varies depending on how well the patient's kidneys work, the amount of fluid accumulation and waste, the size of the patient, and the type of dialysis machine used (National Kidney Foundation, 2012b). On average, the treatments last approximately four hours and occur three times per week.

Peritoneal Dialysis

With peritoneal dialysis, the patient's blood does not leave the body for filtering. Peritoneal dialysis usually takes place four to six times per day and can be done at home, work, or anywhere the patient travels. During a surgical procedure, a surgeon inserts a catheter to create access into the patient's abdomen. Treatment occurs when the catheter transfers a fluid called dialysate into an area in the abdomen called the peritoneal cavity. The peritoneal membrane acts as a filter, and the dialysate absorbs excess fluid and waste products that working kidneys would normally filter. The used cleansing fluid then drains into an empty bag that will be discarded (National Kidney Foundation, 2007b). While there are many types of peritoneal dialysis, the two major ones are continuous ambulatory peritoneal dialysis (CAPD) and continuous cycling peritoneal dialysis (CCPD) (National Kidney Foundation, 2012b).

Transplantation

A kidney transplant is another option for those whose kidneys have failed. A transplant is not a cure for kidney failure; rather, it is another treatment option. When a kidney transplant occurs, surgeons perform an operation where a kidney from a donor is surgically placed into the person whose kidneys have failed. The one transplanted kidney can perform the function of two kidneys.

Following a thorough evaluation at a transplant center, physicians will determine whether the patient is healthy enough for transplant surgery. The transplant kidney can be from a donation by a living, related donor or a living, unrelated donor who is usually a close friend. Nonliving organ donors who have recently died can also provide the necessary kidney (National Kidney Foundation, 2012b). If the patient has a family member or friend willing to donate a kidney, physicians will evaluate the potential donor to determine whether he or she is healthy enough and determine whether the kidney is a match (National Kidney and Urologic Diseases Information

Clearinghouse, 2010). If there is not a potential donor match, the patient will be placed on a waiting list.

There are risks and complications involved in the transplant procedure, such as blood clots, bleeding, leakage from the tube (ureter) that links the kidney to the bladder, blockage of the ureter, infection, and failure or rejection of the donated kidney (Mayo Clinic, 2011). In addition to these risks, after a kidney transplant a patient must take medications that work to prevent the body's rejection of the donated kidney. These medications cause side effects such as bone thinning, high cholesterol, high blood pressure, skin sensitivity, puffiness, weight gain, swollen gums, acne, and excessive hair growth (Mayo Clinic, 2011).

Prevention

Glucose control will reduce the risk of developing diabetic kidney disease. In addition to glucose control, patients should also control their blood pressure and maintain it within normal range. Exercise and weight loss along with reduced salt and alcohol intake also can decrease the risk of developing diabetic kidney disease. Regular visits to the doctor are important and patients should stop smoking to reduce the risk of developing kidney failure. Patients should also have routine screenings for the presence of albumin in the urine, serum creatinine level, and GFR to diagnose kidney disease early.

Summary

Diabetic kidney disease is a serious condition that can lead to kidney failure. The condition is more common in type 1 diabetes patients but can affect type 2 patients as well. In addition to having diabetes, other risk factors include obesity, high blood pressure, high cholesterol, and smoking. Patients generally experience no symptoms until they have lost 70 to 90 percent of their kidney function. The goal of treatment is to slow the progression of the disease, so a diabetic patient's first goal is to keep glucose and blood pressure under control. Once the patient reaches kidney failure, there are only three options available: hemodialysis, peritoneal dialysis, or kidney transplantation. Glucose control is key to reducing the risk and preventing the condition from occurring.

Information Sources

Selected Print Resources

➤ American Diabetes Association. 2010. *Diabetes A to Z: What You Need to Know about Diabetes—Simply Put*. Alexandria, VA: American Diabetes Association.
   The chapter on kidney disease in this title provides a short, easy-to-read explanation of kidney disease. Patients can learn how the kidneys work, the progression of

kidney disease to kidney failure, symptoms of the condition, and tips on how to slow the progression of kidney disease. This book includes illustrations showing where the kidneys are located in the body and a cross-section of a kidney.

➤ Gilligan, Hannah. 2011. *100 Questions and Answers about Liver, Heart, and Kidney Transplantation: A Lahey Clinic Guide*. Sudbury, MA: Jones and Bartlett.
While also covering information about liver and heart transplant, this resource includes information about kidney transplant. Both patients and their family members can learn how to prepare for an upcoming transplant and learn helpful methods for coping with the emotional and medical aspects of life after receiving a transplant.

➤ Levin, Marvin E., and Michael A. Pfeifer. 2009. *The Uncomplicated Guide to Diabetes Complications*. 3rd ed. Alexandria, VA: American Diabetes Association.
This resource provides patients with an introduction to kidney disease by providing an overview of how the kidneys function in the body and their complex operation. This book provides information on risk factors for developing the condition, symptoms associated with kidney disease, the stages of the disease, nephrotic syndrome, chronic kidney disease, and end-stage renal failure. The book provides tips on how to prevent the condition from developing and how to delay its progression in people who have kidney disease. The chapter also presents an overview of treatment options available to people with kidney failure.

➤ Pennington, Jean A. T., and Judith S. Spungen. 2009. *Bowes and Church's Food Values of Portions Commonly Used*. 19th ed. Rev. ed. New York: Lippincott Williams and Wilkins.
Because people with kidney disease and those on dialysis must limit intake of potassium, phosphorus, and sodium, this guide is very useful in providing users with the nutrient content of many common foods.

➤ Stam, Lawrence. 2010. *100 Questions and Answers about Kidney Dialysis*. Sudbury, MA: Jones and Bartlett.
Though not specifically aimed at people with diabetic kidney disease, this book contains information about kidney dialysis that would be helpful for patients who need to undergo kidney dialysis. In addition to providing an overview of the kidneys and how they function, this resource explains how patients can prepare for dialysis and live well while on dialysis. The book also covers basic information regarding diet and nutritional needs while on dialysis as well as how to live a healthy lifestyle.

➤ Townsend, Raymond, and Debbie Cohen. 2009. *100 Questions and Answers about Kidney Disease and Hypertension*. Sudbury, MA: Jones and Bartlett.
The focus of this book is on kidney disease and high blood pressure, and it also contains a chapter on diabetes and kidney disease. The resource covers information

on what microalbuminuria means to someone with diabetes, how patients should control their blood pressure, the effect of glucose on developing kidney disease, prevention, and treatments. Those with diabetes will also find the remainder of the book helpful in its explanation of how high blood pressure and kidney disease are related.

Selected Web Resources

Diabetic Kidney Disease

➤ American Association of Kidney Patients—"Diabetes," http://www.aakp.org/aakp-library/dsp_kidneyCats.cfm?cat=6
This site provides a range of information for kidney disease patients, as well as a specific section for diabetic kidney disease patients. The diabetes section provides a list of links to a variety of articles pertaining to diabetic kidney disease. Articles include topics such as delaying dialysis, diabetes and kidney disease, diet restrictions, hypertension, living with kidney disease, treatment, managing diabetes, and obesity.

➤ American Diabetes Association—"Living with Diabetes: Kidney Disease (Nephropathy)," http://www.diabetes.org/living-with-diabetes/complications/kidney-disease-nephropathy.html
The webpage provides information about how diabetes causes kidney disease to develop. The page discusses who is at risk for developing the condition and how patients can prevent kidney disease. There is also a section that includes signs and symptoms of which diabetes patients should be aware. Discussion includes treatments methods such as self-care, medications, and diet, followed by information about kidney failure, dialysis, and transplant.

➤ Canadian Diabetes Association—"Diabetes and Kidney Disease," http://www.diabetes.ca/diabetes-and-you/living/complications/kidney/
This short but succinct page contains a description of diabetes-related kidney disease followed by information on how the kidneys work and the effect diabetes has on the kidneys. A section of this page also presents information on screening, prevention, and treatment of the condition.

➤ Diabetes UK—"Kidneys (Nephropathy)," http://www.diabetes.org.uk/Guide-to-diabetes/Complications/Kidneys_Nephropathy/
This brief webpage about diabetes-related kidney disease contains information describing what kidney disease is and how high blood pressure contributes to the development of the condition. The page contains information about the symptoms that follow the development of kidney disease, diagnosis of the condition, treatment, and options for when kidney disease worsens, including dialysis and transplant.

➤ dLife—"Kidneys," http://www.dlife.com/diabetes/complications/kidney
The overall website contains information about the various diabetes-related complications including kidney disease. This webpage, which focuses on the kidneys, includes links to various articles relevant to any patient with diabetes. The article topics include general information about kidney disease, how the kidneys work, causes, sodium and fluid consumption, dialysis, statistics, chronic kidney disease, living with the condition, treatment options, and blood pressure.

➤ The Hormone Health Network—"Diabetes High Blood Pressure and Kidney Protection," http://www.hormone.org/Resources/Patient_Guides/upload/FS_DIA_Dia_HBP_Kidney-Protection_EN-6-12.pdf
This is a link to a two-page fact sheet that provides an overview of diabetes-related kidney disease and focuses on how patients can protect their kidneys from becoming damaged. The discussion begins with an overview of the function of the kidneys and then follows up with the causes of kidney disease, diagnosis of the condition, and tips for preventing kidney disease. The resource concludes with a list of additional resources for information.

➤ Joslin Diabetes Center—"High Blood Pressure and Diabetic Kidney Disease," http://www.joslin.org/info/High-Blood-Pressure-and-Diabetic-Kidney-Disease.html
This webpage explains the importance of managing blood pressure to prevent diabetic kidney disease from developing. The article provides information on kidney disease diagnosis and treatment, stressing the importance of lifestyle changes.

➤ Life Options, http://www.lifeoptions.org/
Provided by the nonprofit Medical Education Institute, this website provides resources for those with kidney disease. It provides a kidney glossary, message board, links, and resources, and a toll-free help line for patients to ask questions about kidneys and kidney dialysis. In addition, there is a link to a toolkit titled, "How to Have a Good Future with Kidney Disease." A number of online booklets in PDF form are available through links. Topics include employment and kidney disease, encouragement, exercise, evaluation, and quality of life.

➤ National Kidney and Urologic Diseases Information Clearinghouse—"Kidney Disease of Diabetes," http://kidney.niddk.nih.gov/kudiseases/pubs/kdd/
This detailed resource provides patients with background information about kidney failure followed by a description of the course the disease typically follows. The webpage provides information about how the disease is diagnosed, effects of high blood pressure on the condition, tips for prevention and slowing its progression, information about dialysis and transplantation, and care.

➤ National Kidney and Urologic Diseases Information Clearinghouse—"Nephrotic Syndrome in Adults," http://kidney.niddk.nih.gov/kudiseases/pubs/nephrotic/

This short but informative page presents in-depth information on nephrotic syndrome. Anyone newly diagnosed with nephrotic syndrome will find the information helpful. The page provides information about what causes the syndrome, how it is diagnosed, and how it is treated. There is also a list of resources for finding additional information.

➤ National Kidney Disease Education Program—"At Risk for Kidney Disease?," http://www.nkdep.nih.gov/learn/are-you-at-risk.shtml
While this is a general resource for kidney disease, diabetic kidney disease patients will find substantive information pertaining to their condition. The resources provide general information on kidney disease, diagnostic testing, and ways to keep the kidney healthy; they also encourage working with a health care provider.

➤ National Kidney Foundation—"Anemia and Chronic Kidney Disease, Stages 1–4," http://www.kidney.org/atoz/pdf/anemia.pdf
This sixteen-page booklet explains what anemia is and some of its causes, including kidney disease as a cause. It explains how people with kidney disease develop anemia, symptoms, treatment, erythropoietin (EPO)-stimulating agents, testing, and diet.

➤ National Kidney Foundation—"Diabetes and Chronic Kidney Disease, Stages 1–4," http://www.kidney.org/atoz/pdf/diabetes.pdf
This twenty-eight-page booklet for patients contains comprehensive information on diabetes-related kidney disease. The booklet discusses the risk for diabetic patients developing kidney disease and advice for preventing it, as well as information on how diabetes harms the kidneys and the symptoms of kidney disease. For those who already have developed kidney disease, it includes information on lifestyle behaviors to prolong the life of the kidneys and information on dialysis and transplant. The booklet also addresses kidney disease during pregnancy. This resource also provides a sample menu plan and recipes.

➤ National Kidney Foundation—"Diabetes and Chronic Kidney Disease, Stage 5," http://www.kidney.org/atoz/pdf/DiabCKD_Stg5.pdf
This PDF file is the second booklet in the "Diabetes and Chronic Kidney Disease" booklet series, which focuses on the last stage of kidney disease—kidney failure—and its course of treatment. Beginning with an overview of kidney failure, the brochure contains information on dialysis—both hemodialysis and peritoneal. There is a section on kidney and kidney-pancreas transplant. Those pregnant while experiencing diabetes-related kidney disease will find a section addressing this topic. The resource concludes with sample recipe plans for diabetic kidney disease patients.

➤ National Kidney Foundation—"Diabetes and Kidney Disease," http://www.kidney.org/atoz/content/diabetes.cfm

This webpage provides comprehensive information about kidney disease and its various causes, including diabetes-related kidney disease. This page is an overview of how diabetes affects the kidneys. In addition, there is a list of early and late signs and symptoms of the condition. This resource presents tips and methods for controlling blood pressure as well as information on preventing nephropathy from occurring. The webpage gives information on treatment for the condition and ways people with kidney disease can keep their kidneys healthy through diet. The site also discusses dialysis and kidney transplants and then follows up with information on the future outlook for patients with kidney disease.

➤ National Kidney Foundation—"Quality of Life with Diabetes and Chronic Kidney Disease," http://www.kidney.org/atoz/pdf/QualityLife.pdf
This sixteen-page booklet teaches patients the basics of diabetes and kidney disease and provides information on how patients can lead a better quality of life. The resource begins by covering information on topics such as how diabetes affects the body and the kidneys, chronic kidney disease information, testing to diagnose kidney disease, and understanding risk factors. The resource provides tips patients can use to live better with the condition, as well as information on partnering with diabetes educators, working with the health care team, and tracking and managing lab work are all provided in this resource.

➤ National Kidney Foundation—"Recipes," http://www.kidney.org/patients/kidney kitchen/recipes.cfm
A proper diet is essential to those with diabetes, and those who also have kidney disease must limit protein in their diet to prevent their kidneys from worsening. Identifying foods to eat can be difficult for people with diabetes and kidney disease. This webpage provides patients with recipes for breakfast, lunch, and dinner as well as snacks and vegetable recipes.

➤ Stanton, Robert C.—"How to Prevent Kidney Disease," http://www.joslin.org/info/how-to-prevent-kidney-disease.html
The author of this article is Robert Stanton, chief of nephrology at the Joslin Clinic. Stanton's article provides a background of what diabetic kidney failure is, the importance of early diagnosis, and how doctors diagnose the disease. He provides readers with a prescription for kidney health that contains five tips for anyone who has diabetes to prevent developing kidney problems.

Dialysis

➤ American Association of Kidney Patients—"Dialysis Information," http://www.aakp.org/dialysis-information/
This site provides a wealth of information about kidney disease. Of particular interest for those on dialysis is a list of articles relating to dialysis. Articles cover topics including dialysis comparisons, costs associated with home dialysis, safety,

the reality of home dialysis, dialysis training, preparation for beginning dialysis, and a dialysis diet.

➤ American Kidney Fund, http://www.kidneyfund.org/
In addition to providing basic information about the kidney, kidney disease, tests, problems, kidney failure, and treatment this website provides charitable assistance to dialysis patients. The assistance is to help patients pay for health insurance premiums and other treatment-related expenses not paid for by insurance.

➤ National Kidney and Urologic Diseases Information Clearinghouse—"Eat Right to Feel Right on Hemodialysis," http://kidney.niddk.nih.gov/kudiseases/pubs/eatright/index.aspx
This webpage explains nutrition for people receiving hemodialysis to help them be healthy. It contains information about proper fluid intake, potassium, phosphorus, protein, and sodium so people can make appropriate decisions about which foods to eat.

➤ National Kidney and Urologic Diseases Information Clearinghouse—"Treatment Methods for Kidney Failure: Hemodialysis," http://kidney.niddk.nih.gov/KUDiseases/pubs/hemodialysis/index.aspx
This webpage provides readers with an excellent overview of hemodialysis. The information includes an overview of what happens when the kidneys fail and how hemodialysis replaces the work of the failed kidneys. In addition, the page includes information about adjusting to the changes of living with dialysis, vascular access, equipment, procedures, tests, diet, and financial issues related to dialysis.

➤ National Kidney and Urologic Diseases Information Clearinghouse—"Treatment Methods for Kidney Failure: Peritoneal Dialysis," http://kidney.niddk.nih.gov/KUDiseases/pubs/peritoneal/index.aspx
Providing a succinct overview of peritoneal dialysis, this webpage begins with a brief description of what happens when the kidneys fail and how peritoneal dialysis works to replace some of the actions of the kidneys. The resource provides an explanation of the various types of peritoneal dialysis available and covers information on how to prevent problems. Information on equipment and supplies for peritoneal dialysis is provided as well as information on how to adjust to the change of dealing with peritoneal dialysis.

➤ National Kidney Foundation—"Dialysis," http://www.kidney.org/atoz/atozTopic_Dialysis.cfm
This webpage provides an overview of dialysis through a series of links. It begins with an explanation of what dialysis is, followed by dialysis myths. It provides guidelines on hemodialysis, hemodialysis access, home dialysis, and nutrition. There is also a section on managing anemia. The resource also provides

information on peritoneal dialysis and eating well while using peritoneal dialysis. The resource also covers information on what patients should know about making the decision to stop dialysis and how to work with the dialysis team.

Kidney Transplantation

➤ American Association of Kidney Patients—"Transplant Information," http://www.aakp.org/transplant-information/dsp_transplant.cfm
This site provides a range of information on kidney disease, including treatment. Patients preparing for kidney transplantation will find the transplant information webpage beneficial. The transplant page contains a list of links to information covering tests, support groups, diet tips, anemia, emotional issues, exercise, hypertension, intimacy, rejection, side effects, and travel.

➤ American Society of Transplantation, "Patient Education Brochures," http://www.a-s-t.org/content/patient-education-brochures
This website contains a range of information on transplants of many types, including kidney transplant in its patient education brochure section. Patients can click on a brochure that pertains to their needs. A brochure titled "Getting a New Kidney" is one of the topics available. This brochure includes facts about kidney transplants, an overview of kidney failure, treatment options, steps to getting a transplant, preparing for the operation, having the operation, and staying health after transplant.

➤ National Kidney and Urologic Diseases Information Clearinghouse—"Treatment Methods for Kidney Failure: Transplantation," http://kidney.niddk.nih.gov/kudiseases/pubs/transplant/
This resource provides an excellent overview of transplantation for anyone who may be preparing for a kidney transplant. This information is easy to read and provides a succinct overview of the kidney transplant process. Beginning with an explanation of what happens when the kidneys fail, it covers how transplant works and the process of obtaining a transplant. It also covers information about posttransplant care, financial issues, and organ donations. The resource concludes with a list of additional resources.

➤ Transplant Living, http://www.transplantliving.org/
This patient education website is courtesy of the United Network for Organ Sharing. Here, transplant patients can find a variety of helpful information to guide them through the entire transplant process. There is information on a variety of types of transplants and how to prepare for the procedure before, during, and after the transplant.

➤ United Network for Organ Sharing, http://www.unos.org/
United Network for Organ Sharing (UNOS), a private, nonprofit organization, manages the nation's organ transplant system. Its website provides a wealth of

information about donation and transplantation. Those being considered for kidney transplant will find information on this site to prepare them for the process. There is also a patient education section with links to fact sheets, patient brochures, and the Transplant Living website (*see previous entry*).

Selected Audiovisual Resources

➤ Joslin Diabetes Center—"Know Your GFR to Stop Kidney Disease," http://www .joslin.org/info/know_your_gfr_to_stop_kidney_disease.html
This short video (approximately two minutes in length) features Robert Stanton, chief of Joslin Nephrology, explaining how the kidneys function and how patients can prevent or slow the progression of the condition. He talks about specific kidney tests that should be performed annually to detect the earliest evidence of the presence of kidney disease.

➤ Joslin Diabetes Center—"Overview of Diabetic Kidney Disease," http://www .joslin.org/info/diabetic-kidney-disease.html
This video (approximately five minutes in length) features Robert Stanton, chief of Joslin Nephrology. The doctor discusses the symptoms of kidney disease, diagnostic tests, and the importance of diagnosing the condition early.

➤ Kidney School, http://www.kidneyschool.org/
While not aimed specifically at patients with diabetic kidney disease, those with the condition can learn about kidney disease, how it affects their health, and how to manage the condition. The learning modules contain information presented online and as an audio file. Patients can work at their own pace through the learning modules, which include information on how kidneys work, treatment options, working with the health care team, following the treatment plan, coping with kidney disease, anemia, understanding kidney lab tests, vascular access, nutrition and fluids, dialysis, sexuality, staying active, heart health and blood pressure, patient rights, alternative therapies, and long-term effects of dialysis.

➤ National Kidney Foundation—"Understanding Kidney Disease and Treatment Options," http://www.kidney.org/kidneyDisease/KDVideoSeries.cfm
This video series is not specific to diabetes patients with kidney disease; however, the videos are very helpful for patients with diabetes to help them prevent the condition from developing. The videos are suitable for those who have kidney disease and need to learn more about the condition. The titles of the videos are "Introduction and Program Overview"; "Your Kidneys and What They Do"; "Chronic Kidney Disease Signs and Symptoms"; "Who's At Risk for Chronic Kidney Disease?"; "Diagnosing Chronic Kidney Disease"; "Choosing a Kidney Failure Treatment"; and "Taking Care of Your Kidneys."

References

American Diabetes Association. 2005. *American Diabetes Association Complete Guide to Diabetes.* Alexandria, VA: American Diabetes Association.

———. 2011. "Executive Summary: Standards of Medical Care in Diabetes—2011." *Diabetes Care* 34 (Suppl. 1): S27.

Kidney School. 2012. "Module 6: Anemia and Kidney Disease." Kidney School. Accessed August 9. http://www.kidneyschool.org/m06/.

Levin, M. E., and M. A. Pfeifer. 2009. *The Uncomplicated Guide to Diabetes Complications.* 3rd ed. Alexandria, VA: American Diabetes Association.

Mayo Clinic. 2011. "Kidney Transplant." Mayo Foundation for Medical Education and Research. November 2. http://www.mayoclinic.com/health/kidney-transplant/MY00792/METHOD=print.

Melmed, S., ed. 2011. *Williams Textbook of Endocrinology.* 12th ed. Philadelphia, PA: Saunders.

National Kidney and Urologic Diseases Information Clearinghouse. 2010. "Kidney Disease of Diabetes." National Institute of Diabetes and Digestive Kidney Disease, National Institutes of Health. Last updated September 2. http://kidney.niddk.nih.gov/kudiseases/pubs/kdd/.

———. 2012a. "Glomerular Diseases." National Institute of Diabetes and Digestive Kidney Disease, National Institutes of Health. Last updated March 23. http://kidney.niddk.nih.gov/kudiseases/pubs/glomerular/.

———. 2012b. "Nephrotic Syndrome in Adults." National Institute of Diabetes and Digestive Kidney Disease, National Institutes of Health. Last updated April 19. http://kidney.niddk.nih.gov/kudiseases/pubs/nephrotic/.

National Kidney Foundation. 2007a. "Diabetes and Chronic Kidney Disease, Stages 1–4." National Kidney Foundation. http://www.kidney.org/atoz/pdf/diabetes.pdf.

———. 2007b. "Diabetes and Chronic Kidney Disease, Stage 5." National Kidney Foundation. http://www.kidney.org/atoz/pdf/DiabCKD_Stg5.pdf.

———. 2012a. "Diabetes and Kidney Disease." National Kidney Foundation. Accessed July 6. http://www.kidney.org/atoz/content/diabetes.cfm.

———. 2012b. "Dialysis." National Kidney Foundation. Accessed July 6. http://www.kidney.org/atoz/content/dialysisinfo.cfm.

Chapter 23

Gastroparesis (Delayed Gastric Emptying)

Introduction

High blood glucose can damage the vagus nerve causing gastroparesis, which is delayed gastric emptying or a semiparalysis of the stomach. In patients with gastroparesis, food moves slowly or stops moving through the digestive tract. Gastroparesis can cause complications and even make controlling blood glucose more difficult. This chapter covers a basic background of gastroparesis, including causes, symptoms, complications, diagnosis, and treatment options, followed by resources for finding information.

Gastroparesis and Diabetes

The stomach acts mechanically to make food particles much smaller through multiple contractions so that the food is able to pass through to the small intestine and provide the body with nutrients. For the digestive tract to work optimally, it requires the correct balance of blood glucose, electrical and motor nerve impulses, and food and water intake.

For patients with diabetes, it is sometimes a struggle to maintain proper blood glucose, which in turn can cause nerve damage. One of the essential nerve bundles, which stimulates proper digestion, is the vagus nerve, running from the brain area down through the abdomen (Mayo Clinic, 2012). It controls both the sensory and motor functions of the stomach and abdomen. If the vagus nerve is not working properly, the result can be a compromise of the digestive system.

Approximately 25 percent of patients with diabetes will receive a diagnosis of gastroparesis (Emral, 2002), and it is more frequently found in patients with type 1 diabetes ten years after onset who have poor blood glucose control. Other causes of gastroparesis include stomach surgeries, hypothyroidism, Parkinson's disease, eating disorders such as bulimia or anorexia, connective tissue diseases, tumors, radiation for cancer, and medications, such as narcotics, which have the effect of slowing down the digestive process.

Managing all the physiological aspects of types 1 and 2 diabetes is challenging, especially if people already have other related or unrelated health problems. Because there is no cure for gastroparesis and its effects can be very serious, it is important for patients to be aware of changes in their digestive system, no matter what the underlying causes. Patients should immediately consult with a physician or other health care provider if there is a noticeable change in the timing of stomach emptying or other symptoms of gastroparesis.

Symptoms

According to the National Digestive Diseases Information Clearinghouse (2012), common symptoms of gastroparesis include the following:

- Heartburn
- Bloating
- Pain in the upper abdomen
- Nausea
- Vomiting of undigested food after a meal
- Feeling full after eating very little food
- Weight loss
- Abdominal bloating
- Variable blood glucose levels—high or low
- No appetite
- Gastroesophageal reflux
- Spasms in the stomach area

Complications

One of the common complications of gastroparesis is the development of bezoars. Bezoars are hardened solid masses of food that have not moved along the digestive tract as they should and can completely block the small intestine from receiving proper nutrients because food cannot pass to it as normal (Mayo Clinic, 2012). When bezoars are present, a person will often feel nausea and may even vomit.

Other complications include weight loss, dehydration, electrolyte imbalance, and malnutrition because inadequate nutrients are entering the blood system. This can disrupt glucose levels in patients and require more or less insulin. In addition, undigested food in the stomach can then cause bad bacteria to grow through fermentation, which disrupts the good bacteria and disrupts the normal digestive process.

Diagnosis

To diagnose gastroparesis accurately, it is important for patients to bring all the medications they are taking to their appointment, because some of the side effects could be causing the condition. They should also report their blood glucose readings, which may demonstrate clear fluctuations caused by gastroparesis. In addition, patients should report all past surgeries, which may have contributed to the digestive system's improper functioning. Diagnostic tests include the following:

- Gastric emptying study: For this test, the patient ingests a small amount of radioactive dye with food, which is then measured with a scanner placed on the abdomen. The test results will determine the rate at which food is passing from the stomach to the small intestine (American College of Gastroenterology, 2012).
- Breath test: First, a patient ingests a meal that contains a small amount of radioactive material. Afterward, a breath test measures whether the isotope is present on exhaled breath, which would indicate the rate of gastric emptying (National Digestive Diseases Information Clearinghouse, 2012).
- Upper endoscopy: During this test, the patient receives sedation and a thin tube with a small camera enters the digestive tract through the mouth (American College of Gastroenterology, 2012). If there are other conditions present, such as ulcers, cancer, or inflammations, then this test can rule out gastroparesis as the cause of symptoms. Likewise, the camera can also detect the presence of bezoars in the stomach.
- Barium X-ray: In this test, the patient ingests barium after fasting for at least twelve hours. If the X-ray shows that any food substances are present in the stomach, there is a high probability of gastroparesis because the stomach should empty after twelve hours of fasting (Parrish and Pastors, 2007).
- Small intestine X-ray and ultrasound: By x-raying the small intestine, the results can show whether a blockage in that area is the cause of the delayed gastric emptying instead of gastroparesis (American College of Gastroenterology, 2012). An ultrasound of the area can also determine if the actual cause of the problem is pancreatitis or gallbladder disease.
- Gastric manometry: After the patient receives sedation, a small tube with the capability of measuring electrical activity enters the patient's throat and moves down into the stomach area (Parrish and Pastors, 2007). Measurement results provide information about the electrical impulses and muscle activity of the stomach.
- SmartPill: The patient swallows a SmartPill, which is a small pill with a diagnostic device inside. The diagnostic device travels through the digestive tract and gathers various data that are transmitted to a receiver worn around the patient's waist or neck (National Digestive Diseases Information Clearinghouse, 2012). Upon passing the SmartPill in the stool several days later, the patient then brings the device to the doctor for further examination regarding its rate of progress through the digestive tract.

Treatment Options

While there is no cure for diabetic gastroparesis and it is a chronic condition, patients should be able to manage it adequately so that the body continues to supply nutrients at their proper levels and the levels of blood glucose remain under control.

There are several treatment options available, and two more are experimental and currently undergoing further testing by the U.S. Food and Drug Administration.

- Medications: According to the National Digestive Diseases Information Clearinghouse (2012), several medications can improve gastroparesis:
  - Erythromycin: This is an antibiotic that helps increase gastric emptying.
  - Metoclopramide: This is a stimulant for stomach muscles that can aid in gastric emptying.
  - Antiemetic: This is a medication from a family of drugs that aids in lessening nausea and reducing vomiting.
  - Cisapride: While this medication was temporarily taken off the market because of contraindications in people who had heart or kidney disease, it is available again for those who are experiencing delayed gastric emptying. This medication acts on the muscles of the stomach to aid in contractions, which improves the digestive process.
- Diet: Adjustments to diet can reduce or eliminate symptoms of gastroparesis. The Mayo Clinic (2012) recommends the following changes:
  - Eat smaller meals.
  - Eat more frequently.
  - Drink water throughout meals.
  - Substitute low-fiber equivalents of high-fiber foods, such as eating cooked instead of raw fruits and vegetables.
  - Avoid high-fiber fruits such as oranges and high-fiber vegetables such as broccoli.
  - Eat soups and foods that are pureed.
  - Exercise after eating.
- Feeding tube: For severe cases, the patient can have a jejunostomy procedure in the abdomen, which bypasses the stomach to deliver nutrients directly into the small intestine (National Digestive Diseases Information Clearinghouse, 2012). With this method, glucose levels become stable after receiving proper nutrients into the bloodstream quickly.
- Parenteral nutrition: If a feeding tube does not work, another possibility is inserting a tube directly into a vein in the chest area, which delivers liquid nutrients directly into the bloodstream. This treatment option is undertaken only temporarily during phases of gastroparesis when the symptoms are so severe that nutrients have to be introduced quickly (National Digestive Diseases Information Clearinghouse, 2012).
- Gastric electrical stimulation: Still considered experimental, the gastric stimulation treatment consists of inserting a battery-operated neurotransmitter into the abdomen (Mayo Clinic, 2012). Operating in the same manner as a heart pacemaker, the gastric stimulator sends mild electrical pulses to the

stomach muscles, helping reduce nausea and vomiting, which are associated with gastroparesis.

- Botulinum toxin injections: Still considered experimental, injections of botulinum toxin injections into the outlet of the stomach can help with associated symptoms of nausea and vomiting (MedlinePlus, 2012). Further studies are under way to determine its efficacy and safety.

Summary

One of the serious side effects of improper maintenance of blood glucose is damage to the nerves controlling stomach muscles, resulting in gastroparesis. When digestion does not occur normally because food is moving too slowly, complications such as bezoars develop, which block the small intestine from receiving adequate nutrients. Likewise, while high levels of glucose cause this condition, once it manifests, controlling blood glucose becomes even more difficult. Patients can prevent gastroparesis by being vigilant in maintaining healthy glucose levels, eating a diet high in fiber, eating smaller portions more often, and drinking plenty of fluids. Additional physical activity is also advised.

Information Sources

Selected Print Resources

➤ Beaser, Richard. 2005. *The Joslin Guide to Diabetes: A Program for Managing Your Treatment*. New York: Fireside.
This book contains information about gastrointestinal complications of diabetes, including gastroparesis and how it can be controlled.

➤ Levin, Marvin E., and Michael A. Pfeifer. 2009. *The Uncomplicated Guide to Diabetes Complications*. 3rd ed. Alexandria, VA: American Diabetes Association.
A chapter discusses gastrointestinal complications in patients with diabetes, including gastroparesis. It also provides an overview, diagnosis, and treatment options for the condition.

Selected Web Resources

➤ American College of Gastroenterology—"Gastroparesis," http://www.acg.gi.org/patients/gihealth/gastroparesis.asp
This webpage provides comprehensive information about the disease, including causes, symptoms, and diagnostic procedures. The text discusses treatment options such as medication, electrical gastric stimulation, and surgical procedures. Color illustrations demonstrate various surgical interventions, such as feeding tubes and electrical gastric stimulation. The page offers details regarding how changing diet can alleviate symptoms and improve overall health.

➤ American Diabetes Association—"Living with Diabetes: Gastroparesis," http://www.diabetes.org/living-with-diabetes/complications/gastroparesis.html
This succinct webpage provides an introduction with basic information about the condition, including symptoms, complications, diagnosis, and treatment options. It also discusses how having both diabetes and gastroparesis can affect insulin intake. Dietary changes can alleviate symptoms while maintaining optimal insulin levels. There is an option to listen to the text of the webpage as well.

➤ Mayo Clinic—"Gastroparesis," http://www.mayoclinic.com/health/gastroparesis/DS00612
This webpages offers basic information about the disease, including symptoms, complications, and treatment options. A symptom checker is available, so patients can determine whether further medical advice is necessary. Color illustrations of the digestive tract help the reader understand which areas are affected. Expert answers discuss how certain foods can exacerbate or cause this condition.

➤ MedlinePlus—"Gastroparesis," http://www.nlm.nih.gov/medlineplus/ency/article/000297.htm
This webpage outlines the condition, including causes, risk factors, symptoms, possible complications, medical tests, and treatment options.

➤ National Digestive Diseases Information Clearinghouse—"Gastroparesis," http://digestive.niddk.nih.gov/ddiseases/pubs/gastroparesis/
This webpage provides an easy-to-understand outline of the causes, symptoms, and diagnosis of the condition. There is discussion of the complications of gastroparesis that can occur if a person has diabetes, such as strategies for taking insulin. It also provides contact information for several organizations for further information and assistance.

➤ Parrish, Carol Rees—"Diet Intervention for Gastroparesis and Diabetes Mellitus," http://uvahealth.com/services/digestive-health/images-and-docs/gastroparesis-diet.pdf
This twelve-page guide by University of Virginia Nutrition Services provides a background on the condition and the connection between diabetes and gastroparesis. It includes an outline of the essential nutrients the body needs, along with recommendations for a specific diet that can ameliorate the symptoms of gastroparesis. There are recipes that are nutritious and will be beneficial for gastroparesis patients.

Selected Audiovisual Resource

➤ Mayo Clinic—"Diabetic Gastroparesis—Mayo Clinic," http://www.youtube.com/watch?v=fACDrGb0T-s
This short video introduces the concepts of diabetic gastroparesis and information about a clinical trial taking place at the Mayo Clinic to improve symptoms of gastroparesis.

References

American College of Gastroenterology. 2012. "Gastroparesis." American College of Gastroenterology. Accessed July 6. http://www.acg.gi.org/patients/gihealth/gastroparesis.asp.

Emral, R. 2002. "Diabetic Gastroparesis." *Journal of Ankara Medical School* 24, no. 3: 129–136.

Mayo Clinic. 2012. "Gastroparesis." Mayo Foundation for Medical Education and Research. January 4. http://www.mayoclinic.com/health/gastroparesis/DS00612.

MedlinePlus. 2012. "Gastroparesis." MedlinePlus. Last updated July 27. http://www.nlm.nih.gov/medlineplus/ency/article/000297.htm.

National Digestive Diseases Information Clearinghouse. 2012. "Gastroparesis." NIH Publication No. 12-4348, June. National Institute of Diabetes and Digestive and Kidney Diseases, National Institutes of Health. http://digestive.niddk.nih.gov/ddiseases/pubs/gastroparesis/Gastroparesis_508.pdf.

Parrish, C. R., and J. G. Pastors. 2007. "Nutritional Management of Gastroparesis in People with Diabetes." *Diabetes Spectrum* 20, no. 4: 231–234. http://spectrum.diabetesjournals.org/content/20/4/231.full.

Chapter 24

Ketoacidosis

Introduction

Ketones form when the body starts burning fat for energy instead of glucose. Ketoacidosis can lead to diabetic coma and even death. This chapter provides basic background information about ketoacidosis including causes, warning signs, treatment, and prevention, followed by an annotated list of print and web resources for additional information.

Ketoacidosis and Types 1 and 2 Diabetes

Typically, ketoacidosis occurs in type 1 diabetes patients who cannot produce their own insulin, and the presence of this condition can be the first sign of onset of the disease. In addition, if a person is under nineteen years of age, he or she is at higher risk of developing this condition. Ketoacidosis can also occur in women with gestational diabetes. If there are not sufficient levels of glucose in the body, it begins to search for other sources of energy in body fat. As the fat breaks down and the body uses it for energy, acids known as ketones simultaneously increase in both the blood and urine. This buildup of ketones can become poisonous to the body, which reacts by manifesting warning signs and symptoms (PubMed Health, 2012).

Type 2 diabetes patients can also experience higher levels of ketones in the body, although it is normally seen in people of Hispanic or African American ethnicity. Because ketoacidosis is such a serious condition, sometimes leading to diabetic coma or death, it is incumbent upon both type 1 and type 2 diabetes patients to be aware of the causes and warning signs and to be committed to preventing the condition from occurring.

Causes and Warning Signs

The main cause of ketoacidosis is improper insulin levels. This may be due to maintenance issues like eating an inadequate diet or not recognizing when higher levels of insulin may be necessary due to another illness. The flu, pneumonia, or secondary health problems, like urinary tract infections, can cause insulin levels to drop below the normal range. Likewise, strokes, heart attacks, and even stress or trauma can be the trigger for ketoacidosis because these can negatively affect insulin levels. Adverse reactions to insulin during sleep can also cause the presence of ketones in the morning.

Patients should be aware of the initial warning signs of ketoacidosis. According to the American Diabetes Association (2012), the major symptoms include dryness in the mouth, excessive thirst, frequent urination, high levels of glucose in the blood, and high levels of ketones in the urine. If left untreated, further symptoms begin to manifest including the following:

- Extreme fatigue
- Flushness and dry skin
- Muscle stiffness
- Abdominal pain
- Nausea and vomiting and an inability to tolerate any food or liquid
- Difficulty breathing, both when upright and lying down
- Breath that smells fruity
- Mental stupor

It is important to note that not all symptoms of diabetic ketoacidosis as outlined in this chapter have much lead time because the condition can manifest itself in as little as twenty-four hours. If patients experience any of these symptoms or signs, they should follow through with immediate home testing for high levels of ketones. If their test confirms high levels of ketones, patients should contact their physician's office immediately or emergency services, if necessary.

Testing and Complications

A patient should have adequate testing materials at home to check both blood glucose and ketone levels in the urine when experiencing any of these symptoms. To test for ketoacidosis, patients should test both blood glucose levels and ketone levels in the urine at home using test strips. There are several brands of ketone testing strips available. For example, one brand is Ketostix; generics are also available. Patients can purchase these testing strips without a prescription. If patients are experiencing the flu or secondary infections, they should be vigilant and check their blood glucose every four to six hours. If the glucose reading shows a level higher than 240 mg/dL, they should then check their urine for ketones.

Depending upon the severity of the symptoms, patients should either go to their primary health care provider or contact emergency services immediately. The health care provider or emergency room staff can also perform additional procedures, such as arterial, amylase, and potassium blood tests, to determine whether ketoacidosis is present.

If ketoacidosis goes untreated, fluid can build up to dangerous levels in the brain and cause cerebral edema, which may put a patient in a diabetic coma. The digestive track begins to lose much-needed tissue and functionality. Further, renal failure or heart attacks can occur, which ultimately may kill the patient.

Treatment

Depending on the degree of ketoacidosis, treatment may occur at home, if mild. If severe, however, the situation would require immediate stabilization of insulin to normal levels. At home, patients can inject fast-acting and smaller doses of insulin. Insulin may also be administered intravenously so that it can enter the system as quickly as possible. Because ketoacidosis causes frequent urination, the patient will likely experience excessive dehydration and therefore will require restoration of fluids by drinking sugar-free beverages or through intravenous methods. Finally, the patient will need intravenous replenishment of electrolytes until levels return to normal (Mayo Clinic, 2010). If the health care provider can identify the underlying cause, the patient should try to address it immediately. For example, the causes could be any of the following: an initial diagnosis of type 1 diabetes, not taking insulin as directed to control existing diabetes, not treating secondary infections properly, or eating an unhealthy diet.

Prevention

According to Polin (2011), preventive measures undertaken during any type of secondary illness are vital to avoiding ketoacidosis. Polin recommends the following:

- Have proper testing materials in the house for both glucose and ketones.
- Ensure there is adequate food at home.
- Any illnesses that cause blood glucose levels to elevate and thus cause ketones to appear in the urine should be reported to a physician, and the patient should seek immediate advice if there is no improvement.
- Test blood glucose levels and ketones every two to four hours until normal.
- Seek advice from a physician or other health care provider if blood glucose levels remain greater than 250 mg/dL for more than six hours and write down the patient's levels for reporting purposes.
- Seek advice from a physician or other health care provider if the patient is unable to take fluids or food for more than four hours or if he or she has a fever for more than twenty-four hours.
- Confirm with the patient's physician whether he or she should continue taking insulin even if unable to keep down solid foods because frequency of insulin dosages may need to be increased during the patient's illness.
- To prevent dehydration, the patient should drink at least eight ounces of fluid every hour. If the patient is vomiting, limit fluid to one to two tablespoons every twenty minutes.

- Limit the patient's activity if his or her blood glucose levels are greater than 259 mg/dL and ketones are moderate to large.

Summary

Ketoacidosis is a preventable condition if patients are vigilant in maintaining proper glucose levels, especially when they are sick with other conditions, such as the flu, pneumonia, or secondary infections. While it is typically found in those with type 1 diabetes, those with type 2 diabetes should also be aware of the signs and symptoms because, while rare, ketoacidosis can still occur, especially in Hispanics and African American patients. Those who are on insulin pump therapy need to check both blood glucose and ketone levels, because equipment malfunctions can also lead to ketoacidosis if the machine is not supplying an adequate supply of insulin to the patient.

Information Sources

Selected Print Resources

➤ American Diabetes Association. 2011. *American Diabetes Association Complete Guide to Diabetes.* 5th ed. Alexandria, VA: American Diabetes Association.
This book details information about ketones and how a person can develop diabetic ketoacidosis, as well as the symptoms associated with the condition. The chapter discussing diabetic tools provides information about test strips for urine ketones and how patients can use the strips as indicated to test for ketoacidosis. Another chapter on blood glucose emergencies has a subsection on type 1 diabetes and ketoacidosis.

➤ Beaser, Richard. 2005. *The Joslin Guide to Diabetes: A Program for Managing Your Treatment.* New York: Fireside.
The author stresses the importance of glucose control to prevent ketones from developing. The book provides information on ketoacidosis and how it develops and the symptoms associated with the condition, as well as information on checking for ketones using urine ketone strips.

➤ Betschart-Roemer, Jean. 2011. *American Diabetes Association Guide to Raising a Child with Diabetes.* 3rd ed. Alexandria, VA: American Diabetes Association.
This book is an introduction to type 1 diabetes for parents who want to help their child manage the disease effectively while still maintaining a normal lifestyle. There is a separate section discussing diabetic ketoacidosis, including the telltale symptoms a parent should be aware of regarding the condition. Betschart-Roemer recommends that parents should call a physician immediately if they witness the following symptoms: moderate or high levels of ketones in

the blood; dehydration symptoms such as sunken eyes, cracked lips, and dry mouth; persistent vomiting; changes in alertness or drowsiness; breathing that is hard; breath that smells fruity; and abdominal pain. The book also provides tips on ways to prevent and treat ketoacidosis.

➤ Garnero, Theresa. 2008. *Your First Year with Diabetes: What to Do, Month by Month*. Alexandria, VA: American Diabetes Association.
For those newly diagnosed with diabetes, this book provides an overview of the disease and its associated complications, including diabetic ketoacidosis. It also provides additional information on prevention, symptoms, and how to test for ketones.

➤ Levin, Marvin E., and Michael A. Pfeifer. 2009. *The Uncomplicated Guide to Diabetes Complications*. 3rd ed. Alexandria, VA: American Diabetes Association.
This book provides a chapter with an overview about diabetic ketoacidosis. It begins by explaining what ketoacidosis is, followed by the causes of ketoacidosis and what it means to have the condition. It lists the risk factors along with the symptoms, treatment options, and prevention.

➤ Scheiner, Gary. 2004. *Think Like a Pancreas: A Practical Guide to Managing Diabetes with Insulin*. New York: Marlowe.
Written by a patient who is also a certified diabetes educator and exercise physiologist, this book provides an easy-to-understand framework for patients to manage their condition. It includes a separate chapter on what to do when insulin does not meet a patient's current needs, including too much or too little. While hyperglycemia is something that is easily treated, an extreme case of too little insulin can result in diabetic ketoacidosis. This book also provides strategies for both the prevention and treatment of diabetic ketoacidosis.

Selected Web Resources

➤ American Diabetes Association—"Living with Diabetes: Ketoacidosis (DKA)," http://www.diabetes.org/living-with-diabetes/complications/ketoacidosis-dka.html
This succinct webpage provides a background of diabetic ketoacidosis and describes how the condition is extremely dangerous if untreated. While the condition can progress slowly, when it manifests itself, it does so quickly. The page outlines the warning signs in detail and recommends that patients with diabetes experiencing these symptoms should proceed to an emergency room or call 911 immediately. The resource includes information on how to test ketones in the urine and what the course of action should be if the levels are too high. The pages also discusses the causes of ketoacidosis.

➤ Joslin Diabetes Center—"Ketone Testing: What You Need to Know," http://www .joslin.org/info/ketone-testing-for-people-with-diabetes.html

This succinct information sheet provides the basics on ketone testing, including what ketones are, how to test for ketones, when testing should be done, and the health implications if ketones are present. If patients test and find ketones, Joslin Diabetes Center recommends contacting a physician or diabetes educator to determine if there is a need for additional insulin.

➤ Mayo Clinic—"Diabetic Ketoacidosis," http://www.mayoclinic.com/health/ diabetic-ketoacidosis/DS00674
This webpage presents a basic definition of ketoacidosis as well as an outline of the symptoms, which often mimic other illnesses such as the flu. It recommends when to elevate concerns about symptoms to a medical professional or to seek emergency care. There is a brief section on the causes of ketoacidosis, including illnesses such as pneumonia and urinary tract infections that can lead to the condition. Not managing insulin properly can also lead to ketoacidosis because there is not enough insulin in the body. Discussion includes other triggers for the condition, such as stress, stroke, heart attack, emotional trauma, or alcohol abuse. There is a summary of risk factors and complications as well as details about the various tests that can detect the condition. The section provides a description of the treatment regimen for ketoacidosis along with preventive steps to ensure the condition does not occur.

➤ MedlinePlus—"Diabetic Ketoacidosis," http://www.nlm.nih.gov/medlineplus/ ency/article/000320.htm
This webpage provides a summary of the causes and risk factors associated with ketoacidosis and underscores that while it is normally seen in people with type 1 diabetes, it is also possible for those with type 2 diabetes, especially those of Hispanic or African American ethnicity, to develop the condition. The section outlines the general symptoms and warning signs, such as rapid breathing, flushed face, fruity odor in the breath, stomach pain, fatigue, mental stupor, muscle stiffness, abdominal pain, and frequent urination and excessive thirst lasting more than a day. There is a summary of the signs and tests used to confirm ketoacidosis, with links to more detailed information on arterial blood gas, amylase blood tests, and potassium blood tests. The webpages explains treatment and prognosis, along with resulting complications that can occur. The article provides further guidance on when patients should contact their health care provider or request emergency services.

➤ Penn Medicine—"Health Encyclopedia: Diabetic Ketoacidosis," http://www .pennmedicine.org/encyclopedia/em_DisplayArticle.aspx?gcid=000320&ptid
From the University of Pennsylvania's School of Medicine's health encyclopedia, this webpage provides a summary of the condition, its causes, incidence, risk factors, symptoms, tests to determine if the condition exists, and treatment

options. It is in easy-to-understand language and can be a good starting point when looking for basic information about ketoacidosis.

➤ Polin, Bonnie Sanders—"Ketoacidosis: A Diabetes Complication," http://www .diabeticlifestyle.com/type-1-diabetes/ketoacidosis-diabetes-complication
The article, appearing on the Diabetic Lifestyle website, emphasizes that both diabetic ketoacidosis (DKA) and hyperglycemic hyperosmolar state (HHS) are two serious conditions that patients can avoid with proper maintenance of insulin. The incidence rates of both conditions are increasing, which means that patients need increased education and awareness regarding the signs, symptoms, and preventive measures to help them avoid the onset of these conditions. The page provides an outline of the symptoms patients should recognize and the tests they may need, along with the treatment course of action. There is an emphasis on preventive measures to follow, along with tips on how and when to test for ketones when experiencing another illness, such as the flu or pneumonia.

References

American Diabetes Association. 2012. "Living with Diabetes: Ketoacidosis (DKA)." American Diabetes Association. Accessed July 6. http://www.diabetes.org/living-with-diabetes/complications/ketoacidosis-dka.html.

Mayo Clinic. 2010. "Diabetic Ketoacidosis." Mayo Foundation for Medical Education and Research. May 14. http://www.mayoclinic.com/health/diabetic-ketoacidosis/DS00674.

Polin, B. S. 2011. "Diabetic Lifestyle—Ketoacidosis: A Diabetes Complication." Diabetic Lifestylehttp://www.diabeticlifestyle.com/type-1-diabetes/ketoacidosis-diabetes-complication.

PubMed Health. 2012. "Diabetic Ketoacidosis." U.S. National Library of Medicine. Last reviewed June 4. http://www.ncbi.nlm.nih.gov/pubmedhealth/PMH0001363/.

Chapter 25

Sexual and Urological Problems

Introduction

Urological and sexual complications result from blood vessel and nerve damage caused by diabetes. Both of these conditions commonly occur as people age; however, having diabetes, particularly with high glucose levels, can lead to more severe urological and sexual complications and occurring at a younger age (National Diabetes and Information Clearinghouse, 2008). Improved glucose control can delay or prevent sexual and urological complications from developing. Those patients exhibiting problems with sexual activity or with urologic complications can often improve their condition with improved glucose control. This chapter provides an overview of the urological and sexual problems found in both men and women with diabetes. It concludes with an annotated list of print, web, and audiovisual resources about urological complications and sexual problems in men and women.

Urological Problems

Uncontrolled high glucose in the body can lead to urological problems in both men and women with diabetes. Over time, high blood glucose can cause damage to blood vessels and to nerves. This damage can lead to urinary problems, including bladder and urinary tract complications.

Bladder Problems

Both men and women with diabetes may suffer from nerve damage that leads to bladder complications, severely impacting their quality of life. Some of the bladder complications that can occur due to diabetes are overactive bladder, poor control of sphincter muscles, and urine retention. A physician will use diagnostic testing to evaluate bladder problems and confirm the diagnosis. Treatment will depend on the specific problem and the cause. The medical team may recommend medications, catheterizations, Kegel exercises (which strengthen pelvic muscles), or surgery to control the diabetes-associated bladder problems.

Those patients with overactive bladder feel a strong urge to urinate, urinate frequently day and night, and may have urinary leakage. Overactive bladder results when the damaged nerves errantly send the bladder signals that result in a contraction

273

of the bladder muscle (National Diabetes Information Clearinghouse, 2012). Diabetes may damage the sphincter muscles and cause problems. Patients with poor sphincter muscle control surrounding the urethra (the tube that carries urine from the bladder to the outside) may leak urine, or the muscles may stay tight making urination difficult (National Diabetes Information Clearinghouse, 2012).

Urine retention can also result from diabetic nerve damage. The damaged nerves send the bladder muscles the wrong message about when it is time to urinate, and the muscles are too weak to empty the bladder. The urine remains in the body too long, which may result in an infection in the kidneys or the bladder, or it may cause incontinence when the bladder becomes full and leaks urine (National Diabetes Information Clearinghouse, 2012).

Infections

Urinary Tract Infections

People with diabetes, particularly those with poor glucose control, are at risk for developing urinary tract infections. Infections occur when bacteria enter the urinary tract. High blood glucose causes the cells of the body's immune system to be less effective than normal in destroying bacteria. Bacteria that enter the urethra cause an infection called urethritis; if the bacteria enter the bladder, the resultant infection is called cystitis. Infections that remain untreated can result in a kidney infection, called pyelonephritis. People with urinary tract infections may exhibit symptoms of frequent urination, urinary pain and burning, painful sexual intercourse, cloudy urine, pressure above the pubic bone in women, and a feeling of fullness in the rectum in men (National Diabetes Information Clearinghouse, 2012).

Genital Infections

Genital infections occur even more frequently in people with diabetes and tend to be the result of a fungus that causes yeast infections. Yeast infections may occur more frequently due to the high level of glucose in the bladder; in women, the vaginal fluid may contain a high level of glucose. Yeast infections can affect the vagina in women and the top of the penis in men. Symptoms of a yeast infection include a thick white vaginal discharge similar to cottage cheese, pain during intercourse, painful urination, redness and swelling, and vaginal itching and burning. Over-the-counter medications are available to treat yeast infections (Eisenstat, 2007).

Sexual Problems

Sexual problems result from damage to the nerves and small blood vessels. Diabetic neuropathy (*see* CHAPTER 21, DIABETIC NEUROPATHY) can cause problems with the body's autonomic nervous system. A type of neuropathy, called autonomic neuropathy, affects the autonomic nerve areas of the body that control the heart, blood pressure, perspiration, glucose levels, and specific internal organs. Because this type of neuropathy affects organs, a range of problems may result, including but not limited to gastrointestinal problems, respiratory difficulty, urinary problems, vision difficulty, and sexual problems.

Because the body's response to sexual stimuli is a function of the autonomic nervous system, patients with diabetic neuropathy may develop sexual dysfunction. In addition to neuropathy, patients also have blood vessel damage from high blood glucose levels. Blood vessel damage may cause restricted blood flow through the damaged vessels, also contributing to problems with sexual activity (National Diabetes Information Clearinghouse, 2012).

Sexual problems can occur in both men and women with diabetes. Men may experience complications such as erectile dysfunction or retrograde ejaculation. Women may experience problems such as vaginal dryness, pain during intercourse, or lack of sexual desire. Complicating these problems is the reluctance of men and women to talk to their health care provider if they are experiencing problems with sexual activity. Many men and women find it embarrassing to talk about sexual dysfunction; others believe it is a natural part of aging and no therapies will be able to improve sexual function.

Males

Erectile Dysfunction

Erectile dysfunction (ED) is defined as "the inability to get or keep an erection firm enough for sexual intercourse" (National Kidney and Urologic Diseases Information Clearinghouse, 2012). ED can result in the inability to attain an erection, an ability to sustain only brief erections, or an inconsistent ability to achieve an erection. Erectile dysfunction may sometimes be referred to as impotence; however, this word is often used to describe other sexual problems, such as lack of desire, ejaculation problems, or problems achieving orgasm. Approximately 35 to 50 percent of men with diabetes experience ED (dLife, 2012).

Erectile dysfunction is treatable in men of any age, so men who experience ED should consult with a health care provider. The health care provider may perform a physical exam, consider the patient's medical history and medications, and order lab tests to find the cause of the ED. The physician may also order a test to monitor for sleep erections/nocturnal erections to rule out psychological causes of ED (National Kidney and Urologic Diseases Information Clearinghouse, 2012).

After determining the cause of the ED, the medical team may recommend any of a variety of treatment options, including psychotherapy, medications, vacuum devices, and surgery (National Diabetes Information Clearinghouse, 2012). Before beginning these treatments, health care providers recommend first making lifestyle changes, such as quitting smoking, drinking less alcohol, and losing weight. In addition, if it is thought that a medication may be the cause, the health care provider can look for alternative medications for the patient (National Kidney and Urologic Diseases Information Clearinghouse, 2012).

There are a variety of medications used in the treatment of ED, including both oral and injected medications. Oral medications include a class of drugs called phosphodiesterase-5 (PDE5) inhibitors. PDE5 inhibitors work by relaxing the smooth muscles in the penis and increasing the blood flow during sexual stimulation, which causes an erection. The medications in this class include sildenafil (Viagra), vardenafil HCl (Levitra), and tadalafil (Cialis) (National Kidney and Urologic Diseases Information Clearinghouse, 2012). Patients should take these medications an hour before sexual activity. PDE5 inhibitors do not cause automatic erections but improve the patient's response to sexual stimulation (dLife, 2010).

Injectable medications, however, will cause an automatic, strong erection several minutes following injection into the penis. Injectable drugs include papaverine hydrochloride, phentolamine, and alprostadil, with the injectable form called Caverject. These drugs work by widening the blood vessels in the penis. These drugs sometimes cause side effects such as scarring of the penis and priapism, which is a persistent painful erection (National Kidney and Urologic Diseases Information Clearinghouse, 2012).

Vacuum devices create a partial vacuum that will draw blood into the penis, causing it to expand. Vacuum devices include a plastic cylinder, a pump, and an elastic ring. The patient places the penis in the plastic cylinder, and the pump draws air out of the cylinder. The patient keeps the plastic ring in place at the base of the penis after the cylinder is removed. The plastic ring prevents blood from flowing out of the penis and back into the body and maintains the erection. It can stay in place for no longer than thirty minutes, at which point it should be removed (National Kidney and Urologic Diseases Information Clearinghouse, 2012).

Surgical therapy is also available to treat erectile dysfunction. Surgery is an option for men who are unable to maintain an erection sufficient for sex using other treatment options. Surgical procedures can implant a device to cause an erection; reconstruct arteries, increasing blood flow to the penis; or block veins to prevent blood from flowing out of the penis back into the body (National Kidney and Urologic Diseases Information Clearinghouse, 2012).

Penile implants are an option for patients who are not able to achieve an erection sufficient enough for sex even with other treatment methods. There are two types of penile implants: inflatable implants and semirigid rods. Inflatable implants are the most common implant. There are two types of inflatable implants: the two-piece model and a three-piece model (Mayo Clinic, 2011a). Patients inflate these implants during sexual activity to create an erection and then deflate them at other times. While inflatable implants are less likely to damage the inside of the penis than could be caused by the constant pressure received from semirigid implants, they are complicated to use, harder to place during surgery, and have a higher risk of failure (Mayo Clinic, 2011a).

Semirigid rods are firm rods implanted into the penis, causing a constantly firm penis. The patient can bend the penis toward the body to conceal it when not having sex. This type of implant is less common than the inflatable type of penile implant but is much less complicated (Mayo Clinic, 2011a).

Surgical penile implant risks include infection, implant problems, internal erosion, or adhesion. Patients with diabetes or other chronic medical conditions are generally at a higher risk for developing infections (Mayo Clinic, 2011a).

Retrograde Ejaculation

Normally during orgasm, also known as sexual climax, semen exits the penis. In patients with retrograde ejaculation, during orgasm the semen flows backward and enters the bladder instead of leaving through the penis. In the bladder the semen is destroyed. Retrograde ejaculation causes male infertility because the penis ejaculates little or no semen (Mayo Clinic, 2011b).

Nerve damage from diabetes, prostate surgery, and some medications may cause retrograde ejaculation. Because of diabetic nerve damage, the internal muscles, called sphincters, do not function properly. The sphincter does not open and close properly and instead causes semen to enter the bladder instead of exiting through the penis (National Diabetes Information Clearinghouse, 2012). Symptoms of the condition include little to no semen in the ejaculate, cloudy urine after orgasm, and male infertility (Mayo Clinic, 2011b).

While retrograde ejaculation is not harmful and men are able to have sexual intercourse, men who would like to be able to produce children are likely to seek medical attention to address the resultant infertility from very little semen in the ejaculate. There are medications available to strengthen the muscle tone of the bladder sphincter, which may help reverse retrograde ejaculation. In addition, infertility treatments are available that make it possible to collect sperm from the urine for use in artificial insemination (National Diabetes Information Clearinghouse, 2012).

Females

Sexual complications are common among women with type 1 or type 2 diabetes. Many factors may contribute to sexual difficulty in women, including nerve damage, reduction in blood flow to the genital area, and hormonal changes. Additional causes of sexual problems in women include alcohol abuse, smoking, psychological problems, infections, diseases, pregnancy, and menopause (National Diabetes Information Clearinghouse, 2012). These complications from diabetes can lead to decreased vaginal lubrication and painful intercourse, lack of sexual desire, and decreased sexual responsiveness.

The most common sexual problem in women with diabetes is vaginal dryness. During sexual activity, natural lubrication of the vagina does not occur, which leads to painful sexual intercourse and decreased ability to have an orgasm (Eisenstat, 2007). Some medications and lower estrogen levels after menopause can also increase the risk for vaginal dryness (Eisenstat, 2007). A common treatment for vaginal dryness is the use of prescription or over-the-counter water-based lubricants, such as K-Y Brand Jelly, during sexual intercourse.

Some women with diabetes may experience decreased sexual desire. Researchers are uncertain why this decreased sexual drive occurs, but some speculate having a chronic condition may cause anxiety, stress, or depression, which can then lead to low or no sexual desire (American Diabetes Association, 2012b). Sometimes medication or counseling can ameliorate the anxiety or depression that may lead to this condition.

Another common problem is decreased sexual response or lack of sexual response. Again, researchers are unaware of the cause in some women with diabetes. Anxiety and depression could be causes, and women may have a better response after drug therapy or counseling. Some find Kegel exercises, which strengthen the pelvic muscles, improve sexual response (National Diabetes Information Clearinghouse, 2012).

Hormones and Menstrual Cycle

Many women with diabetes experience difficulty in controlling glucose levels the week before and the week of their period. The rise in hormone levels about a week before a woman's period may cause blood glucose to increase, making glucose control difficult. In addition, women typically eat more sweets and carbohydrates before their period, exercise less, and feel bloated, which can all lead to difficulty with glucose control. Women who experience premenstrual syndrome (PMS) have difficulty with glucose control near the time of their periods (Eisenstat, 2007). Women with diabetes, especially younger and obese women, often have more irregular periods than women who do not have the condition. Poor glucose control can lead to the absence of periods for one or more cycles. Some women may also experience heavy bleeding, lengthy periods, and longer than normal cycles (Eisenstat, 2007). The American Diabetes Association (2012b) recommends that women who experience hormonal problems talk to their health care team to develop a plan to keep glucose levels under control.

Contraception

Women with diabetes should carefully plan any pregnancy to prepare for the safest pregnancy possible. Women in their forties or fifties can still become pregnant. Women who do not wish to become pregnant should continue to use birth control until periods have stopped for more than a year. For women who wish to avoid pregnancy, several contraceptive choices are available for patients with diabetes;

there is no one ideal contraceptive available to use. The contraception choices currently available for women have their advantages and disadvantages (Cleveland Clinic, 2012). Types of contraception include hormonal, barrier methods, intrauterine devices, and tubal ligation (Eisenstat, 2007).

Hormonal contraceptives block ovulation through the use of hormones, specifically estrogen and progestin. Hormonal contraceptives today deliver much less estrogen than they did in the past and so are considered much safer to use. Contraceptives in this category include the pill, patch, vaginal contraceptive ring, and injection (Eisenstat, 2007).

Barrier methods include male condoms, female condoms, diaphragms with spermicide, cervical caps, and contraceptive sponges. These contraceptive devices work by forming a barrier to prevent the man's sperm from reaching the woman's egg. The most commonly used type of contraception is the male condom, which is the only contraceptive that offers some protection against sexually transmitted diseases. Female condoms, diaphragms, cervical caps, and contraceptive sponges have a high failure rate (Cleveland Clinic, 2012).

Intrauterine devices (IUDs) are the most effective form of birth control. IUDs are small, plastic, T-shaped devices that are inserted into the uterus by a gynecologist or health care professional and are left in place for up to ten years. There are two types of IUDs. The hormonal IUD releases small amounts of progestin into the uterus, which thickens cervical mucus. The thickened cervical mucus decreases the mobility of the sperm entering the cervix, makes the sperm less active, and thins the lining of the uterus, keeping the fertilized egg from attaching (American College of Obstetricians and Gynecologists, 2012). The other type of IUD, the copper IUD, works by releasing small amounts of copper into the uterus. The copper prevents the egg from fertilizing, prevents the egg from attaching to the uterine wall, and prevents sperm from entering the fallopian tubes (American College of Obstetricians and Gynecologists, 2012). In the past, IUDs were not recommended for women with diabetes due to risk of pelvic inflammatory disease (PID). However, today's IUDs are much safer and are available for women with diabetes (Eisenstat, 2007).

Tubal ligation, also known as female sterilization, is a permanent surgical procedure that blocks the fallopian tubes, preventing the egg from traveling to the uterus and becoming fertilized. The surgeon will either burn the tubes or clamp them off with a clip or ring. The failure rate for tubal ligation is very low. Even though the procedure is considered permanent, a surgeon can reverse it with another surgical procedure (Eisenstat, 2007).

Pregnancy

Women with type 1 or type 2 diabetes should carefully plan pregnancies to prevent diabetes-related complications (Alkon, 2010). Though considered a high-risk pregnancy, with proper planning and collaboration with the diabetes health care team, women with preexisting type 1 or type 2 diabetes can have a safe and healthy pregnancy. Gestational diabetes, different from type 1 or type 2 diabetes, is diabetes that occurs in women who do not have type 1 or type 2 diabetes during pregnancy. For information on gestational diabetes, *see* CHAPTER 5, GESTATIONAL DIABETES.

Just a few years ago, it was very common for women with diabetes to miscarry during pregnancy or for the baby to be born with birth defects. Keeping blood glucose levels within normal range can help prevent these complications from occurring. If blood glucose levels are not well controlled before and during pregnancy, there are risks to both the mother and the baby (American Diabetes Association, 2012a). In addition to miscarriage and birth defects, other risks to the baby include premature delivery, macrosomia (larger than normal baby), hypoglycemia at birth, jaundice, premature labor, and respiratory distress syndrome. Risks to the mother include risk of diabetic ketoacidosis, preeclampsia (high blood pressure with protein in the urine), progression of diabetic eye and kidney disease, urinary and vaginal infections, and difficulty delivering (Eisenstat, 2007).

The American Diabetes Association (2012a) recommends keeping blood glucose and glycated hemoglobin (A1C) levels within the target range both before becoming pregnant and during the pregnancy to ensure the proper development of the child and reduce the risk of birth defects. The target blood glucose level before meals is 60 to 119 mg/dL and after meals is 100 to 149 mg/dL (American Diabetes Association, 2012a). Women planning to become pregnant should also lead a healthy lifestyle to help reduce the risk of complications developing during pregnancy. Women should eat a healthy diet and exercise to maintain a normal body weight before and during pregnancy.

In addition to healthy lifestyle habits, women planning to become pregnant should collaborate with their diabetes health care providers to properly plan for the pregnancy. A nutritionist or registered dietitian can also help with meal planning. Patients should also undergo an examination that includes A1C testing and physical, checking for high blood pressure and heart, kidney, nerve, and eye complications, because pregnancy can worsen these complications (Eisenstat, 2007). Women should use a reliable form of birth control while in the pregnancy planning stage until blood glucose levels are under control and healthy lifestyle habits are in place.

A pregnant woman with diabetes should seek an obstetrician with experience handling high-risk pregnancies. It is important during the pregnancy to monitor blood glucose levels regularly. As the baby grows and develops, these changes will also affect blood glucose levels and the symptoms of hypoglycemia become more difficult to notice. Women should strive to stay within normal blood glucose levels to prevent complications. Too much glucose during the second and third trimesters will cause the baby to grow too large, a condition called macrosomia. Macrosomia increases the risk of trauma during birth and may necessitate the need for a cesarean section (dLife, 2010).

During pregnancy, the body will need more insulin, particularly during the last trimester. In that third trimester, the placenta releases hormones that block the action of insulin, causing a need for increased insulin. Women with type 1 diabetes will need to take this into consideration to properly manage their insulin treatment plan. Insulin is safe for the baby.

Those with type 2 diabetes need to consult with their doctor about treatment. Some oral diabetes medications may be unsafe to take during pregnancy and the effectiveness of some drugs decreases during pregnancy as insulin resistance increases. Because of these reasons, some patients may be prescribed insulin during pregnancy (American Diabetes Association, 2012a).

Many health care facilities offer classes to help mothers prepare for labor by explaining what to expect during the delivery process. The health care team will determine the best delivery method based on the health of the mother, glucose levels, blood pressure, kidney function, and diabetes-related complications. The physicians will also take into consideration the health of the baby, size and movements, heart rate, and quantity of amniotic fluid in the uterus (American Diabetes Association, 2012a). Women with properly controlled glucose levels usually will carry their baby to full term without any complications. Because babies born to mothers with diabetes are usually larger, the doctor may decide to deliver through cesarean section. Some doctors may decide to induce labor early instead of waiting forty weeks (Eisenstat, 2007).

Labor is a form of exercise and, as happens because of exercise, the patient's insulin needs will decrease. The medical team will frequently monitor blood glucose levels during and directly after labor, but patients usually do not need insulin during this time period. During the weeks following delivery the patient may find it increasingly difficult to control blood glucose levels, so regular monitoring is important to avoid levels becoming too high or too low.

Menopause

When a woman enters menopause, she can no longer become pregnant. If a woman has not had a menstrual period for a period of one year, she is entering menopause. Up until this time, women should use a reliable form of birth control to avoid becoming pregnant. Menopause usually occurs between the ages of forty-two and fifty-eight, with the average age being fifty-one (Eisenstat, 2007).

During menopause and perimenopause (the years before menopause), the body gradually produces less of the hormones estrogen and progesterone. The reduction of these hormones produces symptoms of hot flashes, vaginal dryness, mood changes, and in women with diabetes, fluctuating blood glucose levels (American Diabetes Association, 2012b). The resultant fluctuation of blood glucose levels can be challenging for women trying to control their levels. Women may experience increased occurrences of low blood glucose levels during this time. During menopause, many women with diabetes may need to make adjustments to their insulin or diabetes medications to properly manage their blood glucose (Eisenstat, 2007).

Summary

Blood vessel and nerve damage from high glucose levels can cause urologic and sexual complications. Urological problems can occur in both men and women with diabetes and result in bladder and urinary tract complications, such as overactive bladder, poor sphincter muscle control, urine retention, and infections. Sexual problems can also result from poor glucose control and affect both men and women. Patients who are experiencing problems with sexual activity or urological complications can often improve their condition when they achieve greater glucose control.

Information Sources

Selected Print Resources

➤ Alkon, Cheryl. 2010. *Balancing Pregnancy with Pre-existing Diabetes: Healthy Mom, Healthy Baby.* New York: Demos Health.
This book is a resource for women with diabetes who are or wish to become pregnant. The resource does not include information about gestational diabetes. The author begins by describing the differences between type 1 and type 2 diabetes. The book emphasizes the importance of developing a diabetes management plan before becoming pregnant. It also provides information on finding the right doctors and working collaboratively with the diabetes health care team. In addition, the book provides information for those who are pregnant and guidelines for expectant moms to follow during each trimester of pregnancy. The author provides information on achieving glucose control and suggests foods to eat during pregnancy.

➤ American College of Obstetricians and Gynecologists. 2010. *Your Pregnancy and Childbirth: Month to Month.* Washington, DC: American College of Obstetricians and Gynecologists.
This general pregnancy resource provides information for women with pregestational diabetes. It discusses risk factors, how diabetes can affect pregnancy, and managing diabetes during pregnancy. Although only one chapter covers diabetes during pregnancy, other parts of the book will also be useful to someone who is pregnant.

➤ American Diabetes Association. 2011. *American Diabetes Association Complete Guide to Diabetes.* 5th ed. Alexandria, VA: American Diabetes Association.
This resource contains information about diabetes and sex and also includes information about vaginal infections that often occur in women with diabetes.

The book contains a chapter about the sexual complications of diabetes and includes the following topics: menstruation, sex hormones, menopause, birth control, lack of desire, erectile dysfunction, and pregnancy.

➤ Beaser, Richard. 2005. *The Joslin Guide to Diabetes: A Program for Managing Your Treatment*. New York: Fireside.

In addition to a chapter about diabetes and pregnancy, this resource also contains a chapter covering information about diabetes-related sexual issues. The pregnancy chapter covers information about how diabetes affects pregnancy, pregnancy planning, managing diabetes during pregnancy, the course of the pregnancy, nutrition, insulin, and delivery. The chapter about sexual problems provides information for both men and women. It covers problems such as erectile dysfunction, retrograde ejaculation, menstruation, birth control options, vaginal dryness, hormone replacement therapy, urinary tract infections, sexual dysfunction, and sexual activity.

➤ Collazo-Clavell, Maria. 2009. *Mayo Clinic The Essential Diabetes Book: How to Prevent, Control, and Live Well with Diabetes*. Rochester, MN: Mayo Clinic.

This resource provides a chapter detailing sexual health issues for men and women. It provides information about erectile dysfunction, menstruation, menopause, and pregnancy. The chapter contains some illustrations, showing how some treatments for erectile dysfunction work.

➤ Eisenstat, Stephanie. 2007. *Every Woman's Guide to Diabetes: What You Need to Know to Lower Your Risk and Beat the Odds*. Cambridge, MA: Harvard University Press.

This book provides a chapter detailing the issues and concerns for women with diabetes regarding sexual, reproductive, and urological health. In addition to information about pregnancy while having diabetes, this book provides information on yeast infections, vaginitis, urinary tract infections, and urinary incontinence. In addition, the resource provides information on sexual health concerns of women with diabetes, including vaginal dryness, painful sexual intercourse, and decreased sexual drive.

➤ Levin, Marvin E., and Michael A. Pfeifer. 2009. *The Uncomplicated Guide to Diabetes Complications*. 3rd ed. Alexandria, VA: American Diabetes Association.

Men and women will find this book a valuable resource for learning more about diabetes-related sexual complications. The chapter regarding men's sexual health contains information about erectile dysfunction, its diagnosis, and treatment options. The chapter about women's sexual health contains information about sexual dysfunction, menstrual periods, contraception, and pregnancy.

➤ Mercer, Amy Stockwell. 2012. *The Smart Woman's Guide to Diabetes: Authentic Advice on Everything from Eating to Dating and Motherhood*. New York: Demos Health.

The intended audience for this resource is specifically women with diabetes. The book contains information about sexual health and pregnancy, as well as sexual issues related to diabetes complications, such as inability to achieve orgasm, decreased lubrication, pain during intercourse, reduced libido, and self-esteem issues. It also contains a chapter about pregnancy in women with diabetes. It covers information about infertility, pregnancy planning, nutrition and exercise during pregnancy, gestational diabetes, and what to expect during each trimester of pregnancy, at birth, and after birth.

➤ Yu, Winnie. 2004. *What to Do When the Doctor Says It's Diabetes: The Most Important Things You Need to Know about Blood Sugar, Diet, and Exercise for Type 1 and Type 2 Diabetes.* Gloucester, MA: Fair Winds.
This resource contains a chapter overviewing sexual health in patients with diabetes. It covers blood glucose control during menstruation, impact of diabetes on menstruation, sexual challenges for men and women, contraception, and pregnancy.

Selected Web Resources

➤ American College of Obstetricians and Gynecologists—"A Healthy Pregnancy for Women with Diabetes," http://www.acog.org/~/media/For%20Patients/faq176.ashx?dmc=1&ts=20111220T1635024332
This resource provides questions and answers about diabetes during pregnancy. It begins by providing an explanation of what diabetes is and how it can affect pregnancy and the baby. The resource also provides information about planning a pregnancy and how to control diabetes during pregnancy. It stresses communicating with the health care team in planning for a pregnancy and during the pregnancy.

➤ American Diabetes Association—"Living with Diabetes: Pregnant Women," http://www.diabetes.org/living-with-diabetes/complications/pregnant-women/
The webpage provides women who have diabetes the information they need to plan for and have a safe and healthy pregnancy. Information is in sections: before pregnancy, prenatal care, delivery, and after delivery.

➤ American Diabetes Association—"Living with Diabetes: Sexual Health (Men)," http://www.diabetes.org/living-with-diabetes/complications/mens-health/sexual-health/
This section of the website provides information for men suffering from sexual problems due to diabetes. The page begins with an overview of the effects of diabetes on sex and provides links to information, including erectile dysfunction, low testosterone, and sexual implications of emotional health. An audio version of the text is also available.

➤ American Diabetes Association—"Living with Diabetes: Sexual Health (Women)," http://www.diabetes.org/living-with-diabetes/women/sexual-health.html

This article provides information for female diabetes patients who are concerned about sexual function and for those experiencing difficulty with sexual function due to their diabetes. It covers information about depression and anxiety, family planning, birth control, hormones, menstrual cycle, menopause, and hormone replacement therapy. An audio version of the text is also available.

➤ Centers for Disease Control and Prevention—"Take Charge of Your Diabetes: Pregnancy and Women's Health," http://www.cdc.gov/diabetes/pubs/tcyd/pregnant .htm
This easy-to-read resource explains how women with diabetes should plan ahead before becoming pregnant. It encourages women to strive for a near-normal glucose level before becoming pregnant. The resource also provides tips on staying healthy during pregnancy.

➤ Cleveland Clinic—"Diabetes and Female Sexuality," http://my.clevelandclinic .org/disorders/Diabetes_Mellitus/hic_Diabetes_and_Female_Sexuality.aspx
The webpage provides information for women with diabetes regarding sexuality. The resource begins with an overview describing sexuality, then follows with information on various topics, including contraception, fertility, sexual function, and depression.

➤ dLife—"Neurogenic Bladder," http://www.dlife.com/diabetes/complications/ neuropathy/neurogenic-bladder
This webpage explains how diabetic nerve problems can cause bladder control problems. It discusses overactive bladder issues, including urinary frequency, urinary urgency, and urge incontinence. The webpage also includes information on tests to diagnose bladder control problems and the treatments available.

➤ dLife—"Planning a Pregnancy," http://www.dlife.com/diabetes/lifestyle/diabetes-women/women_pregnancy
This webpage provides information for women with type 1 or type 2 diabetes to help them plan for a healthy pregnancy. It explains some of the risks associated with diabetes and pregnancy.

➤ dLife—"Sex and Relationships," http://www.dlife.com/diabetes/complications/ sex
The webpage provides a short overview of diabetes-related sexual problems. Following the overview are links to additional information, including articles on erectile dysfunction, heart disease and sexual health, intimacy with diabetes, female sexual dysfunction, and romantic relationships. Each article provides details regarding diabetes sexual complications, including information about the diagnosis and treatment options for diabetes patients suffering from the complication.

➤ JDRF—"Type 1 Diabetes and Pregnancy," http://www.jdrf.org/index.cfm?page_ id=103524

This article explains the steps that women should take to ensure a safe pregnancy. It stresses good glucose control before becoming pregnant and working with the medical team. The resource provides advice for women to follow during and after pregnancy. It also provides a link to a type 1 diabetes and pregnancy online support group.

➤ Joslin Diabetes Center—"Sexual Dysfunction and Diabetes," http://www.joslin .org/info/sexual_dysfunction_and_diabetes.html
The webpage begins with an overview of the problem and statistics regarding the occurrence. The page links to information about causes, symptoms, treatment options, and communication with the health care team and family. Patients can take a quiz to see if the problems they are experiencing may be symptoms of sexual dysfunction.

➤ March of Dimes—"Pregnancy Complications: Preexisting Diabetes," http:// www.marchofdimes.com/pregnancy/complications_diabetes.html
Women with diabetes who are pregnant or wishing to become pregnant can use this webpage to learn more about managing their diabetes during pregnancy. It covers tips on diabetes management before pregnancy, during pregnancy, and after the baby arrives.

➤ Mayo Clinic—"Penile Implants," http://www.mayoclinic.com/health/penile-implants/MY00358
For men who are considering penile implants to treat their erectile dysfunction, this webpage provides an overview of the procedure. Basic information describes why the procedure may be performed and the explains the risks of the surgery. Information follows on how the patient should prepare for the procedure and what can be expected before, during, and after the procedure. It also compares and describes the different types of implants.

➤ Mayo Clinic—"Pregnancy and Diabetes: Why Lifestyle Counts," http://www .mayoclinic.com/health/pregnancy-and-diabetes/DA00042
Diabetic women can use this site to learn more about pregnancy through each trimester. This site provides women with diabetes information about managing glucose and working with the health care team to have a healthy pregnancy.

➤ Mayo Clinic—"Retrograde Ejaculation," http://www.mayoclinic.com/health/ retrograde-ejaculation/DS00913
This article provides a description of retrograde ejaculation. Beginning with a background of the condition, it then provides information on the symptoms, causes, risk factors, complications, tests, diagnosis, treatments, drugs, coping, and support.

➤ National Diabetes Information Clearinghouse—"Sexual and Urologic Problems of Diabetes," http://diabetes.niddk.nih.gov/dm/pubs/sup/

This webpage provides information for both men and women with diabetes regarding the sexual and urological problems associated with the condition. There is an overview of the types of sexual problems that can occur in men, including erectile dysfunction and retrograde ejaculation, as well as information about lack of arousal and painful sexual intercourse that can occur in women. The page also discusses urological complications such as bladder problems and urinary tract infections.

➤ National Kidney and Urologic Diseases Information Clearinghouse—"Erectile Dysfunction," http://kidney.niddk.nih.gov/kudiseases/pubs/ED/index.htm
While not specifically addressing diabetes-related erectile dysfunction, this webpage provides beneficial information about the disorder. Beginning with an overview of erectile dysfunction, a list of causes follows. The resource provides information about diagnosis and treatments. Men with diabetes-related erectile dysfunction can learn about the various therapies available, including psychotherapy, drug therapy, oral medications, injectable medications, vacuum devices, and surgery.

➤ The Official Foundation of the American Urological Association—"Non-surgical Management of Erectile Dysfunction," http://www.urologyhealth.org/urology/index.cfm?article=60
The site contains general information about nonsurgical treatments for erectile dysfunction. It explains information about erectile dysfunction pills, sildenafil citrate (Viagra), vardenafil HCl (Levitra), and tadalafil (Cialis), which are a class of medications known as phosphodiesterase-5 (PDE5) inhibitors. The page links to patient education booklets that delve into further discussion of treatment, including the following titles:
  • "Erectile Dysfunction: Primary Treatment Options," http://www.urology health .org/content/moreinfo/edprimtreatment.pdf
  • "Erectile Dysfunction: Secondary Treatment Options," http://www.urology health.org/content/moreinfo/edsectreatment.pdf

Selected Audiovisual Resources

➤ dLife—"Men's Issues," http://www.dlife.com/dlifetv/video/playlist/mens_issues
This webpage contains links to several short videos regarding diabetes-related sexual problems in men. These videos cover topics such as low testosterone, erectile dysfunction, and the effects of diabetes on romance in relationships.

➤ dLife—"Relationships," http://www.dlife.com/dlifetv/video/playlist/relationships
This webpage, which lists the relationship videos available on dLifeTV, provides links to a variety of short videos. Videos include topics such as intimacy and diabetes, sex, erectile dysfunction, and relationships.

➤ dLife—"Women's Issues," http://www.dlife.com/dlifetv/video/playlist/womens_issues

This webpage provides links to a range of short videos about sexual, urological, and gynecologic issues affecting women with diabetes.

➤ MedlinePlus—"Erectile Dysfunction—Your Choices," http://www.nlm.nih.gov/medlineplus/tutorials/erectiledysfunctionyourchoices/htm/index.htm
This resource provides an interactive audiovisual tutorial. It explains erectile dysfunction in general, not just those conditions caused by diabetes; however, this resource will help men suffering from erectile dysfunction learn about the different treatment methods. It provides information about psychological counseling, oral medications (Viagra, Levitra, and Cialis), urethral suppositories, penile injections, vacuum devices, and surgery. There is also a text summary of the tutorial's information.

References

Alkon, C. 2010. *Balancing Pregnancy with Pre-existing Diabetes*. New York: Demos Health.

American College of Obstetricians and Gynecologists. 2012. "The Intrauterine Device." FAQ014: Contraception. The American Congress of Obstetricians and Gynecologists. January. http://www.acog.org/~/media/For%20Patients/faq014.pdf?dmc=1&ts=20120709T1416172307.

American Diabetes Association. 2012a. "Living with Diabetes: Pregnant Women." American Diabetes Association. Accessed July 9. http://www.diabetes.org/living-with-diabetes/complications/pregnant-women/.

———. 2012b. "Sexual Health." American Diabetes Association. Accessed July 9. http://www.diabetes.org/living-with-diabetes/women/sexual-health.html.

Cleveland Clinic. 2012. "Diabetes and Female Sexuality." The Cleveland Clinic. Accessed August 9. http://my.clevelandclinic.org/disorders/Diabetes_Mellitus/hic_Diabetes_and_Female_Sexuality.aspx.

dLife. 2010. "Planning a Pregnancy." dLife. Last modified February 18. http://www.dlife.com/diabetes/lifestyle/diabetes-women/women_pregnancy.

———. 2012. "Erectile Dysfunction." dLife. Last modified July 10. http://www.dlife.com/diabetes/complications/sex/erectile-dysfunction.

Eisenstat, S. 2007. *Every Woman's Guide to Diabetes: What You Need to Know to Lower Your Risk and Beat the Odds*. Cambridge, MA: Harvard University Press.

Mayo Clinic. 2011a. "Penile Implants." Mayo Foundation for Medical Education and Research. February 25. http://www.mayoclinic.com/health/penile-implants/MY00358.

———. 2011b. "Retrograde Ejaculation." Mayo Foundation for Medical Education and Research. February 17. http://www.mayoclinic.com/health/retrograde-ejaculation/DS00913.

National Diabetes Information Clearinghouse. 2012. "Sexual and Urologic Problems of Diabetes." National Institute of Diabetes and Digestive and Kidney Diseases, National Institutes of Health. Last updated June 29. http://diabetes.niddk.nih.gov/dm/pubs/sup/.

National Kidney and Urologic Diseases Information Clearinghouse. 2012. "Erectile Dysfunction." National Institute of Diabetes and Digestive and Kidney Diseases, National Institutes of Health. Last updated March 28. http://kidney.niddk.nih.gov/KUDiseases/pubs/ED/index.aspx.

Index

About the Authors

Alyssa Altshuler, MLIS, MA, is the senior manager of library services for Ropes and Gray, LLP. Altshuler received her bachelor of science degree and master of library and information science degree from the University of South Carolina. In 2003, she received a master of arts in liberal studies from Georgetown University. Altshuler received a master of arts degree in instructional technology from Virginia Tech in 2012.

Dana Ladd, MS, SLIS, AHIP, manages the Community Health Education Center (CHEC) at Virginia Commonwealth University Health System and is an assistant professor on the faculty of VCU libraries. Ladd received her bachelor of arts degree from the College of William and Mary and graduated from the University of Tennessee School of Information Science in 2000. In 2007 Dana completed a specialist degree in library and information science from the University of South Carolina. At CHEC, Ladd assists patients and their family members in finding reliable health information at about their illnesses or conditions. She is currently pursuing a PhD in social and behavioral health at Virginia Commonwealth University.

You may also be interested in

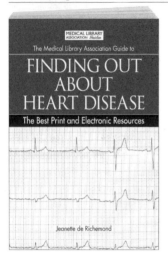

THE MEDICAL LIBRARY ASSOCIATION GUIDE TO FINDING OUT ABOUT HEART DISEASE
JEANETTE DE RICHEMOND

An indispensable, comprehensive guide to heart disease and related information resources available to patients, caregivers, and librarians.

ISBN: 978-1-5557-0750-7
464 pp / 6" × 9"

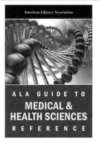

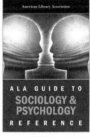

THE MLA's MASTER GUIDE TO AUTHORITATIVE INFORMATION RESOURCES IN THE HEALTH SCIENCES
EDITED BY LAURIE L. THOMPSON, ESTHER CARRIGAN, MORI LOU HIGA AND RAJIA TOBIA
ISBN: 978-1-5557-0719-4

ALA GUIDE TO MEDICAL & HEALTH SCIENCES REFERENCE
AMERICAN LIBRARY ASSOCIATION
ISBN: 978-0-8389-1023-8

ALA GUIDE TO SOCIOLOGY & PSYCHOLOGY REFERENCE
AMERICAN LIBRARY ASSOCIATION
ISBN: 978-0-8389-1025-2

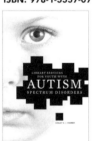

LIBRARY SERVICES FOR YOUTH WITH AUTISM SPECTRUM DISORDERS
LESLEY S. J. FARMER
ISBN: 978-0-8389-1181-5

THE MLA GUIDE TO FINDING OUT ABOUT COMPLEMENTARY AND ALTERNATIVE MEDICINE
GREGORY A. CRAWFORD
ISBN: 978-1-5557-0727-9

THE MLA GUIDE TO MANAGING HEALTH CARE LIBRARIES, 2ND EDITION
EDITED BY MARGARET MOYLAN BANDY AND ROSALIND FARNAM DUDDEN
ISBN: 978-1-5557-0734-7

Order today at **alastore.ala.org** or **866-746-7252!**
ALA Store purchases fund advocacy, awareness, and accreditation programs for library professionals worldwide.